KING ALFRED'S COLLEGE
WINCHESTER

———

To be returned on or before the day marked
below :—

PLEASE ENTER ON ISSUE SLIP:

AUTHOR MANNING

15 DEC 2006
18 MAY 2010

TITLE Politics, religion, & the English Civil War

ACCESSION No. 13651

14 DEC 2011

Politics, Religion and
The English Civil War

Politics, Religion and The English Civil War

edited by

Brian Manning

EDWARD ARNOLD

Printed in Great Britain by
Butler & Tanner Ltd, Frome and London

Contents

Abbreviations

B.M.	British Museum
C.J.	*Journals of the House of Commons*
C.C.C.	*Calendar of the Committee for Compounding*
C.C.D.R.O.	Chester County and Diocesan Record Office
C.S.P.D.	*Calendar of State Papers Domestic*
C.S.P. Venetian	*Calendar of State Papers Venetian*
D.N.B.	*Dictionary of National Biography*
H.M.C.	Historical Manuscripts Commission
J.R.L.	John Rylands Library
L.J.	*Journals of the House of Lords*
M.C.R.L.	Manchester Central Reference Library
P.R.O.	Public Record Office
S.P.D.	*State Papers Domestic* (in P.R.O.)
V.C.H.	*Victoria County History*
Y.B.I.H.R.	York. Borthwick Institute of Historical Research

Note: seventeenth-century orthography, capitalization and punctuation have been retained in quoted matter, except that contractions and abbreviations have been spelt out.

General Preface

No one historian can hope to master all aspects of a period such as the English Civil War: he has to specialize in a limited field. The work of specialists is commonly confined to articles in learned journals and to large scholarly monographs. This present volume brings together the work of several specialists in a convenient form. The contributions are derived from larger, monographic studies, and they are more substantial than short articles. But a volume such as this is liable to lack background and unity, and therefore, in order to fill in some of the background and to link the essays together, I have written a short preface to each essay. It is also hoped that the volume achieves some coherence through a unity of theme. The relation between religion and politics is the most crucial and difficult problem of this period. While some of the essays are concerned primarily with religion, and others with politics, I hope that together they will make a contribution to understanding the connection between the two, and to disentangling on occasions the one from the other. At the same time this volume reflects some of the recent trends in research, and fills in some gaps. The study of ideas has been proving one of the most successful methods of understanding attitudes and issues in this period and Colin Davis exemplifies this in his essay. Our knowledge of the civil war has been greatly increased by the study of local history, which is represented in this collection by the essays of R. C. Richardson and Keith Lindley; and the latter's contribution also reflects the stress which historians now place upon compiling statistics. But concentration upon the gentry has resulted until recently in neglect both of the aristocracy and of 'the middle and poorer people', and I hope that my own essays will help to redress the balance. The role of women in history is beginning to receive serious attention and Patricia Higgins's essay contributes to this development. The essays in this volume have arisen from studies undertaken in the History Department at Manchester University. If the contributors learnt anything from me when I supervised their early researches, I learnt far more from them. I am grateful to them for their contributions; and to my wife for compiling the index

BRIAN MANNING

I

Puritanism and the Ecclesiastical Authorities

The Case of the Diocese of Chester

R. C. Richardson

Preface

There was both a religious and a political background to the English civil war. Of the many discontented groups in England in the 1630s, the puritans were one of the most important; and of the many sources of discontent, puritanism was one of the most significant in the long run. In order to explore the causes of the English civil war, it is as well to begin with puritans and puritanism. Puritans disliked some parts of the Prayer-Book, and they objected to the wearing of the surplice, to the sign of the cross in baptism, to kneeling at the communion and other ceremonies. They were strict sabbatarians, who objected to the traditional sports and recreations which the government permitted and encouraged on Sundays. Some, but by no means all, puritans condemned the government of the church by bishops; and some puritans carried their dislike of the official church services to the lengths of attending illegal services in private houses. But puritanism needs to be studied in the local context and at different periods, for it varied from place to place and from time to time. The attitude of the government towards the puritans was not uniform. In the diocese of Chester the government aided the growth of puritanism in order to combat Roman Catholicism (for political as much as for religious reasons). But in a state church nonconformity was a challenge to the state and so a political matter, and for political as well as religious reasons the toleration of puritans in the diocese of Chester did not last. Efforts were made in the 1630s to force them to conform, by a government that was seeking to assert its authority over the provinces. The efforts failed, even before the crisis of 1640, because the ecclesiastical authorities lacked the machinery to enforce their authority; just as the state authorities failed to get the localities to conform to the edicts of the central government because they lacked the machinery to enforce cooperation. But without lay support, reflected in the non-cooperation of the churchwardens, puritanism would not have survived.

BRIAN MANNING

IN stark contrast to the situation in the south of England, the existence of puritanism in the diocese of Chester, in Elizabeth's reign at least, was in no sense regarded by the authorities as a threat to the well-being of the church. On the contrary, the prevailing attitude was that puritanism was far too useful and necessary to be persecuted. This region, after all, was one of the 'dark corners of the land' faced with the constant and alarming threat of Catholicism on the one hand and irreligion on the other: church and government needed to enlist the able and energetic support of the puritan preachers. The ministers' patrons, therefore, could always offer in their defence the effective argument that without them the reformed religion in the diocese stood virtually unprotected against the old faith.

This was a view which was generally shared by the ecclesiastical authorities. For the religious condition of the diocese—and of Lancashire particularly—made preaching not only desirable but essential. Bishop Aylmer of London, for example, in 1577 saw the attractive possibility of ridding London of its numerous puritan clergy by using—and exhausting—them in active service elsewhere: 'They might be profitably employed in Lancashire, Staffordshire, Shropshire, and other such like barbarous counties, to draw the people from Papism and gross ignorance.'[1] Similarly, in 1582, the Earl of Huntingdon, Lord President of the Council in the North, declared to the Bishop of Chester that: 'the want of diligent and faithful preachinge doth wonderfullie hinder the buildinge of oure churche, and in these north parts yt is most apparent.'[2] In the following year, a similar reminder was given to the same bishop—William Chaderton—by the Privy Council: 'It is a principall part of your pastoral charge, to appoint some learned and godly ministers to repair unto such places where it shall be needful, to instruct the people the better to know their duty towards God and her Majestys laws and to reduce them to such conformitie as we desire.'[3] And in like manner, Walsingham told the Earl of Derby in 1583 that 'there can be no sounder way and surer in my opinion to redress this mischief [i.e. Catholic

---

1 J. Strype, *Life and Acts of Bishop Aylmer* (Oxford, 1821) p. 36.
2 F. Peck, *Desiderata Curiosa* (1779) p. 130. In 1630, for example, it was noted that at Baldeston Chapel, Blackburn, there was no minister 'which is the cause of the increase of popery'. (York. Borthwick Institute of Historical Research: 1630 visitation: *R.V.I.A.* 22, f. 62*v*.)
3 Peck, *op. cit.* p. 113.

recusancy] than by diligent and public preaching.'[4] Thus, while in the south at this time puritan divines were being harried to conform, in the diocese of Chester—as in that of York[5]—a working cooperation evolved between the authorities and the puritan clergy. The puritan onslaught on Catholicism in the diocese of Chester was a part of the wider, official, campaign to extirpate the old religion.

Around 1584, James Gosnell, lecturer at Bolton in Lancashire, wrote to the Leicestershire divine Anthony Gilby about the contrast between official ecclesiastical policy in the north and that in the province of Canterbury. Gosnell was from Leicestershire himself and he had good news to tell his brother in the ministry. '. . . The Bishop of Canterbury [i.e. Whitgift] has not yet, God be thanked, stung us with his articles,[6] which in the south parts have so great power that by report, they have quenched the Lords lights nearly to the number of two hundred.'[7] But ecclesiastical policy towards puritans in the north, it should be stressed again, was not merely one of unwilling or passive toleration. For example in the same year a system of preaching Exercises—regular monthly meetings at fourteen centres—was set up to cover the whole diocese of Chester.[8] Its purpose was to win over the people from popery and at the same time improve the educational standards of the lower clergy. The scheme took effect with full official approval and direction.

The Exercises of 1584 arose out of an arrangement made in 1582 which provided for thrice-yearly synods which the Lancashire clergy were to attend. The privy council wrote to Bishop

---

4 Peck, *op. cit.* p. 138.
5 The development of puritanism in Yorkshire is discussed in R. A. Marchant, *The Puritans and the Church Courts in the Diocese of York, 1560–1642* (1960) and in J. A. Newton *Puritanism in the Diocese of York, 1603–40* Ph.D. thesis, University of London, 1956.
6 Whitgift's Three Articles of 1583 are quoted in P. Collinson, *The Elizabethan Puritan Movement* (1967) pp. 244–5. It was above all the second article—which required submission to the view that the Prayer-Book contained nothing contrary to the word of God—to which puritans took exception.
7 Quoted in J. C. Scholes and W. Pimblett, *History of Bolton* (Bolton, 1892) p. 314.
8 Full details of these preaching Exercises are to be found in Gonville and Caius (Cambridge) MS. 197, ff. 175–85.

Chaderton in April 1584 praising the original scheme and recommending its extension. They fully approved of the fact that the clergy 'have heretofore used an Ecclesiasticall Exercise in some fewe places of those countryes and that onlie thrice in ye whole yeare. Forasmuch as ye good proceedinge or slacknes in religion is a cure of no small consequence, especiallye in those remote parts of ye realme standinge dangerouslye for ye enemie and where ye Gospell as yet hath not bene thoroughlie planted, we have thought good for increase of knowledge and zeale in ye common people, as lykewyse for ye establishinge of a learned ministerie in ye countrye to commend unto your Lordship's good consideracon some further enlargement . . . to have ye said exercises of religion hereafter more frequentlie used and in more places of ye diocesse. . . .'[9] Moreover, their Lordships appended a list of clergy in the diocese with whom they wished the bishop to confer. These were not, as might be imagined, those renowned for their orthodoxy, but some of the most prominent nonconformists. Listed here, for example, were Christopher Goodman of Chester, John Caldwell of Winwick, Richard Midgley of Rochdale, William Langley of Prestwich and Edward Fleetwood of Wigan.

Arrangements for the enlarged version of the preaching Exercises were accordingly made. Significantly the document listing them was signed not only by the bishop but by the puritans Edward Fleetwood, Leonard Shaw of Bury, William Langley and Richard Midgley.

The bishop now wrote to the various deans of his diocese informing them of the privy council's instructions concerning the enlargement of the scheme of preaching Exercises and of his own discussions with the leading preachers in his charge. He accordingly commanded them to 'acquainte all ye parsons, vicars, curats, readers and scholemasters within your deaneries with the same, and especiallie ye moderators and to let them have copies of the same at theire owne charges, so as they maye observe and kepe ye saide order for there owne benefyte. Moreover these shalbe to require you to deliver one perfecte note of the names of all ye saide parsons, vicars, curats, readers and scholemasters within your deaneryes whether they be publique or private at ye first daye of your meeting and that you also send me another imediatelie after, that ye absents may be noted and used as they

9 *ibid.* f. 179.

deserve. Fayle you not hereof as you will answer the contrarie at your perill.'[10]

This was by no means the only decisive intervention from above in favour of the puritan divines of the diocese. In 1599 the four Queen's Preachers for Lancashire—each worth £50 a year —were established as part of the official effort to win over the county to the reformed religion.[11] 'I have seated the Queen's Preachers in Lancashire,' wrote Chaderton's successor, Bishop Vaughan, to Cecil in 1600, after the first appointments had been made, 'with as much care as I could, and following the records of presentments made to me and the Judges of Assize of late years, I have put one in every part of the county where there are most recusants . . .'[12] Although it was with Cecil that the scheme originated, the Bishop of Chester had an important share in making the first appointments and thereafter, in fact, was left in complete control of the nominations. Bishop Vaughan particularly wanted Richard Midgley, formerly vicar of Rochdale, to take up one of the preacherships in view of 'his well deserving of the churches in these parts'.[13] Midgley, of course, was a strict nonconformist, and the bishop's choice of him may possibly have caused some official concern in the southern province. But Bishop Vaughan stood firm: 'As to Mr. Midgley,' he declared in the following year, 'whatever exception may be taken to him, considering the good he has done in the last forty years and the respect in which he is held, I am resolved for his continuance unless by superior authority I am pressed to the contrary.'[14]

Bishop Vaughan's choice of Richard Midgley provides a further indication of the peculiarities of the situation in the diocese of Chester. The endowment of the four Queen's Preachers was a royal attempt to further orthodoxy in Lancashire, and of the four

10 *ibid.* f. 184.
11 The history of the preacherships—which survived until 1845—is outlined in E. Axon, 'The King's Preachers in Lancashire', *Transactions of the Lancashire and Cheshire Antiquarian Society* Vol. 56 (1944) pp. 67–104.
12 *Salisbury MSS.* H.M.C., x, p. 41. 20 February, 1600. Leigh, Huyton, Ormskirk and Garstang were the places chosen for the preacherships. Appropriately enough, the preachers' stipends, it was agreed, were to come from recusancy fines levied in the county. Catholics were to pay to be converted!
13 *Salisbury MSS.* H.M.C., x., p. 91.
14 *ibid.* p. 41.

first appointed, three—Midgley, William Harrison and William Forster—were inclined to puritanism.[15]

In view of their usefulness to church and government, the Elizabethan puritan divines of the diocese of Chester were very rarely troubled for their nonconformity by the ecclesiastical authorities. In contrast, Giles Wigginton, incumbent of Sedbergh in the archdeaconry of Richmond—a Yorkshireman and a graduate and later Fellow of Trinity College, Cambridge—aroused the personal animosity of none other than Archbishop Whitgift. Such at least is the impression gained from Wigginton's own full, although very biased, account of the archbishop's dealings with him, which he gave to Sir Walter Mildmay, his patron.[16]

According to Wigginton the feud was of long standing and had begun during his student days at Cambridge. Whitgift became Master of Trinity in 1567 when Wigginton was still an undergraduate. 'What time (he), makeinge diligent enquirie after such schollers and boyes as durst be bold to reprove sinne and to call for reformation—whom he then and ever since hath called sawcy boyes, busie bodies and medlers with matters of estate, etc.—founde me, as happie it was, to be one of that number.' Thereafter, Wigginton told Mildmay, Whitgift did all in his power to hinder his advancement. He tried first of all to prevent his election to a fellowship. Then in 1571 when Wigginton received his M.A., the Vice Chancellor—at the instigation of Whitgift, the preacher felt sure—gave 'a generall admonition and reproofe to certaine over busie fellowes', and especially mentioned one, 'whom he termed Whittington, for God would not suffer him to utter the worde plainely'. But this was not all: 'At sundrie tymes and in sundrie sorts I suffered many like injuries at his hands,' Wigginton went on, 'and at the hands of his cheife adherents, schollers and frends, procured and encouraged by him to molest and trouble me, namely for wearing my hatt instead of a square

15 Of the remaining Queen's Preacher—Barnard Adams—virtually nothing is known, save that he was well liked by the bishop (*Salisbury MSS.* H.M.C., x, p. 84).
16 Wigginton's letters to Mildmay are printed in A. Peel, ed., *The Seconde Parte of a Register* . . . (1915) Vol. ii, pp. 238–58. Collinson reminds us that 'every allowance (must be made) for the warped mind of this unbalanced and quarrelsome man' (*Puritan Movement* p. 130).

capp, and for not wearing of a surplice when I went to the chappell, for speakinge againste nonresidents, stage playes and popery
or prelacie, and such like matters.'[17]

Wigginton claimed that the archbishop's calculated opposition
towards him continued unabated after he had left Cambridge.
Even after he had settled at Sedbergh, Wigginton was convinced
that Whitgift was trying to stir Archbishop Sandys of York and
Bishop Chaderton of Chester to take action against him. And certainly Sandys was aware of what a firebrand he had in his midst.
As early as 1582, he had written to the Bishop of Chester that:
'Your Lordship shall doe well to better Mr. Wigginton, a young
man verie farre out of frame, who in myne opinion will not
accept of you as of his ordinarie, a bishop. Neither woulde I
accept of him beinge in your place as a preacher of my dioces.
*He laboreth not to builde, but to pull downe, and by what meanes he can to
overthrowe the state ecclesiasticall.*'[18] The opportunity for which, in
Wigginton's opinion, Whitgift had long been waiting came two or
three years later when complaints were lodged against him by
members of his congregation. Whitgift, Wigginton told Mildmay, enthusiastically acted upon this information and urged
the Archbishop of York and the Bishop of Chester to deprive
him.

Wigginton was indeed deprived of his living and a successor
introduced. But his patron, Mildmay, intervened on his behalf and
he was restored. He had in any case ignored his deprivation and
continued to preach. Later, however, in 1586, Wigginton was
imprisoned in London at Whitgift's instigation and was subsequently deprived and degraded. The immediate cause of this
action, as Wigginton himself admitted, was that he had 'preched
diverse sermons in sundrie churches never prayinge for nor
praisinge any prelate nor any part of their prelacye, dealings nor
proceedings, but on the contrary prayinge and prechinge in every
one of my sermons commonly againste anti-christe, and againste
all popish prelates and usurpers such as had no warrant from Gods
[Word] to deale in his church, and yett did Tyranniz and over-
rule the same. And sometimes prayinge in my sermons that God

17 *Seconde Parte of a Register* pp. 241–2.
18 Letter of 7 March 1582, printed in Peck, *op. cit.* p. 115. (My italics.)
   Clearly then Wigginton—unlike most other puritan divines in the diocese
   —was of no use to the authorities.

would confounde the councelles of Achitophell, and that God would send and establish true pastors, teachers, elders and deacons, with the wholl righte government of Christ in every severall congregation of his churche. Also I used to praye . . . that God would blesse all hir majesty's faithfull councellors and namely my Lord the Earle of Leicester [Whitgift's great adversary] in his expedition and warrfare for the church and for the gospell.'[19] Having preached such inflammatory matter, it is hardly surprising that attempts—according to Wigginton, by the Earls of Warwick and Huntingdon among others—to secure his release were unsuccessful. Wigginton remained in gaol.

But even detention in prison could provide an ardent Presbyterian like Wigginton with ample scope for his talents. Here he came into contact with the religious fanatics Hacket and Coppinger,[20] and Whitgift—perhaps not unjustly—came also to suspect Wigginton of being in some way involved in the Marprelate tracts. But although he vigorously denied the accusation Wigginton refused to answer questions on oath, and he was not restored to Sedbergh until 1592.

Wigginton's experience has been described at some length since it provides one of the very few instances of Elizabethan attacks on the nonconformist clergy of the diocese of Chester. But although Wigginton himself and the case against him were quite untypical, this was not the only occasion in Elizabeth's reign on which an attempt was made to reverse the normal policy of toleration in the diocese and to impose a tighter control over the puritan clergy of this region and particularly those of Lancashire.

A more general, but at the same time isolated and apparently short-lived, effort to bring the puritan divines of Lancashire to conformity was made in 1590. On this occasion, as in Wigginton's case, the initiative behind the action came from outside the diocese. Archbishop Piers of York used his metropolitan visitation of this year as a weapon against the puritans, though in this he may only have been acting on instructions from Whitgift.[21]

19 *Seconde Parte of a Register* p. 247.
20 Some account of Hacket's activities and of his execution in 1591 is given in J. E. Neale, *Queen Elizabeth I* (Pelican edn., 1960) p. 320. Like Wigginton, Hacket was a native of Oundle, Yorkshire (*D.N.B.*).
21 Collinson argues that 'the whole episode should probably be understood as an effort by Whitgift to bring the administration of the northern province into line with his own.' (*op. cit.* p. 406.)

However, it was not with the Bishop of Chester that the 1590 drive against puritanism originated.

The most puritan region of the whole diocese was the deanery of Manchester,[22] and it was with the clergy of this area that Piers was most concerned. His metropolitan visitation had revealed that the use of the surplice was almost entirely neglected throughout the whole deanery. The clergy of the collegiate church in Manchester were perhaps the most obstinate offenders in this respect, and they were singled out for separate comment: 'forasmuch as it appeared to the commissioners that none of the Fellowes, ministers or choristers do wear surplices in time of prayers and ministration of the sacraments, which is indecent and offensive in such a collegiate church and contrary to her majesty's laws and injunctions in that case provided, therefore the commissioners did monish them all to provide surplices and wear them in time of prayers and ministration of the sacraments in the same church before Michaelmas next or else to appear . . . before my Lord Archbishop and others his associates Her Majesty's Commissioners for causes ecclesiastical at York.'[23]

The preachers involved, however, were quite capable of defending themselves. A letter was drawn up and delivered to the archbishop—a letter which contained an admission of their nonconformity but which also proclaimed their fundamental loyalty to the church. They emphasized that the peculiarities of the religious state of Lancashire were such that special treatment was necessary. Ceremonies, they wrote, 'however otherwise they may be thought lawfull and tolerable els where, yet assuredly in these partes of our countrey they may seeme lesse expedient then in anie other part of the realme.' '. . . these consideracons . . . being well knowen and duely weighed of our owne Bisshop have hitherto caused him to deale favourably with us in these matters, in which favourable course we doubt not but of himself hee purposeth to continue, as finding it most expedient for our state, which consideracons also no doubt have drawen heertofore the like grace towards us from yor Lordships most worthy predecessor.'[24] They

---

22 See my book *Puritanism in North-West England: A Regional Study of the diocese of Chester to 1642* (Manchester, 1972) *passim*.

23 F. R. Raines, ed., *Miscellany* Vol. V, *Chetham Society*, Old Series, 97 (1875) p. 4.

24 Raines, *op. cit.* pp. 11–12. Piers's predecessor as Archbishop of York was the moderate Edwin Sandys. Bishop Chaderton of Chester wrote of the

did not forget, of course, to remind the archbishop of their usefulness as preachers. They had 'continually been called both by the
ecclesiasticall comission when it was, and also by the civill authoritie ever since the other hath ceased, to make presentments of the
papists amongst us, by meanes wherof manie of them have been
reformed, but the most of them therby stirred up in rancour and
malice against us.' By their ceaseless activity on behalf of the
reformed religion, therefore, the puritan preachers had made many
enemies among the Catholic population who were only waiting
for an opportunity for revenge. Having thus forcefully stated their
case, the preachers' request was that since: 'in all wee have carried
one tenor, to wit, a quiet and peaceable course in the faithfull
work of or ministry, we trust yor good Lordship upon this full
intelligence of our state will not varie from the former favourable
proceedinges which hitherto have been taken with us, wherein
wee doubt not but yor Lordship shall finde a far greater blessing
to the good reformacon of our country from the grosse idolatry
and heathenish prophanacons which yet continue with many
amongst us, then yf a more strict course were taken in these
smaller matters of inconformitie in the preachers.'[25]

Piers, probably under instructions from Whitgift, stood firm.
He wrote to Edmund Hopwood of Hopwood, a J.P. and a puritan sympathizer: 'Whereas they alleage that they speake not
against the co(mmun)ion boock their accons and examples are
witnesses to the contrary . . . In their other allegacons I see no
sufficient reason to warrant the breaking of the order of the
church established by auctoritie and not being contrary to God
his word. Therefore I do require that according to the order of
the communion boock they have divine service celebrated in their

---

puritan divines of his diocese that 'I have alwayes loved them dearlie,
favoured them greatlie and geven them the best of intertaynment and
countenance in their honest causes.' (Letter to Walsingham, 12 May
1586. P.R.O. *S.P.D.*, S.P. 12/189/12.)
25 Raines, *op. cit.* p. 12. Those who signed the letter to the archbishop were
Oliver Carter of Manchester, Edward Fleetwood of Wigan, William
Leigh of Standish, Edward Assheton of Middleton, Peter Shaw of Bury,
Edward Walsh of Blackburn, William Langley and John Hill of Prestwich,
John Buckley of Manchester, Thomas Hunt of Oldham and Richard
Midgley of Rochdale. Biographical details of all these preachers are given
in Raines's edition, mentioned above, of the material relating to the
1590 metropolitan visitation.

churches and the sacraments administered in a surplus.'[26] There could be, then, no question of treating Lancashire as a special case. Laws were laws, and there could be no exemptions. 'I see no sufficient reason alleaged,' the archbishop wrote to Chaderton, 'either in your letters or to the preachers, to warrant you to use any such tolleracon or for them to take anie such tolleration at your handes for the breaking of the orders of the Church established by auctoritie. . . . And this order my trust is and request that you will see observed not onely there but in all your dioces and that you will first beegin with your owne colledge at Manchester. If anie bee desirous to bee further satisfied in these poinctes yor godly learned wisdome can doe it. Yf anie of them bee disposed to conferre with mee, they shalbee heartily welcome; I will do it in most charitable and brotherlike manner. [But] yf anie man be contentious, wee have no such custome, nor the Church of Christ.'[27]

But the issuing and enforcement of orders in sixteenth-century England were two entirely different things. Despite the archbishop's determination, there is no evidence that conformity was enforced in the diocese of Chester: the use of the surplice continued to be neglected by puritan divines.

At the Hampton Court Conference in 1604 a plea for a continuation of the traditional policy of studied lenience towards the puritan clergy of his native county was made by Laurence Chaderton, brother of the bishop and Master of Emmanuel College, Cambridge. William Barlow reported that Chaderton had begged James I that 'the wearing of the surplis might not be urged upon some honest, godly and painful ministers in some parts of Lancashire, who feared that if they should be forced to them, many whom they had won to the Gospel would slide back and revolt unto popery again. . . .' His request met initially with a not unfavourable response. The king promised that moderation would be shown to those preachers who 'by their pains and preaching had converted any from popery and were withall men of quiet disposition, honest of life and diligent in their calling. . . .' To those, on the other hand, who were 'of a turbulent and opposite spirit, both they and others of that unquiet humour, should presently be

26 Raines, *op. cit.* p. 19.   27 *ibid.* p. 16.

enforced to a conformity. . . .'[28] In the end some sort of time-limit was agreed upon, before which, it was hoped, the nonconformist divines of Lancashire would have seen the error of their ways.

Although proceedings were taken against individual ministers, the puritan clergy of the diocese were still obstinately persisting in their 'errors' in 1616 when Thomas Morton succeeded George Lloyd as Bishop of Chester.[29] Faced with this situation, one of Morton's earliest actions was to cite the main puritan clergy of the diocese to appear before him and demand a reasoned explanation of their continuing opposition to the ceremonies. Bishop Morton, wrote John Barwick, 'was content himself to endeavour their satisfaction in a publick and solemn conference with them upon . . . these . . . poynts. But their perversness frustrating his expectation and desires, in relation to their own good, his next care was to make his endeavours more publick for the common good of the rest of their partie. And therefore he printed a relation of that conference.'[30] This work was his *Defence of the Innocencie of the three ceremonies of the Church of England*.[31] It was prefaced by an 'Epistle to Nonconformists', in which the bishop told the puritan divines of 'the extreme injurie you do unto the Church. But you pretend peace because forsooth you preach not against conformitie—as though there were not a Preaching as well in the eare as on the house top, or not as well an exemplarie

28 William Barlow, D. D. Dean of Chester, *The Summe and Substance of the Conference at Hampton Court* . . . in E. Cardwell, *A History of Conferences* (Oxford, 1840) pp. 210–11.

29 According to S. B. Babbage, *Puritanism and Richard Bancroft* (1962) pp. 213–214, there were two deprivations of puritan clergy in Lancashire in 1606—Edward Walsh of Blackburn and Joseph Midgley of Rochdale. A total of eighty to ninety puritan ministers in fifteen different dioceses were deprived at this time, including fourteen from the see of London, thirteen or fourteen from Peterborough, thirteen from Chichester, nine from Lincoln and eight from Norwich. In the diocese of York, there were four deprivations. (Fuller details are given in the chapter on 'Deprivations' in Babbage, *op. cit.*)

30 John Barwick, *Life . . . of Thomas, late Lord Bishop of Duresme* (1660) p. 79.

31 The three ceremonies defended in the bishop's book, published in 1618, were the surplice, the cross after baptism and kneeling at communion. Barwick, in his biography of the bishop, mistakenly substituted the ring in marriage for the last of these three. Opposition to the use of the ring does not seem, however, to have been expressed by the puritans of the diocese, and there is no mention of the subject in the locally written sermon and devotional literature.

as there is an oratorie seducement ... And that which herein doth double your offence is that your opposition is grounded upon a sinister conceit that our Church observeth these ceremonies in an opinion of Holinesse and Necessitie, which is altogether contrarie to her owne expresse protestation. ...' To the general contention of William Hinde, preacher at Bunbury,[32] that the imposition of the ceremonies was unlawful since it deprived men of their christian liberty, the bishop scornfully answered: 'You stand either chargeable to proove this Assumption, or else compellable to confesse it no better than a false and impious Slander against the Church.'[33] He buttressed his position *vis-à-vis* the ceremonies by ample quotation from scripture, the Church Fathers and from the leading protestant theologians.

Challenging the arguments put forward by the puritan divines against the use of the surplice, the bishop asked: 'If distinct apparell may be used of magistrates, why not of ministers?'[34] He roundly criticized them for their 'fierce and factious opposition' on this point, and contended that it worked 'nothing but Schisme, Scandall and a great Prejudice against the liberty of Christian Churches'.[35]

Again, on the question of the use of the sign of the cross, the bishop claimed that the puritan divines of the diocese were misrepresenting the official position. To those clergymen who failed to see any great difference between the sign of the cross in baptism and the popish practice of crossing, he declared: 'there is a great difference betweene the manner of Protestants crossing the foreheads of Infants, and the Papists crossing their Breastes, because even if there were no other oddes, the practice of the Protestants is joyned with an interpretation of their meaning shewing to what end the crosse is used.'[36] Moving now to the question of kneeling at the communion, Morton refuted the opinion of those who held that the sacrament was like a banquet where the most natural gesture was that of sitting. The communion service, he argued, was a mystical banquet only: 'therefore you are not to require or expect therein the very forme and fashion of an ordinary banquet, where it will become men to talke, eate and drinke, to invite and

32 Hinde (1569–1625), is chiefly remembered as the author of *The Life of John Bruen* (1641).
33 Morton, *op. cit.* p. 175.
34 *ibid.* p. 204.
35 *ibid.* p. 220.   36 *ibid.* p. 233.

pleadge one another; and how then can you exact of us the manner of sitting?'[37] And so, in conclusion, the bishop exhorted them: 'but to permit your internall reverence to become visible by bodily gesture. . . .'[38]

Morton's defence of conformity was published in 1618. In 1617 James I had issued the famous *Declaration of Sports*, a document which attacked the puritan position but from a different angle. Morton was its author. The declaration was issued with Lancashire in mind and only became generally applicable in the following year.[39] Its avowed purpose was to make certain that: 'our good people bee not letted or discoraged from anie lawfull recreacon such as Pypinge, Dansinge, either men or women, archerie for men, leapinge, valtinge or anie such harmles recreation, and the women to have leave to carrie rushes to the church. . . .'[40] The holding of bull and bear baitings, plays and bowling on Sundays, however, was expressly prohibited.

The declaration was intended to contribute towards the solution of Lancashire's Catholic problem. Over-strict regulation of the sabbath, it was argued, could only persuade Catholics that the reformed religion was dull and joyless. The document, of course, was not an edict of toleration for the Catholic population. Recusants, in fact, were denied all these Sunday pastimes since they were 'unworthie of anie lawfull recreation after the [said] service that will not first come to the church and serve God'.

There is no doubt, however, that the *Declaration of Sports* was designed to weaken the puritan position and to undermine the authority of the preachers, who by now were beginning to be considered almost a greater nuisance than the Catholics they opposed. It was a direct attack on the puritan insistence upon the godly discipline.[41] Moreover, the Bishop of Chester was authorized to take: 'straight order with all the puritanes and precisians within (his diocese) either constraininge them to conforme (them) selves or to leave the cuntrie according to the lawes of our

37 *ibid*. pp. 251–2.   38 *ibid*. p. 308.
39 J. Tait, 'The Declaration of Sports for Lancashire', *English Historical Review* Vol. XXXII (1917).
40 E. Axon, ed., 'Manchester Quarter Sessions', *Lancashire and Cheshire Record Society* Vol. 42 (1901) p. xxv.
41 The 1617 *Declaration* was far more permissive than, say, the Manchester regulations made by the J.P.s in the previous year. These orders had forbidden all dancing and music at any time on the Sabbath. (Axon, *op. cit*. p. 17.)

kingdome and canons of our church, and so to strike equallie on both hands against the contemners of our authoritie and adversaries of our church'.

How successful the declaration was in achieving its objects and how much difference it made to the local situation, is difficult to determine. But since it had to be re-issued in 1633, it can hardly have achieved all that had been intended. The 1633 declaration was necessary 'because of late in some counties of our kingdom we find that under pretence of taking away abuses, there hath been a general forbidding, not only of ordinary meetings, but of the Feasts of the Dedication of the churches, commonly called Wakes.'[42] And so that none should be ignorant of the declaration, it was required to be read in all parish churches.[43] But it is certain that the main effect of the declarations was not to weaken the hold of puritanism but to identify the latter even more closely with sabbatarianism in such a way that the two became virtually inseparable.[44] By the civil war, it was reasonable to assume that an individual who was a sabbatarian would also be a puritan.

The official attitude to puritanism and Catholicism in the diocese of Chester was beginning to change in the early seventeenth century. But puritanism still continued to develop, and a general conformity was not enforced. It was not until the Archbishop of York's metropolitan visitation in 1633 that a determined and systematic attempt was made to defeat the puritans of this region. For Richard Neile (1562–1640), who became Archbishop of York in 1631, soon proved himself 'the great adversary of the puritan faction'[45] in the north.

Neile's visitation articles for 1633—with which all parishes

---

42 S. R. Gardiner, ed., *Constitutional Documents of the Puritan Revolution* (Oxford, 1906) p. 102. Admittedly, it was the situation in Somerset, not in Lancashire, which on this occasion was the immediate cause of the declaration.

43 A similar provision had been made in James's Declaration—in the 1618 version—but had been withdrawn; Christopher Hill, *Society and Puritanism in Pre-Revolutionary England* (1964) p. 200.

44 The earlier suppression of Nicholas Bownde's treatise on *The True Doctrine of the Sabbath* (1595) had had a similar effect. (Collinson, 'The Beginnings of English Sabbatarianism', *Studies in Church History* Vol. I (1964).)

45 The phrase is Neile's own.

were required to equip themselves—show the extent of his pre-
parations against the puritans. In them he demanded that churchwardens should tell him, for example, 'whether doth your minister observe the orders, rites and ceremonies prescribed in the
books of common prayer, in reading holy Scriptures, prayers and
administration of the Sacraments without diminishing, in regard
of preaching or any other respect, or adding anything in the
manner or somme thereof.'[46] The archbishop also wanted to
know 'whether hath your minister administered the Communion
to any but such as kneele, or do you know any that refuse to
kneele; hath he administered to any that are under Ecclesiasticall
Censure, as for refusing to be present at publike Prayer, or who
hath depraved the Booke of Common Prayer and administration
of the Sacraments, or the Rites and Ceremonies prescribed, or the
Articles of religion agreed upon, or the Book of ordering
Deacons, Priests and Bishops, or against his Majesties Supremacy. . . .'[47] Turning now to the subject of fasts and lectures,
Neile asked 'whether hath your minister held or appointed any
publike fast not appointed by Authority, or beene present at such:
doth he or any other in your parish hold any lecture or exercise?'
Still on the question of lectures, the archbishop inquired 'whether
have you in your parish any weekeday Lecture or not. And if you
have, by whom is the same performed, whether by one particular
man thereto licensed or by sundry neighbour Ministers, and
whether are the publike prayers alwaies read before such lectures
and sermons, in his surplesse and hood, according to his Majesties
injunctions lately set forth?'[48]

Concentrating next on the laity, Neile wished to know from
the churchwardens whether members of the congregation had
refrained from standing or kneeling as prescribed in the church
service and whether any of them had kept on their hats in
church.[49] The archbishop also asked 'whether hath any in your
parish spoken against or impugned the forme of making and
consecrating Bishops, Priests, or Deacons, or have separated
themselves from the society of the congregation, and combined

46 Neile's Visitation Articles (1633). B.M. copy 5155, C. 17, pp. 231-2, no. 2.
47 ibid. p. 233, no. 8.   48 ibid. p. 237, no. 38.
49 There is some evidence to suggest that among puritans, as later
   among Quakers, the practice of keeping on the hat in church can be
   viewed as an expression of dissent. Discussion of this point can be found
   in Richardson, op. cit. pp. 80-81.

in a new Brotherhood or depraved the Sinods of the Church of England, held by the Kings Authority.'

Inquiries were also made about puritan practices at baptisms, and churchwardens were instructed to inform the archbishop 'whether hath any parent beene urged to be present or admitted to answere as Godfather for his owne child, or hath any God-father or godmother made any other answer or speech than is prescribed by the Booke.'[50]

The visitation articles thus show both the archbishop's full awareness of the forms in which puritanism was expressed by both clergy and laity, and his determination to control them.

The visitation took place in the autumn of 1633 and was con-ducted not by Neile himself, but by his three equally anti-puritan commissioners, John Cosin, William Easdall and Henry Wick-ham.[51] It marked the turning point in the official policy towards the puritans of the diocese of Chester. The change, as has been shown, had been coming for some time, but both the scope and effects of earlier dealings with the puritans (such as Morton's) had been limited—a fact clearly shown by Neile's visitation report.

The commissioners had found the Prayer-Book 'neglected and abused in most places by chopping, changing, altering, omitting and adding . . . so unregarded (in fact) that many knew not how to reade the service accordinge to the Booke.' 'Many were found,' the archbishop continued in the account he gave to Charles I, 'that thought themselves well deserving and conform-able men, though they observed not the Booke and orders prescribed so long as they did not oppose them. . . .'[52] But the dividing line between conformity and nonconformity had been left deliberately vague for so long in the diocese of Chester that Archbishop Neile ought not to have been surprised to find that 'the country is full . . . of puritans . . . though they will not endure to be thought any such.'[53]

50 Neile, *op. cit.* p. 240, no. 10. Puritan opinion on the subject of godparents was to some extent divided. Those divines, however, who opposed the practice of having godparents, were above all reluctant to allow an individual to take a solemn oath on behalf of others. At baptism, only a father could confidently make a promise concerning the upbringing of his child—a position which was perfectly in accord with the general emphasis in puritanism on the authority of the heads of households.
51 Marchant, *op. cit.* p. 54.
52 P.R.O. *S.P.D.* S.P. 16/259/78.
53 Bradford MSS (the Bridgeman Papers) Weston Park, Salop, 9/8—

On no occasion before 1633 had puritanism in the diocese of
Chester been subjected to such a penetrating investigation. But
what was the subsequent experience of those who were presented
in this year? In a great many cases, unfortunately, the visitation
records give no indication—a fact which may in itself imply
that proceedings were not taken against them. Further details are
available, however, of some of those puritan clergymen and laymen whose nonconformity was discovered in 1633. For example,
George Willis, curate at Broughton Chapel in Amounderness, was
charged in the visitation for not wearing the surplice and for not
reading prayers on Wednesdays and Fridays, and for these acts of
nonconformity he was inhibited.[54] Robert Shaw, vicar of Cocker-
ham, presented on similar charges, was sternly warned 'hereafter
to observe the orders and ceremonies of the Book of Common
Prayer'.[55] William Gregg of Bolton, having been presented as a
nonconformist, was then enjoined: 'to catechise diligently . . .
and that he doe not administer the communion to any but those
that kneele. . . .'[56] Thomas Bewersall, the puritan curate at
Blackley Chapel, was presented on a variety of charges: then he
too was enjoined 'to observe the rites and ceremonies of the
Church of England to weare the surplice and read prayers according to the booke of common praier and to certify'.[57] Hugh
Burrows, vicar of Runcorn, Cheshire, was enjoined 'to read the
letanie and wear the surplice constantly'.[58] At Witton the curate,
Richard Mather, was presented for failing to wear the surplice
and read the canons, but he too was later dismissed with a
warning.[59]

The nonconformist clergy of Bunbury in Cheshire posed a
special problem, however, in view of their connection with the
London Haberdashers' Company. Neile described his difficulties
in his report to Charles I, emphasizing the Haberdashers' claim
that their authority over the clergy they appointed there was

Bridgeman's copy of the 1633 visitation report, f. 4. These important
documents were consulted in the Cheshire Record Office, and for this
facility I am grateful to the County Archivist, Mr B. C. Redwood, who
negotiated their temporary transfer.
54 Y.B.I.H.R. (1633) vis. R.V.I.A. 23, f. 194.
55 ibid. f. 199v.   56 ibid. f. 560.
57 ibid. f. 597.
58 ibid. f. 407v.
59 ibid. f. 413v.

lawfully exercised 'without any respect of episcopall jurisdiction'.[60] Neile's commissioners, however, took a firm line with the two Bunbury clergymen—Samuel Torshell and John Swan—and suspended them. Finding themselves in this position, the two puritans expediently submitted.[61]

At Richmond in Yorkshire, the nonconformity of the incumbent Thomas Rokeby was fully noted in the visitation, but as the commissioners declared: 'we have so dealt with him that he will not dare the like againe in any kind.'[62] Stern treatment was also extended to another clergyman from the archdeaconry of Richmond: the commissioners recorded that 'we suspended here one Mr. Shaw, parson of Aldingham, against whom there was many complaints' (concerning his nonconformity).[63] At Wigan, a curate (unnamed) being presented for his failure to wear the surplice was: 'openly suspended . . . but afterwards upon his submission and promise of due observance hereafter, he was released.'[64]

The commissioners' dealings with Richard Mather of Toxeth near Liverpool are known in more detail. According to Mather's biographer: 'these visitors being come into the country kept their courts at Wigan where amongst many other unrighteous proceedings and having Mr. Mather convened before them, they passed a sentence of suspension against him merely for his nonconformity to the inventions of men in the worship of God.' Mather himself describes the interview he had with the commissioners: 'In the passages of that day I have this to bless the name of God for, that the terror of their threatening words, of their pursuivants and of the rest of their pomp, did not so terrify my mind but that I could stand before them without being daunted in the least

60 P.R.O. *S.P.D.* S.P. 16/259/78. Charles I wrote in the margin that he would not 'endure that anie lay persons, much lesse a corporation, have power to place and displace curates or beneficed preestes at their pleasur. . . .'

61 The link between Bunbury and the Haberdashers dated from 1594 when Thomas Aldersey, a Cheshire-born merchant tailor of London, having purchased the tithes of Bunbury, used them to endow a preachership and curacy there. He appointed the London company of Haberdashers as his trustees. Bunbury was the first of several church livings of which the Haberdashers gained control. See D. Williams Whitney, 'London Puritanism: the Haberdashers' Company', *Church History* Vol. XXXII (1963).

62 Bradford MSS., Weston Park, Salop, 9/8—Visitation report, f. iv.

63 *ibid.* f. 3*v.* Shaw refused to wear the surplice, re-arranged the prescribed service at his pleasure and preached against bowing at the name of Jesus.

64 *ibid.* f. 4*v.*

measure, but answered for myself such words of truth and sober-
ness as the Lord put into my mouth, not being afraid of their
faces at all: which supporting and comforting presence of the
Lord I count not much less mercy than if I had been altogether
preserved out of their hands.'[65] Attempts were made by some of
Mather's lay supporters to secure his release—without success.
But the situation was hardly eased by the fact that Mather freely
admitted that he had never worn the surplice. ' "What!" said the
visitor, swearing as he spake it, "preach fifteen years and never
wear a surplice? It had been better for him that he had gotten
seven bastards!" ' 'This,' declared Mather's biographer, 'was a
visitors judgement.'[66]

When the commissioners came to the Collegiate Church in
Manchester, they found—not surprisingly—that 'all things and
all men were out of order.' To resist the intended reforms of the
visitation, some of the Collegiate clergy even 'pleaded . . . exemptions from the canons and had common lawyers' opinions for
them.'[67] The commissioners, however, overrode this resistance:
'We behaved ourselves so among them,' they wrote, 'that we gott
them all to put on their Quire habit—all but Mr. Bourne—and
some of the Fellows to execute at service, which no man there
alive ever saw so fully performed before.' William Bourne, Fellow
of the College, as the commissioners emphasized, presented the
greatest problem. Although after much cajoling, he was eventually
persuaded to read service from the Prayer-Book—for the first
time in his thirty years at the College!—he could not be prevailed
upon to wear the surplice being 'ashamed to putt on that which
he hath not worne heretofore. . . .' This being the case, Bourne
was suspended.[68]

Never before had so many puritan laymen been presented at
Manchester in the course of a visitation. Twenty-seven were
charged on this occasion with failing to kneel at the communion.

65 Increase Mather, *Life and Death of Richard Mather* (Cambridge, Mass,
    1670) pp. 10, 11.
66 *ibid*. p. 11. Mather was presented in this year at Prescot—where he gave a
    regular lecture—for refusing to put on the surplice when offered to him
    by the churchwarden. (Y.B.I.H.R. (1633) vis. *R.V.I.A.* 23, f. 345v.)
67 Bradford MSS. Visitation report, f. 5v.
68 P.R.O. *S.P.D.* S.P. 16/259/78. William Bourne, B. D., described by a noted
    local historian of the nineteenth century as 'the John Knox of Manchester',
    had been presented on no less than six occasions between 1608 and 1633
    for his failure—indeed refusal—to wear the surplice.

Sixteen of the congregation were presented for keeping on their hats in church, and fifty-three for not kneeling at the reading of the prayers. In addition, Thomas Worsley, gentleman, his wife and daughter were 'credibly reported to be Brownists'.[69]

In view of the incompleteness of the evidence, no meaningful statistics can be given concerning the treatment of lay puritans presented in the visitation of 1633; and as in the case of the clergy, illustrations must again suffice. Edmund Fazakerley of Hale, for example, who was presented for his nonconformity, was merely ordered: 'to forbear the putting on of his hatt and to stand up' (at the saying of the Belief).[70] Many of those non-kneelers at Bolton, however, were excommunicated.[71] At Burton in Kendal, Edward Preston, an unlicensed schoolmaster, though charged with organizing conventicles and with making extemporary prayers, was none the less dismissed with a warning. Charged along with him were three other lay puritans—separatists, in fact—and they were enjoined to attend their parish church diligently and to certify the fact.[72]

In 1633, as in 1590, the initiative behind the drive against puritanism came from outside rather than from within the diocese of Chester. It was Archbishop Neile of York, rather than John Bridgeman, Bishop of Chester, who was responsible for the change of policy. All the available evidence suggests that Bridgeman, who had been bishop since 1619, was moderate in his own dealings with the puritans.[73] He was content to follow the traditional policy of his predecessors—as long, that is, as he was permitted to do so. 'I must ingeneously confess I can neither justify nor excuse them,' wrote Neile of the Bishops of Chester and Carlisle in his visitation report, 'yet this I know they will say, that finding their Dioceses so distracted with Papists and Puritans, they thought by a mild way to recover the puritan part, lest yt by carrying a severer hand upon the puritans then they had power to carry upon the Papists, the Popish party might take heart and opinion of favour....'[74] Bridgeman's basically moderate

69 Y.B.I.H.R. (1633) vis. R.V.I.A. 23, ff. 601–2v, 610–10v, 611–12v, 607v.
70 ibid. f. 330v.   71 ibid. ff. 560–60v.   72 ibid. ff. 113, 111v.
73 Bridgeman's wife may even have been inclined to puritanism herself for she seems to have had a great respect for the Lancashire nonconformist divine John Angier of Denton. (Oliver Heywood, 'Life of John Angier' Chetham Society, New Series Vol. 97 (1937) p. 57.)
74 P.R.O. S.P.D. S.P. 16/259/78. Bridgeman, however, made known that he

approach to puritanism, although the policy of most of his predecessors, was quite unacceptable at York, Lambeth and Whitehall in the changing climate of the Laudian years. 'The neglect of
punishing puritans,' commented Charles I on Neile's visitation
report, 'breeds Papists.' A new doctrine indeed so far as the
diocese of Chester was concerned!

Only because of pressure from his superiors did Bridgeman's
attitude to the puritans of his diocese begin to harden, and
though personally well-disposed towards them he was bullied
into taking at least some action against them.[75] What must have
helped to make Bridgeman more amenable to pressures from
York and Canterbury in 1633 was the fact that he had himself
very recently been the subject of a case heard before the High
Commission. The investigation into the bishop's alleged mal-
practices had been conducted only a matter of months before
Neile's metropolitan visitation took place.[76] In the end Bridgeman's
accusers—James Martin, John Lewis (both clergymen) and Henry
Reynolds (a lawyer)—and their claims that the bishop had mis-
appropriated funds and conspired with the puritans of his diocese were all discredited, and the bishop acquitted.[77] But even
so, when Neile's visitation of the diocese of Chester took place
in the autumn of 1633, Bridgeman can hardly have been in a
confident mood.

After the visitation, puritans in the diocese at Chester never
again enjoyed that almost complete immunity from official interference which they had known before. Neile tried to keep a

---

took a critical view of the activities of the archbishop's commissioners.
But in effect the dispute concerned the respective boundaries of episcopal
and archiepiscopal jurisdictions, and as such was by no means peculiar
to the diocese of Chester. The pro-puritan Bishop Potter of Carlisle also
grumbled about the 1633 visitation, and in the following year Bishop
Williams of Lincoln challenged Laud's right to conduct a metropolitan
visitation of his diocese. E. R. C. Brinkworth, 'The Laudian Church
in Buckinghamshire', *University of Birmingham Historical Journal* Vol. 5
(1955) p. 31.

75 Some of the puritan divines of the diocese realized that Bridgeman
was being pushed into the role of persecutor. See, for example, the preface to John Paget's *Defence of Church Government* (1641) and Oliver
Heywood's *Life of John Angier* p. 57.

76 The case against Bridgeman was dealt with in the first half of 1633.
Neile's visitation took place in the autumn of that year.

77 Martin and Lewis had both been earlier suspended by Bridgeman for
their inadequacies. Documents concerning the case are in the Bradford
MSS., Weston Park, Salop (18/2), and in *S.P.D.* (P.R.O. S.P. 16/236/27).

watchful eye on the diocese through an extended use of the northern High Commission and was always ready when necessary to prod Bridgeman into taking action against the nonconformists in his charge.[78] 'I might not runne the race of one year at Ringley Chapel,' wrote John Angier, one of the victims of the changed situation, 'whither I was first called, and in that year was twice inhibited. . . . In nine or ten years at Denton Chapel,' he continued, 'I preached not above two separated years, to my best remembrance, without interruption and in that time was twice excommunicated. . . . Sabbath assemblies were sundry times distractedly and sorrowfully broken up and my departure from habitation and people often forced [and] no means left in sight of returne.'[79]

A very rough indication of the increased effort against the puritans in the 1630s is provided by the Consistory Court Papers.[80] Although the series is by no means complete, the fact that no sixteenth-century records of proceedings against puritans in the Consistory have survived would seem to be a genuine reflection of episcopal policy during that period. Between 1601 and 1610, two cases—both involving laymen—were heard by the Consistory Court, while in the following decade, four cases—two concerning laymen—were dealt with. The decennial total rose slightly in the years 1621–30 to six, of which one involved a layman. But in the decade 1631–40, the much higher total of fourteen cases was heard by the Consistory—four of these concerning the laity. And, significantly, all but one of these proceedings were opened after 1633.

The Prynne episode of 1637 is of considerable relevance to this discussion of changed official attitudes towards the puritans. Full details of the case are not necessary in this context, and it will

---

78 Dr Tyler has shown that the northern High Commission did not actively oppose puritanism until after Neile's accession to the archbishopric. P. Tyler, 'The Ecclesiastical Commission for the province of York, 1561–1641', D.Phil. thesis, University of Oxford (1965) pp. 344–65. A pursuivant was specifically appointed to deal with the affairs of the diocese of Chester: Marchant, *op. cit.* p. 54.

79 John Angier, *An Help to Better Hearts for Better Times* (1647) Epistle Dedicatory. The sermons in this volume were originally preached in 1638.

80 The very numerous series of Court Papers at Chester, though generally arranged chronologically, are often incomplete and the records themselves are in a decayed and disorderly condition. Any calculations based upon these documents must necessarily be tentative.

suffice to say that William Prynne, newly tried, convicted and mutilated in London and being escorted to Caernarvon where he was to serve his term of imprisonment, was met and hospitably entertained in Chester and his portrait painted by a local artist. Bridgeman played a part in examining the offenders, Calvin Bruen, Peter and Robert Ince and Thomas Aldersey, all prominent citizens,[81] and was thanked for his services by Archbishop Neile in December of that year when the case was over.[82] But the Bishop of Chester had professed his inability to deal with the matter without outside help. 'I myself,' he told Neile in August 1637, 'have no authority in Chester to punish them, but what my Consistory doth afford, not so much as a Justice of the Peace to bind them to the good behaviour.'[83] So the archbishop and the northern High Commission at York took over. A pursuivant was sent to Chester, further examinations arranged and the accused summoned to York. In the course of these examinations, further names were added to the original list of offenders, and they too were dealt with by the High Commission.[84] It did not take long to deal with the affair, and on 26 December 1637, Neile was able to write to Bridgeman that the guilty parties had all been tried, fined and ordered to make public confession of their crimes.[85] Calvin Bruen was fined £500, Peter Ince and Richard Golborn £300 each, Peter Leigh £200, William Trafford £150 and Thomas Hunt £100. Although Pulford, the painter, was not fined, his portraits of Prynne were publicly burnt.

So far as the authorities were concerned, the Prynne affair had been successfully dealt with. Such firm treatment of puritans was,

81 Bridgeman to Neile, 20 August 1637 and 20 November 1637. Letters printed in *Cheshire Sheaf* Old Series Vol. 3 (1883) pp. 9, 32. The whole episode is described in Canon Blomfield, 'Puritanism in Chester in 1637', *Chester Archaeological Journal* Old Series Vol. 3 (Chester, 1885).

82 Bradford MSS. Weston Park, Salop, 9/8. Neile to Bridgeman, 5 December 1637.

83 *Cheshire Sheaf* Old Series Vol. 3 (1883) p. 9. A telling comment, this, on the weakness of ecclesiastical authority.

84 These were Peter Leigh, Thomas Hunt, William Trafford and Richard Golborn.

85 Bradford MSS. 18/2. Neile to Bridgeman, 26 November 1637. A copy of Bruen's confession is in the Harleian MSS. (B.M., 165, f. 22). In 1640, Bruen complained to the House of Commons about the treatment he had received at the hands of the High Commission (*ibid*. f. 21).

however, as has been shown, by no means universal. In 1633, Neile had aimed to undermine the hold of puritanism in the diocese of Chester and to bring official policy in the region belatedly in line with that in the southern province. But to be successful, the archbishop's efforts presupposed an existing system of effective church discipline. This, however, was quite clearly lacking, and in consequence the actual achievements of Neile's great metropolitan visitation were less than his many and far-reaching intentions. The fact that he never secured the full and willing cooperation of Bishop Bridgeman must be counted as a reason for this. But equally important, as Neile himself realized, was the opposition he encountered from churchwardens. He had no illusions about the fact that it was 'in a manner impossible for the Bishop to know how the publick service is performed in every church and chappell of his Dioces. The Bishop can but enquire by the othes of churchwardens and sidesmen who make no conscience of dispensing with their othe, and can hardly be brought to present anythinge, be things never so farr out of order.'[86] Neile was convinced that puritans abounded in the diocese of Chester, but his commissioners 'could not gett the churchwardens to present any; and till some of these wilfull churchwardens be exemplarily punished,' they concluded, 'the rest will never take care to discharge their duties, their othes. We threatened them much but they are moved at nothing.'[87]

It was upon churchwardens that the enforcement of church discipline ultimately depended. As the representatives of the parish, they were responsible for the provision of the surplice and they were required to equip themselves with the bishop's or archbishop's visitation articles. Visitation presentments could, of course, come from other quarters—from private informers and from the bishop's or archbishop's apparitors—but none the less the churchwarden was the most usual source of presentment. If churchwardens were sympathetic towards or actively involved in puritanism, then puritanism was naturally more difficult to detect at parochial level.

The puritan sympathies of churchwardens in the diocese of Chester, however, had been observed long before the 1630s. At

86 P.R.O. *S.P.D.* S.P. 16/259/78.
87 Bradford MSS. Weston Park, Salop, 9/8. Visitation report, f. 4.

Rochdale, for example, the churchwardens were asked in 1595 whether their puritan vicar Richard Midgley 'signed children in baptism with the sign of the cross or not; the churchwardens and swornmen say they know not.'[88] Undoubtedly their reply was based on more than mere ignorance!

The churchwardens of Manchester, too, accurately reflected the town's religious sympathies. In 1622, the three wardens were charged for refusing to present those laymen who failed to kneel at the communion.[89] Their act of defiance, however, did not go unnoticed, for Archbishop Abbot complained about these wardens in the same year: 'I have received advertisement that in the church of Manchester, which should be a president of virtue and obedience to the whole country, there are many disorders concerning ecclesiastical affairs, and I am let to understand that a great reason wherof is because the churchwardens who do have the care of that place are such as are contented to wink at disorders and do never present them to the Bishop of the diocese. I marvel how these persons can dispense with the oath which they do take wherby it behoveth them to take notice of such inconformities to the canons and orders of the church and so to seek to redress them. I know his Majesty will be much offended when he shall hear therof. And it shall be no pleasure for those which transgress this way to be called up hither to be censured by the High Commission for their misdemeanour.'[90]

At Runcorn, the puritan incumbent, Hugh Burrows, and his curate enjoyed the support of their churchwardens in 1633. Churchwardens, however, were elected annually, and in the previous year Burrows and his assistant had been struggling against opposition from the parish officers. Accordingly, when the time of the metropolitan visitation came round, Burrows desperately tried to prevent the former, anti-puritan wardens from making a presentment against him. The attempt was unsuccessful: a full charge was made by them against Burrows and his curate, and the vicar was sternly reproved 'for his note of citation he sent up to forbyd the old churchwardens not to come to the visitacon, for they knew they would present them'. And the two new,

88 Y.B.I.H.R. (1595) vis R.V.I.A. 14, f. 22v.
89 C.C.D.R.O. (1622) vis. E.D.V. 1/24, f. 129v.
90 Quoted in F. R. Raines and C. W. Sutton, eds., 'Life of Humphrey Chetham' *Chetham Society*, New Series Vol. 49 (1903) p. 37.

27

pro-puritan wardens were themselves charged 'they being addicted to Puritanisme. They presented not any sitters at the communion, nor anything worth presenting.'[91]

Churchwardens such as these were hardly likely to cooperate with any policy—episcopal or archiepiscopal—which attacked puritanism. But even if from a religious point of view the churchwardens of a parish were reliable, they still lacked sufficient authority and respect to be effective agents of ecclesiastical government.

Cases concerning the difficulties experienced by churchwardens in exercising ecclesiastical jurisdiction regularly occur in the church records—so regularly that one suspects that some historians have tended to exaggerate both their prestige and efficiency.[92] For example, at Mobberley, Cheshire, in the visitation of 1601, one Humphrey Paulden was presented 'for abusing the churchwardens in the church'.[93] While at Leigh in Lancashire in 1604, George Higson was charged with 'brawlinge with John Lunt, churchwarden, at the church dore', and Robert Haughton was said to have 'used undecent speeches to the churchwarden at service tyme'.[94] At Mobberley again in 1605, Richard Leigh was presented for having 'abused the churchwardens in the church and rayled against William Hardy one of the churchwardens in marketts and publique places'.[95] In the 1630 visitation, a presentment was made from Poulton parish in Lancashire which concerned John Fisher, who having been reproved by the wardens for irreverence in church, 'gave them evill words, using also scornful gestures towards them saying he would talke in despight of them and what had they to do with it'.[96] Finally, it may be noted that at the Quarter Sessions in 1632 a case was heard which involved

91 B.R.I.H.R. (1630) vis. *R.V.I.A.* 22, f. 162. During Laud's visitation of Salisbury diocese in 1634, it was noted that 'there is still a puritane and an honest man chosen churchwardens together (and that) the puritane always crosses the other . . . in the presentment of unconformityes. . . .' *Wiltshire Notes and Queries* Vol. I (1893) p. 75, partly quoted in Hill, *op. cit.* p. 23.

92 See, for instance, 'The Churchwardens and the Parish' in W. Notestein, *The English People on the Eve of Colonisation, 1603–1630* (New York, 1954). Peter Laslett, *The World We Have Lost* (1965) p. 27, takes a completely opposite view.

93 C.C.D.R.O. (1601) vis. E.D.V. 1/12a, f. 92.

94 C.C.D.R.O. (1604) vis. E.D.V. 1/13, f. 92v.

95 C.C.D.R.O. (1605) vis. E.D.V. 1/14, f. 82v.

96 Y.B.I.H.R. (1630) vis. *R.V.I.A.* 22, f. 44.

a man who had assaulted a churchwarden in the church at Guilden Sutton, Cheshire.[97]

Although in the nature of things, the conscientious church-warden was no doubt always likely to arouse opposition and hostility, it is tempting to speculate whether the disrespect in which wardens seem often to have been held may have been partly due to the fact that they themselves lacked social standing. Sir Thomas Smith in *The Commonwealth of England*, it may be noted, says of 'the fourth sort of men who do not rule' that 'they are commonly made churchwardens. . . .'[98] Smith's view is supported by the fact that at Barnard Castle in 1587 one of the wardens was a husbandman who was apparently unable to write.[99] The churchwarden's office, as its duties became more onerous, seems to have become correspondingly more unpopular among those eligible to hold it, and it may be that the 'electors' were obliged, or preferred, to choose wardens who were socially not of the best in the village community. Refusals to take office when once elected churchwarden are fairly common in the records.

The responsibility for choosing churchwardens usually lay jointly with incumbent and congregation, although this function of the Easter parish meeting at which the election took place had by the seventeenth century occasionally fallen into the hands of a select vestry.[100] Sometimes churchwardens were chosen not as the result of an 'election' at all. It was deponed in 1611, for example, that at Lawton in Cheshire 'it hath beene a custome . . . that two men were yearely chosen churchwardens of Lawton accordinge as their turne did falle oute by the house rowe.'[101]

The rank or occupational status of churchwardens, unfortunately, are rarely given in the records—but even bearing this in mind, it still seems to have been quite exceptional for a gentleman

---

97 C.C.D.R.O. Quarter Sessions Records. Q.S.F. 1632, 3/37.
98 Quoted in Laslett, *op. cit.* pp. 30–1. Smith's group, however, did not include the lowest sections of society, those classified by Gregory King as 'labouring people' and 'cottagers and paupers'.
99 E. Trotter, *Seventeenth-Century Life in the Country Parish* (Cambridge, 1919) p. 32. But his fellow warden was in fact a labourer.
100 J. C. Cox, *Churchwardens' Accounts* (1913) p. 14; Trotter, *op. cit.* p. 18. For details of the operation of one select vestry, see R. Cunliffe Shaw, ed., *Records of the Thirty Men of the Parish of Kirkham* (Kendal, 1930).
101 C.C.D.R.O. Consistory Court Papers E.D.C. 5, 1611, Miscellaneous. It was by an arrangement of this kind that a woman became a church-warden at Moreton-in-Marsh in 1635. Hill, *op. cit.* p. 428. Other examples of women being elected wardens are given in Cox, *op. cit.* p. 17.

to undertake the office. At Wigan in 1618 the churchwardens were Robert Markland and John Wakefield, a shoemaker and panner respectively,[102] and in Liverpool in 1642 Edward Ryle, a sadler, is known to have been one of the wardens.[103]

Churchwardens, then, being either 'addicted to puritanism' themselves, or else simply incapable—for whatever reason—of enforcing the orders of the church, severely compromised the effectiveness of ecclesiastical government. The weakness of church discipline in the diocese of Chester, in fact, was everywhere apparent, and was certainly no new phenomenon in 1633.[104] In the 1580s, as noted earlier in this essay, Giles Wigginton of Sedbergh ignored his suspension and continued to preach, either in his home or in the churchyard.[105] Similarly in 1636, Joseph Smithson, a non-wearer of the surplice in his ministry at White-gate, Cheshire: 'being cyted by a citacion under the seale of our office to appeare before us at a day and place therein assigned did irreverently scorne and scoffe at the said processe and called it an Hue and Crie, and did laugh at it to the manifest contempt of our Authority and the Jurisdiction.'[106]

Nor was it only the puritan clergy who defied the ecclesiastical authorities. Puritan laymen, too, were quite capable of behaving in a similar manner—a fact which can be well illustrated by the case of Thomas Constable. Constable, a wheelwright, had been charged at Acton, Cheshire, in the 1625 visitation for determinedly refusing to kneel at the receiving of the communion. He proclaimed on this occasion that he would ' "never kneele at the communion whilest I live and yf I bee torne in peaces with horses". This he spake publiquelie in courte.'[107]

Constable meant what he said. Sixteen years later, this resolute

---

102 G.V.O. Bridgeman, 'History of the Church and Manor of Wigan' Vol. 2, *Chetham Society*, New Series Vol. 16 (1888) p. 233.

103 G. Chandler, *Liverpool under James I* (Liverpool, 1960) p. 95.

104 Interesting for comparative purposes are the chapter on 'The Rusty Sword of the Church' in Hill, *op. cit.* pp. 354–81, and for a specific aspect of the question, F. D. Price, 'The Abuses of Excommunication and the decline of ecclesiastical discipline', *English Historical Review* Vol. LVII (1942). As a local illustration of the declining fear of the spiritual penalties of the church, it can be noted that at Bowdon, Cheshire, in 1619 there were twelve excommunicated persons who 'seeke not to be absolved'. C.C.D.R.O. (1619) vis. E.D.V. 1/22, f. 48.

105 *Seconde Parte of a Register* p. 248.

106 C.C.D.R.O. Consistory Court Papers, E.D.C. 5 (1636) Miscellaneous.

107 C.C.D.R.O. (1625) vis. E.D.V. 1/26, f. 40v.

nonconformist was still defying the authorities. By this time he had removed to Winwick in Lancashire, and it was witnesses from that parish who deponed in 1641 that they had heard him 'utter and give out speeches . . . that he did not value or care for any presentment that could bee made against him by any of the churchwardens or sworne men, for that for space of twentie yeares past hee had stood in the chancellor's teeth in defyance of his Authoritie, and that for all the Bishopps they are as they have proved themselves, the very scum of our countrie.' The other deponents made known that Constable had also declared that 'the Bishopps are an accursed herarkye [and] that he careth not for a binding to the good behaviour no more than grasse or docks which he puld from the grownd and spurnd itt with his foote. . . .'[108]

Some indication has been given in the present essay of the contrasts in the regional history of puritanism in England in the period before the civil war. These variations and contrasts existed not so much in the field of puritan ideas: the puritan clergymen— the main retailers of religious beliefs and practices—shared to a considerable extent a common educational background at the universities.[109] The differences between regions—especially between north and south—consisted principally in the chronology of the development of puritanism, in the impact it made not only within but outside the area in question, and in the attitude of the authorities towards its growth. So far as the chronology is concerned, in the diocese of Chester the reformed religion took hold later than in the south, and when the 'real' as opposed to the statutory Reformation came it was in the form of puritanism.[110] In the last analysis, however, the puritanism of this region was primarily local in character although it was not—and could not

---

108 Lancashire Record Office, Preston, Quarter Sessions Records Q.S.B. 1/246/30 (1641).
109 'Clerical puritanism, as a cohesive national movement, was created in the universities. It was here that the various regional and social origins of the Elizabethan preachers were submerged in a common brotherhood.' Collinson, op. cit. p. 127.
110 Attention is drawn to earlier differences between the religious situation in Lancashire and elsewhere in C. Haigh, 'The Last Days of the Lancashire Monastries and the Pilgrimage of Grace' Chetham Society, Third Series Vol. 17 (1969).

have been—entirely self-contained physically and intellectually. And for this state of affairs, the limited character and scope of patronage within the diocese was chiefly responsible: it was through effective patronage that the puritan divine could achieve national importance. But the puritan patrons in this diocese were only local figures themselves and could exert little outside influence. So although about a sixth of the puritan preachers of the diocese of Chester got into print, very few of their names occupy a central place in the history of English puritanism.

This essay has particularly emphasized some of the very real regional variations in the attitude of the authorities to the growth and consolidation of puritanism. It has been shown here that in Elizabeth's reign, official support and encouragement was extended to puritanism in the diocese of Chester—thus providing an atmosphere conducive to its growth. This encouragement came not only from sympathetic bishops of Chester but also from the privy council. Puritanism, they were all convinced, was the only possible counter which could effectively be used against Catholicism. Only in 1590 was a general, but short-lived, attempt made to reverse this policy.

But for related reasons the official attitude to both puritans and Catholics in this region began to change in the seventeenth century. Bishop Morton, during his brief episcopate, made some attempt to weaken the hold of nonconformity in the diocese of Chester, and so also did James I and Charles I by their *Declarations of Sports*. But John Bridgeman, who succeeded Morton in 1619, was as moderate as Bishop Chaderton had been in the previous century. As in 1590, it was only determined outside intervention—this time from Archbishop Neile of York in 1633—that brought puritanism in the diocese really under attack.

It has been shown, however, that even when the attack came the results fell short of intentions. Although the official attitude to puritanism had changed and had hardened by the 1630s, much of the machinery for enforcing church discipline was as inefficient, unworkable and aweless as ever. In any case, the growth of puritanism in the diocese of Chester had been unobstructed for far too long for a relatively sudden reversal of policy to uproot it successfully.

There are, therefore, significant regional variations in the chronology of the development of puritanism, in the impact it made locally and nationally, and in the attitude of the authorities towards its growth. It is surely difficult to speak meaningfully—except perhaps, in an ideological sense—of a single, monolithic and national 'Puritan Movement', even at any given moment in time. 'Puritan Movement', on the whole, is probably best regarded merely as a convenient generic term, for in practice puritanism was expressed differently, evolved in different ways and at different speeds, and indeed meant something different to different people in different areas and circumstances and in different periods. The civil war faithfully mirrored these as well as other peculiarities in its regional settings.

2

The Aristocracy and the Downfall of Charles I

Brian Manning

Preface

In 1640 Charles I was almost powerless. The Scots had rebelled against his attempt to impose a new form of church service upon them, and against episcopacy, and he had tried and failed to restore his authority in Scotland by force of arms. The army which he had raised to invade Scotland had been defeated in a trivial skirmish and the Scots had invaded England and occupied Newcastle upon Tyne. The king was forced to conclude a truce with the Scots and to summon a parliament in England. There were thus two armies in England: the Scots army in Northumberland and Durham, the English army in Yorkshire, and both were paid by the English parliament. So the king could not dissolve the parliament and had to consent to its demands, for if payments to the armies ceased, the English army would mutiny and the Scots would continue their advance southwards.

By the time the Long Parliament met in November 1640 a great many complaints and grievances had accumulated in many different sections of English society against the government of Charles I in both church and state. Perhaps the fatal weakness of the king's position was that he had antagonized so many of the English nobility. The opposition to the king was not confined to the peers who lived in the country and did not hold court or government offices, for many peers who did hold places at court and in the government were critical of the king's policies. The aristocracy still dominated politics, and the politics of the aristocracy were concerned with the struggle for place and power, but they recognized in 1640 that popular discontents were so widespread and so strong that changes of the king's advisers would not be sufficient without changes of the king's policies and reforms in church and state. In 1640 the aim of the aristocrats, of court and country, was to take over the power which fell from the hands of the king's two great ministers Strafford and Laud, to oblige the king to govern in future with and through his nobles, and to redress their own grievances and such of those of other sections of the community as did not conflict with the interests of the nobility. But, of course, the aristocrats fell out among themselves, since there were not enough places to satisfy all of them, nor could they all take power. The king's stratagems in this crisis not only failed to unite the aristocracy behind the crown but positively drove sections of it towards rebellion.

BRIAN MANNING

36

CHARLES I increased rather than reduced the cost of the court,[1] and the burden of paying for this expensive establishment fell more heavily on the lesser gentry and the richer peasants and the tradesmen than on the aristocracy and the greater gentry.[2] Nevertheless, the latter had grievances of their own against the Personal Government of Charles I: '. . . All the rich families of England, of noblemen and gentlemen, were exceedingly incensed' by the intensification of the exactions of the Court of Wards under the administration of Lord Cottington, which made them 'even indevoted to the Crown, looking upon what the law had intended for their protection and preservation to be now applied to their destruction. . . .'[3] But, above all, the fines for encroachments on the royal forests 'brought more prejudice upon the court, and more discontent upon the King, from the most considerable part of the nobility and gentry in England, than any one action that had its rise from the King's will and pleasure. . . .'[4] However, it was rather the style of government in the 1630s than specific grievances that offended an aristocracy which had become hypersensitive to slights and threats to its rights and privileges and social superiority. 'There were very few persons of quality who had not suffered or been perplexed by the weight or fear' of the 'censures and judgements' of the Court of Star Chamber.[5] Worse than that, 'persons of honour and great quality . . . were every day cited into the High Commission Court, upon the fame of their incontinence, or other scandal in their lives, and were there prosecuted to their shame and punishment . . . (which they called an insolent triumph upon

1 F. C. Dietz, *English Public Finance 1558–1641* (reprinted, London, 1964) pp. 100–8, 398–424; Menna Prestwich, *Cranfield: Politics and Profits under the Early Stuarts* (Oxford, 1966) p. 211.
2 *Considerations Touching Trade* (1641) pp. 11–14; [William Prynne], *An Humble Remonstrance to His Majesty, Against the Tax of Shipmoney* (1641) p. 23; M. D. Gordon, 'The Collection of Ship-Money in the reign of Charles I', *Transactions of the Royal Historical Society* Third Series Vol. IV (1910) pp. 146–50; Lawrence Stone, *The Crisis of the Aristocracy* (Oxford, 1965) pp. 496–9.
3 Edward, Earl of Clarendon, *History of the Rebellion* ed. W. D. Macray (6 vols., Oxford, 1888) Vol. I, p. 199; Vol. V, p. 288; Prestwich, *op. cit.* pp. 240–1.
4 Clarendon, *History* Vol. II, pp. 14–18; Stone, *op. cit.* p. 499.
5 Clarendon, *History* Vol. I, p. 374.

their degree and quality, and levelling them with the common people). . . .'[6]

The king's two chief ministers in the 1630s did nothing to conciliate the aristocracy in court or country. Wentworth (who was made Earl of Strafford in 1640) combined 'too elate and arrogant' a nature with too rapid a rise to power, which 'made him more transported with disdain of other men, and more contemning the forms of business' than was tactful. He 'too much neglected' the opinions of other ministers and he engaged 'too often, and against too many' great men; even Laud warned him to be careful of 'being over-full of personal prosecutions against men of quality'. His 'sour and haughty temper' led him to expect 'to have more observance paid to him, than he was willing to pay to others, though they were of his own quality; and then he was not like to conciliate the good will of men of the lesser station'. He was 'a man of too high and severe a deportment, and too great a contemner of ceremony, to have many friends at Court . . .'. 'It was a great infirmity in him, that he seemed to overlook so many, as he did; since everywhere, much more in court, the numerous or lesser sort of attendants can obstruct, create jealousies, spread ill reports, and do harm: for as 'tis impossible, that any power or deportment should satisfy all persons: so there a little friendliness and openness of carriage begets hope, and lessens envy.'[7]

Laud 'was a man . . . of too warm blood and too positive a nature towards asserting what he believed a truth, to be a good courtier; and his education fitted him as little for it, as his nature; which having been most in the university . . . gave him wrong than right measure of a Court.' He had 'usually about him an uncourtly quickness, if not sharpness, and did not sufficiently value what men said or thought of him. . . .' 'He could not debate anything without some commotion when the argument was not of moment nor bear contradiction in debate, even in the Council where all men are equally free, with that patience and temper that was necessary. . . .' While he insisted on being treated with respect himself, and kept a 'state and distance . . . with men' that 'he

6 Clarendon, *History* Vol. I, p. 125; Christopher Hill, *Society and Puritanism in Pre-Revolutionary England* (London, 1964) pp. 349, 353.

7 Clarendon, *History* Vol. I, pp. 197, 341–2; Sir Philip Warwick, *Memoires of the reigne of King Charles I* (London, 1701) pp. 109–17; W. Knowler (ed.), *The Earl of Strafforde's Letters and Dispatches* (2 vols., London, 1739) Vol. I, p. 479.

thought . . . not more than was suitable to the place and degree he held in the church and state', he would not treat others with their due respect. He 'did court persons too little' and was unceremoniously short with 'those persons, who thought their quality, though not their business, required a patient and respectful entertainment'. Edward Hyde tried to give him a friendly warning of the danger of speaking sharply and ungraciously to 'persons of the best condition': 'that this kind of behaviour of his was the discourse of all companies of persons of quality.' He advised him 'that he would more reserve his passion towards all persons, how faulty soever; and that he would treat persons of honour and quality, and interest in their county, with more courtesy, and condescension. . . .'[8] An arrogance that might be more excusable in a gentleman like Wentworth was less excusable in a plebeian like Laud: 'a man of mean birth, bred up in a college,' Viscount Saye called him; 'a fellow of mean extraction and arrogant pride,' wrote Mrs Hutchinson.[9]

Laud tried to uphold the authority and defend the wealth of the church by encouraging the clergy to be less subservient to the nobility and gentry. This was seen by the Long Parliament as incitement 'of ministers to despise the temporal magistracy, the nobles and gentry of the land'.[10] When the Earl of Portland died in 1635 and the Lord Treasurership became vacant—which 'is the greatest office of benefit in the kingdom, and the chief in precedence next the archbishop and the Great Seal'—'the eyes of all men were at gaze who should have this great office; and the greatest of the nobility who were in the chiefest employments looked upon it as the prize of one of them, such offices commonly making way for more removes and preferments.' But Laud secured the appointment of Juxon, the Bishop of London, 'a man so unknown that his name was scarce heard of in the kingdom,

8 Clarendon, *History* Vol. I, pp. 120–32, 196; *The Life of Edward Earl of Clarendon* (Oxford, 1759) pp. 32–3; Warwick, *op. cit.* pp. 78–82; Bulstrode Whitelock, *Memorials of the English Affairs* (4 vols., Oxford, 1853) Vol. I, p. 99.
9 *Two Speeches of the Right Honorable William, Lord Viscount Say and Seale* (1641) B.M. E. 198(16); Lucy Hutchinson, *Memoirs of the Life of Colonel Hutchinson* ed. J. Hutchinson and revised C. H. Firth (London, 1906) p. 71.
10 S. R. Gardiner (ed.) *The Constitutional Documents of the Puritan Revolution* (3rd edn. revised, Oxford, 1947) p. 138; Clarendon, *History* Vol. I, p. 130; Christopher Hill, *Economic Problems of the Church from Archbishop Whitgift to the Long Parliament* (Oxford, 1956) pp. 220–3.

who had been within two years before but a private chaplain to the king and the president of a poor college in Oxford.' Laud rejoiced at this coup, thinking he had secured the church: 'And now if the church will not hold up themselves under God, I can do no more'; but it 'inflamed more men than were angry before . . .' who now looked on the church 'as the gulf ready to swallow all the great offices' that rightfully belonged to the nobility.[11]

The peers were obsessed with the need to preserve respect for their order. The Earl of Arundel affected the antique dress of the time when the nobles 'had been most venerable'. 'He was a great master of order and ceremony, and knew and kept greater distance towards his sovereign than any person I ever observed,' wrote his secretary, 'and expected no less from his inferiors. . . .' 'He was a person of great and universal civility, but yet with that restriction as that it forbade any to be bold or saucy with him. . . . He was not popular at all, nor cared for it, as loving better by a just hand than flattery to let the common people to know their distance and due observance.'[12] The Earl of Northumberland 'was the proudest man alive' and 'was in all his deportment a very great man, and that which looked like formality was a punctuality in preserving his dignity from the invasion and intrusion of bold men, which no man of that age so well preserved himself from.'[13] The Earl of Clare 'was of a most courteous and affable disposition, yet preserved exactly the grandeur and distance of his quality.'[14] The Earl of Southampton 'had a great spirit, and exacted the respect that was due to his quality. . . .'[15] The Earl of Essex, though unlike the Earl of Arundel he 'too immoderately and importunately' affected popularity, yet he 'set as great a price upon nobility as any man living did . . .';[16] and 'no man valued himself more upon his title' than the puritan Lord Saye.[17] Sir John Suckling 'did not much care for a lord's converse', Davenant

11 Clarendon, *History* Vol. I, pp. 131–2.
12 Sir Edward Walker, *Historical Discourses* (London, 1705) pp. 221–3; Clarendon, *History* Vol. I, pp. 69–71.
13 Clarendon, *History* Vol. II, pp. 537–9; Vol. III, p. 495.
14 Gervase Holles, 'Memorials of the Holles Family', *Camden Society* Third Series Vol. LV (1937) p. 113.
15 Clarendon, *History* Vol. II, pp. 529–31.
16 *ibid.* Vol. III, p. 224; *The Life of Edward Earl of Clarendon* (The Continuation) p. 412.
17 Clarendon, *History* Vol. II, pp. 547–8.

recalled after the Restoration, 'for they were in those days damnably proud and arrogant. . . .'[18] The Earl of Arundel regarded his function as Earl Marshal as being to support 'ancient nobility and gentry, and to interpose on their behalfs' and to keep the common people in their proper place. A waterman pressing a citizen of London for a fare, showed his badge, which was a swan, the crest of an earl whose servant he was; and the citizen, thinking the fare excessive, said 'Begone with thy Goose', and was fined and imprisoned by the Earl Marshal's court for insulting the crest of an earl. A tailor, trying to get a gentleman to pay his bill and being called a 'base fellow' for his pains, answered 'that he was as good a man as the other', but was forced by the Marshal's court to pay damages to the gentleman for the insult. Hyde thought that the Marshal's court was one of the greatest grievances of the people in 1640.[19]

The unpopularity of the war with Scotland in 1640 gave the aristocracy the opportunity to assert itself in more popular ways. On 31 August 1640 Secretary of State Windebank wrote from London to the king, who was with his army in Yorkshire, to report 'the resort hither to this town of some lords, and other persons of quality, who have been observed not to be very well contented with the time: namely, the Earls of Essex, Warwick and Bedford, the Lords Saye, Russell and Brooke, Pym and Hampden. These have had their meetings . . .', and Windebank heard that they intended 'to join in a petition to your Majesty' and he feared some dangerous practice or intelligence with the 'rebels of Scotland'. The privy council sent the Earl of Arundel to try to persuade the Earl of Bedford to return to the country; but they were more worried about the Earl of Essex and they advised the king to write 'with your own hand' a 'most obliging' letter to Essex, calling him to York and offering to employ him in the army. Windebank stressed that this advice 'is of extraordinary consequence to your Majesty's present affairs; and therefore I most humbly beseech your Majesty to take it to heart. . . . If this lord were taken off, the knot would be much weakened, if not dissolved. And besides that it will be of great importance to sever him from that ill-affected company; he is a popular man, and it

18 John Aubrey, *Brief Lives* ed. A. Clark (2 vols., Oxford, 1898) Vol. II, pp. 240-5.
19 Walker, *op. cit.* pp. 222-3; *The Life of Edward Earl of Clarendon* pp. 37, 39.

will give extraordinary satisfaction to all sorts of people to see him in employment again.' So important did the privy council think this advice that they asked Henry Percy, the courtier brother of the Earl of Northumberland, to persuade the queen to support it. Percy reported back to Windebank: 'I thought time very important in this matter, therefore I waited on her Majesty this night, and according to their instructions represented those reasons to her that might conduce most to make her a party in this design, which she apprehended so rightly that she instantly wrote as one much concerned and gave them many thanks for preparing this which she believes will prove much for his Majesty's service.'[20] The factions of the Earl of Bedford and the Earl of Warwick were the core of the aristocratic opposition to the king in the country;[21] but Essex, as the privy council recognized, was more formidable. As the son of Queen Elizabeth's fallen favourite, the great Earl of Essex who was executed as a traitor in 1601, he was heir both to a following and to a popular legend of heroism, royal injustice and martyrdom. He was both the champion of the rights of the nobility and the champion of the rights of the people. He was both 'the darling of the swordmen' and 'the most popular man of the kingdom'.[22] He was connected with the discontented country magnates—his ally the Earl of Southampton, his cousin the Earl of Warwick—and with the discontented court lords—his cousins the Earl of Northumberland, the Earl of Holland, the Earl of Newport. He was the link between Country opposition and Court opposition, and between aristocratic opposition and popular opposition; he stood between the Court and the Country and held the balance between them.[23] But the king feared and disliked him; he was unmoved by the pleas of his wife and his councillors and replied that he had already asked Essex to come to him, and would write again, but he would not employ him.[24]

20 *State Papers Collected by Edward, Earl of Clarendon* (2 vols., Oxford, 1767–1773) Vol. II, pp. 94–5; *C.S.P.D. 1640* pp. 652, 653.
21 A. P. Newton, *The Colonising Activities of the English Puritans* (London, 1914); J. H. Hexter, *The Reign of King Pym* (London, 1941) Ch. IV.
22 V. F. Snow, 'Essex and the Aristocratic Opposition to the Early Stuarts', *Journal of Modern History* Vol. XXXII (1960); Clarendon, *History* Vol. I, p. 150.
23 *The Life of Edward Earl of Clarendon* (The Continuation) pp. 412–13; Francis Peck, *Desiderata Curiosa* (London, 1735) Vol. II, Bk. xii. pp. 13–16.
24 *State Papers Collected by Edward, Earl of Clarendon* Vol. II, pp. 95, 96, 99.

On 28 August the country lords drew up a petition to the king, which was signed by the Earls of Essex, Hertford, Bedford, Warwick, Exeter and Rutland, and by the Lords Saye, Brooke, Mandeville, Mulgrave, Bolingbroke and Howard of Escrick. They complained of innovations in religion, the increase of popery, shipmoney, monopolies, the long intermission of parliaments and the precipitate dissolution of the Short Parliament. They demanded the summoning of a parliament to remove these grievances, to punish the authors of them, and to make peace with the Scots.[25] Lord Mandeville and Lord Howard took the petition to the king at York; the Earl of Bedford and the Earl of Hertford went to the privy council in London and asked 'the Lords to join with them in it'. Every day more nobles were arriving in London to give their support to the petition.[26] The privy councillors considered advising the king to appoint 'some of the country nobility' to the privy council, 'if it be but to engage them'.[27] But the situation was becoming too urgent and the movement among the nobility too widespread to be dealt with in this manner. So when the council met on 2 September the Earl of Manchester, the Lord Privy Seal, put forward a proposal to advise the king to summon a Great Council of all the peers. The Earl of Berkshire objected that such an assembly would do no more than demand a parliament. Lord Newburgh and Sir Thomas Roe thought that the only solution to the crisis was to call a parliament, but that if it were thought that an immediate assembling of the peers would have some good effects, then they should advise the king to summon a parliament and in the meantime to hold a Great Council of the peers. The Earl of Dorset objected that it would take just as long to assemble the peers as to call a parliament. Manchester replied that he was 'wholly averse from advising a parliament, and wholly for calling the peers, the council of the kingdom, consiliarii nati; Edward III called his great council upon a like occasion; they raised great sums of money without a parliament, and assisted the king. The kingdom will follow the peers.' Lord Cottington was also against advising the king to summon a parliament, and he supported

25 *C.S.P.D. 1640* pp. 639–41.
26 *State Papers Collected by Edward, Earl of Clarendon* Vol. II, pp. 110–112; *C.S.P.D. 1640–1641* pp. 15, 23, 79.
27 *C.S.P.D. 1640* p. 634; *C.S.P.D. 1640–1641* p. 2.

Manchester's proposal, but on the grounds that if the peers
declared for a parliament, it would be more acceptable to the king
as the request of the whole of the nobility than as the advice
merely of the privy council. Dorset objected that the privy
councillors might do better to earn for themselves popular
approval by advising the king to call a parliament. Laud could
give no lead: he agreed with Manchester's proposal but recognized that such a Great Council could not be an alternative to a
parliament and would be bound to lead in the end to the summoning of a parliament, and he concluded that they should 'put
to the king, that we are at the wall, and that we are in the dark,
and have no grounds for a counsel.' But Sir Thomas Jermyn
supported Manchester's proposal on the grounds that it would
be a means to redress the grievances of the discontented lords
and to engage them against the Scots; and the Earl of Arundel
declared that a Great Council was 'the only way, the best and the
shortest way'. The privy council voted by a majority to advise
the king to summon a Great Council of the peers.[28]

Windebank forwarded this advice to the king with a covering
letter which is an interesting revelation of how the councillors
saw their constitutional position: they were only advisers to the
king, but the language of Windebank's letter does not conceal
that they were giving the king an ultimatum. 'Your Majesty will
please to understand that the proposition I have sent from the
Lords is only a mere humble advice of theirs . . .; it is the best
they could think upon for the present; that it is no way binding,
but that, if your Majesty dislike it, or shall in your wisdom advise
or command some other way, they will in all humility submit to
it, and lay it aside; that the ground and motive of it hath been the
uniting of your Majesty and your subjects together, the want
whereof the Lords conceive is the source of all the present
troubles; and they are confident, if your Majesty and your people
had been well together, the rebels durst not have thus insolently
affronted your Majesty and the nation; that in probability the
Lords being made sensible of your Majesty's and their own
danger, and participants of your counsels, will be won to lay
aside all private animosities and discontentments, and unani-
mously join to save the monarchy, and to repel the common
enemy by a present assistance; that the lords, thus gained, will in

28 *Hardwick State Papers* Vol. II, pp. 168–71; *C.S.P.D. 1640–1641* pp. 3, 8.

all likelihood train with them their friends and adherents and many of the people; besides the satisfaction that is conceived the people will receive by this calling of the lords to your counsels; that it is likely these lords, when they shall be called, and shall meet . . . will fall upon grievances, and the present calling of a parliament, which also are the pretences of the rebels. And the question is, whether your Majesty will not rather give the glory of redress of grievances, and of a parliament, to your own lords, or rather to yourself by their common advice, than to the rebels, if your power and force be inferior to theirs; that in outward appearance, considering the constitution of the city and the generality of the kingdom, without some such sweetening of the lords and people as this, it is to be doubted, if your Majesty should receive a blow . . . monies and forces will be raised very coldly and slowly; and without a voluntary assistance of both these, the kingdom must be in danger; for to force supplies of either in this conjuncture is not held practicable. . . .'[29] Thus the privy councillors saw the gravity of the crisis to lie in the discontent of the peers; they pointed out the dependence of the Crown upon the peers; and they spoke to the king as the representative of the peers. They told the king that he was beaten: the prospect of defeat at the hands of the Scots combined with mounting popular discontent at home meant that the king must reconcile the peers and follow their advice in dealing with his discontented subjects in Scotland and England.

The advice of the privy council reached the king just as he was considering what reply to make to the petition of the Twelve Peers for a parliament, and he seized upon the alternative and summoned a Great Council of the Peers to meet at York on 24 September.[30] On 7 September the privy council in London met the Earl of Bedford and the Earl of Hertford and informed them of the king's decision. The two earls approved of a Great Council, providing that it was not intended as an alternative to a parliament nor as a means of raising money without a parliament; but Windebank reported that 'the Earl of Bedford seemed not to like it so well as the Earl of Hertford; and I have heard since, he hath let fall discourses against it. . . .'[31] There was activity at

29 *State Papers Collected by Edward, Earl of Clarendon* Vol. II, pp. 97–8.
30 *C.S.P.D. 1640–1641* p. 15.
31 *State Papers Collected by Edward, Earl of Clarendon* Vol. II, pp. 111–12, 115.

court: Sir John Suckling and Henry Jermyn were urging the queen to advise her husband to summon a parliament; and when the Earl of Essex and the Earl of Hertford came to see her they were able to persuade her to support the demand for a parliament.[32] The action of the Twelve Peers had released a popular agitation. On 10 September three hundred citizens of London met and drew up a petition for a parliament, and obtained 10,000 signatures, including those of four aldermen; and the efforts of the privy council to get the Lord Mayor and aldermen to suppress or condemn this petition were unsuccessful.[33] It became obvious to the whole of the aristocracy, as it had been before to Bedford and his friends, that the lords themselves would be endangered by the popular discontent if concessions to the peers were not accompanied by concessions to the people as well. The Earl of Arundel changed his mind and Laud gave in: at the meeting of the privy council on 16 September Arundel moved that they advise the king to summon a parliament, he was seconded by Laud, and the rest of the councillors agreed.[34] When the peers assembled in the Great Council at York on 24 September the king announced that parliament would meet on 3 November.

With the meeting of the Long Parliament, and the fall of Strafford and Laud, the great aristocrats began to grasp at the power which had fallen from the hands of those two great ministers. The court magnates like Arundel, the Earl Marshal, and Northumberland, the Lord Admiral of the Navy and General of the Army, who held great offices but were critical of the government in the 1630s, seem to have expected this power to come to them. Arundel began to play a more dominant role in the government;[35] and Northumberland discussed with his sisters, the Countess of Carlisle and the Countess of Leicester, whether the Earl of Leicester should be Lord Deputy of Ireland or Lord Treasurer of England.[36] They do not seem at first to have expected to share their power with the country magnates,

32 Alfred Harbage, *Sir William Davenant* (London, 1935) pp. 84–5; *The History of England during the Reigns of the Royal House of Stuart* (London, 1730) p. 151.
33 *C.S.P.D. 1640–1641* pp. 40, 60, 67–8, 72, 73–4, 77, 79, 84, 90, 95; *State Papers Collected by Edward, Earl of Clarendon* Vol. II, pp. 116, 117, 123.
34 *C.S.P.D. 1640–1641* pp. 67–8.
35 *C.S.P. Venetian 1640–1642* p. 139.
36 *De L'Isle and Dudley Manuscripts* Vol. VI, H.M.C. (1966) pp. 340, 342–3, 346, 348.

who had not held offices in the 1630s. When rumours were heard, early in December 1640, that the Earl of Bedford would be Lord Treasurer, the Countess of Carlisle thought it could be 'neither true or possible without such a change as I dare not think of. They have disposed and changed all the officers of this kingdom. The king makes himself merry at it, though I believe there is not much cause for that. . . .'[37] But by the middle of January 1641 the story had become general, not only that Bedford would be Lord Treasurer, but that John Pym, Bedford's closest political adviser, would be Chancellor of the Exchequer; the Earl of Bristol would be Lord Privy Seal and his eldest son, Lord Digby (Bedford's son-in-law) would be Secretary of State, and the Earl of Essex Lord Deputy of Ireland.[38] By 14 January the Countess of Carlisle was persuaded that 'we shall have great change of officers, and contrary to what I thought that Bedford will be treasurer. . . .'[39] This pointed to a serious effort to come to terms with the parliamentary opposition. Sir John Temple wrote to the Earl of Leicester: '. . . I understand the king is brought into a dislike of those counsels that he hath formerly followed, and therefore resolves to steer another course. . . . And I do believe some ways are laid upon the bringing in of those men to make up an entire union between the king and his people, and so to moderate their demands as well as the height of that power which hath been lately used in the royal government.' This was connected with the two main aims of the king—to save the life of Strafford, who had been charged with treason by the House of Commons, and to preserve episcopal government of the church: on both these issues there were good prospects that the House of Lords would support the king, provided that he would take new ministers that they could trust and make some concessions to the complaints of lords and commoners against the bishops. Temple understood that 'His Majesty is well enough inclined to lessen' the power of the bishops, 'and take away the abuses introduced into the church by them', and 'to have them moulded into the ancient primitive way, and to see them reduced into the same state wherein they continued many hundred years after Christ . . . These preparatives make us now hope for a happy success of this parliament. . . .'[40]

37 *ibid.* p. 346.   38 *ibid.* pp. 366, 367-8; *C.S.P.D. 1640-1641* p. 439.
39 *De L'Isle and Dudley Manuscripts* Vol. VI, p. 361.   40 *ibid.* pp. 367-8.

The initiative in fact came from the queen, who opened 'a negotiation with some of the leading members of both Houses'.[41] The person with most influence over the queen was her Master of Horse, Henry Jermyn, who, as the Countess of Carlisle observed, was in her favour 'to a strange degree'.[42] His elder brother sat in the House of Commons, and his father, Sir Thomas Jermyn, was the Comptroller of the King's Household and the senior privy councillor in the Commons. According to Temple it was Henry Jermyn 'who hath powerfully moved in the bringing in those men . . . and is now so great with the King as he and the Queen are locked up alone with him many hours together. It is not unlikely, if our affairs settle, but that he may prove a great favourite. He hath laid a shrewd foundation, and, in my judgement, advances apace towards it, holding secret intelligence with the new officer that shall be made.'[43] The influence of Jermyn and the queen was reinforced by that of the Marquis of Hamilton, who, according to Clarendon, advised 'that, his Majesty having declared to his people that he really intended a reformation of all those extravagancies which former necessities, or occasions, or mistakes, had brought into the government of church or state, he could not give more lively and demonstrable evidence, and a more gracious instance, of such his intention, than by calling such persons to his Council whom the people generally thought most inclined to, and intent upon, such reformation. . . .'[44] Hamilton was Master of the Horse to the king, a Gentleman of the King's Bedchamber and a privy councillor. 'The King used him with so much tender kindness, that his carriage of him spoke more the affection of a friend than of the power of a master; he called him always James, both when he spoke to him and of him, as an expression of his familiarity with him; and . . . none had more of the king's heart than he possessed.' He accompanied 'the king in his hard chases of the stag, and in the toilsome pleasure of a racket. . . .' After the death of Buckingham he had been looked upon 'as the rising favourite' but in the 1630s, though 'he continued about his Majesty in the highest character of favour',

41 S. R. Gardiner, *History of England* (10 vols., London, 1899) Vol. IX, pp. 259–60.
42 *De L'Isle and Dudley Manuscripts* Vol. VI, pp. 204, 360.
43 *ibid.* p. 369.
44 Clarendon, *History* Vol. I, pp. 258–62, 279–82, 333–5; *De L'Isle and Dudley Manuscripts* Vol. VI, p. 367.

he did not use his position 'to engross things to himself nor his kindred' but restricted himself to procuring occasionally 'a particular kindness to his friends'; and 'he kept himself much out of business', and 'abstracted himself from public affairs . . . meddling no further than in giving general advices when called for. . . .' Though he was more 'a courtier than a statesman', he 'had a large proportion of his Majesty's favour and confidence, and knew very dexterously, how to manage both . . . and though he carried it very modestly and warily, yet he had a strong influence upon the greatest affairs at Court. . . .'[45] In 1638 the king had turned to him to manage his policy towards the Scottish rebels, and it may be that Hamilton was anxious to conciliate the opposition in England in order to divert from himself attack in parliament as the man, who with Laud, had been chiefly responsible for the king's disastrous policy towards Scotland.[46]

The alliance between Hamilton and the queen may have been forged by Sir Henry Vane, 'a busling subtil forward Courtier', who was both 'a creature of the Queen's' and Hamilton's 'great confidant'.[47] The queen and Hamilton had joined forces to secure the appointment of Vane as Secretary of State in February 1640, against the opposition of Strafford and in face of the efforts of the Percy–Sidney connection to get the place for the Earl of Leicester.[48] This appointment marked the growing ascendancy of the alliance of the queen and Hamilton, and it boded ill for Strafford, who was not 'in any degree acceptable to' the queen.[49] Her side of the court had always been the focal point of opposition to Strafford, and her friend the Earl of Holland was the leader of opposition to Strafford from inside the court. Holland had quarrelled bitterly with Strafford in 1638–9. Strafford had accused Sir Piers Crosby of slander and obtained the king's permission for Holland and Henry Jermyn, in whose presence the alleged offence had taken place, to be examined by the Court of Star Chamber, believing in fact that Holland was as guilty as Crosby. Holland objected to

45 Gilbert Burnet, *The Memoires of the Lives and Actions of James and William Dukes of Hamilton* (London, 1677) pp. 4, 25, 27, 38; Warwick, *op. cit.* pp. 102–9.
46 Clarendon, *History* Vol. I, pp. 200–2; Burnet, *op. cit.* p. 188.
47 Warwick, *op. cit.* pp. 107, 141; Burnet, *op. cit.* pp. 52, 173.
48 Clarendon, *History* Vol. I, pp. 165–6; David Mathew, *The Age of Charles I* (London, 1951) pp. 319–21.
49 Clarendon, *History* Vol. I, p. 217.

Strafford's discourtesy in not approaching him first before applying to the king, and that the questions that Strafford proposed to ask him were unfit for a peer and a privy councillor to answer. The Court of Star Chamber did rule that the questions were too general, but they did still examine Holland, but on a different set of interrogatories. Strafford complained to the king: 'I had much rather indeed it were to be tried betwixt the Earl of Holland and myself, which of us could or should furthest seek your Majesty's greatness and triumph amidst your enemies. . . . In all humility I beseech your Majesty I may have some right against this great lord, that seems to magnify himself in nothing more desirously, than in putting slights and casting aspersions upon me. . . .'[50] It is significant that Henry Jermyn, the queen's favourite, was involved in this quarrel between Holland and Strafford. Similarly, Strafford made a bitter enemy of Vane, not only by opposing his appointment as Secretary of State, but also, when he was created Earl of Strafford in January 1640, taking as a subsidiary title Baron of Raby, which was an estate belonging to the Vanes and a title to which they had aspired.[51] According to Clarendon, the queen was 'persuaded, by those who had most credit with her [no doubt Vane, Jermyn and Holland] to believe that by the removal of the great ministers her power and authority would be increased, and that the prevailing party would be willing to depend on her, and that, by gratifying the principal persons of them with such preferments as they affected, she would quickly reconcile all ill humours. . . .'[52] Vane was the key man, for he drew in not only Hamilton but also Northumberland who, under Vane's influence, in 1639 began to drift away from his earlier alliance with Strafford.[53] Vane was 'a confidant both of Marquis Hamilton's and of the Earl of Northumberland's'.[54] The efforts of Northumberland to get the place of Secretary of State for Leicester instead of Vane did not cause a breach, and the Countess of Carlisle told her sister, the Countess of Leicester, that

50 Knowler, *op. cit.* Vol. II, pp. 189, 230, 252–3, 258, 259, 276, 277, 282–4, 286, 307, 328, 341, 375, 378.
51 *De L'Isle and Dudley Manuscripts* Vol. VI, pp. 221, 224; Warwick, *op. cit.* pp. 141–2; Clarendon, *History* Vol. I, p. 197; Vol. II, pp. 548–9; Walker, *op. cit.* pp. 304–5.
52 Clarendon, *History* Vol. I, p. 217.
53 *De L'Isle and Dudley Manuscripts* Vol. VI, pp. 201, 204, 207–8.
54 Warwick, *op. cit.* p. 141.

Northumberland and Vane 'are much united and ever of one opinion', and that Strafford had failed to detach Northumberland from Vane.[55] Northumberland secured for Vane's son, Sir Henry Vane the younger, the place of Joint Treasurer of the Navy, and a seat for Hull in both the Short and Long Parliaments.[56] The Vanes were neighbours in Kent of the Earl and Countess of Leicester, and the Countess was said to take her political views from Sir Henry Vane the younger.[57] The elder Vane had influence with most of the great court magnates who were after the inheritance of Strafford and Laud. He 'had a great and a long interest in' the Earl of Arundel, and owed his own seat in parliament to the patronage of the Earl of Pembroke.[58] He was the essential intermediary in the aristocratic alliance against Strafford.

A number of courtiers on the queen's side, led by Henry Jermyn, were urging her to intervene actively in this crisis. One of these was Sir John Suckling, who 'was a dependant of the marquis of Hamilton and a follower of Sir Henry Vane the Elder',[59] and more particularly a friend of Henry Jermyn, to whom he addressed a letter 'in the beginning of Parliament' (published as a pamphlet in 1641), which reveals the views and aims of the queen's party. He pointed out that the king was 'in an eclipse' and that at this time it was almost impossible for him 'to have right counsel given to him': 'His party for the most part . . . have so much to do for their own preservation, that they cannot . . . intend another's. Those that have courage have not perchance innocence, and so dare not show themselves in the King's business; and if they have innocence, they want parts to make themselves considerable, and so consequently the things they undertake. Then in Court, they give as much counsel as they believe the King is inclined to. . . .' The critical problem was to reunite the king with his people and regain their love. 'Certainly the great interest of the King is a union with his people, and whosoever hath told him otherwise . . . was a seducer from the first. If there ever had been any one Prince in the world, that made

55 *De L'Isle and Dudley Manuscripts* Vol. VI, pp. 207–8.
56 *ibid.* p. 159; M. F. Keeler, *The Long Parliament* (Philadelphia, 1954) p. 371.
57 G. Brennan, *A History of the House of Percy* ed. W. A. Lindsay (2 vols., London, 1902) Vol. II, p. 243.
58 Warwick, *op. cit.* pp. 129–30; Keeler, *op. cit.* p. 72, 370.
59 David Mathew, *The Social Structure in Caroline England* (Oxford, 1948) p. 115, *n.* ii; Prestwich, *op. cit.* p. 548.

a felicity in this life, and left fair fame after death, without the love of his subjects, there were some colour to despise it. There was not among all our princes a greater courtier of the people than Richard the third; not so much out of fear as out of wisdom. And shall the worst of our Kings have striven for that, and shall not the best?' Suckling argued that in this situation the queen should supply the king's lack of good counsel and reunite him to his people. 'She is to consider with herself, whether such great virtues and eminent excellencies (though they be highly admired and valued by those that know her and are about her), ought to rest satisfied with so narrow a payment as the estimation of a few, and whether it be not more proper for a Queen so great to aim at universal honour and love than private esteem and value? Besides, how becoming a work for the sweetness and softness of her sex is composing of differences and uniting hearts: and how proper for a Queen, reconciling King and People.'[60] The same thoughts were expressed in verse by another of the queen's courtiers, William Davenant, in a poem which his friends Jermyn and Suckling presented to the queen:

> Madam; so much peculiar, and alone
> Are Kings, so uncompanion'd in a Throne:
> That through the want of some equality
> (Familiar Guides, who lead them to comply)
> They may offend by being so sublime;
> As if to be a King might be a crime;
> All less than Kings no more with Kings prevail. . . .
> To cure this high obnoxious singleness
> (Yet not to make their power but danger less)
> Were Queens ordain'd; who were in Monarch's breasts
> Tenants for life, not accidental guests;
> So they prevail by Nature, not by chance;
> But you (with yours) your virtue does advance;
> When you persuade him (in the People's cause)
> Not to esteem his Judges more than laws.
> In Kings (perhaps) extreme obdurateness
> Is as in Jewels hardness in excess;
> Which makes their price: for we as well call stones

---

60 *The Works of Sir John Suckling* ed. A. Hamilton Thompson (London, 1910) pp. 322-4.

For hardness as for brightness, Parragons
And 'tis perhaps so with obdurate Kings
As with impenitrable things.
No way to pierce or alter them is found,
Till we to Di'monds use a Diamond,
So you to him, who, to new-form his Crown,
Would bring no aids less precious than his own: . . .
Whilst you (whose virtues make your counsels thrive)
Look't on that mystic word, Prerogative,
As if you saw long-hid uncurrent Gold;
Which must (though it prove good) be tried
Because it long has lain aside;
And rather too, because the Stamp is old:
Which in the Metal's trial some deface,
Whilst you by polishing would make is pass.
When you have wrought it to a yieldingness
That shows it fine but makes it not weigh less.
Accurst are those Court-Sophisters who say
When Princes yield, Subjects no more obey.[61]

Davenant, like Suckling, called upon the queen to supply the
king's lack of good counsel. Davenant later claimed that he had
always been in favour of the king governing with parliament,
and that his friends Suckling and Jermyn, 'both in their writing,
and speech', had 'often extolled the natural necessity of parliaments here, with extreme scorn upon the incapacity of any that
should persuade the King he could be fortunate without them'.[62]
Both Davenant's poem and Suckling's letter were critical of the
king's policies in the 1630s. The main aim of Davenant's poem
was to persuade the queen to advise the king that great concessions to the opposition were needed if the king were 'to new-
form his crown' on the love of his people. This was also the main
aim of Suckling's letter, which argued that the king should not
wait until demands were made by parliament and let himself be
forced to concede them under pressure, but that he should seize
the initiative and 'do something more . . . something of his own,
as throwing away things that they call not for, or giving them
things they expected not.' In this way he would prove that he

61 Sir William Davenant, *Works* (London, 1673) pp. 298–9.
62 Harbage, *op. cit.* pp. 84–5.

was sincere in saying that he wished to reform church and state, and he, rather than parliament, would get the credit for the reforms. If this meant relinquishing some of his power, the love of his people would compensate for the loss and in the long run make him stronger than ever, 'as you may see in Queen Elizabeth'. Concessions would be necessary in 'Religion and Justice' in order to satisfy the people—not 'by any little acts, but by royal and kingly resolutions'. Suckling did not specify the concessions but it may be guessed that in religion he had in mind the reduction of the power of the bishops. Concerning justice he drove closer to the real issue: 'There is but one thing remains, which whispered abroad busies the King's mind much (if not disturbs it) in the midst of these great resolutions; and that is the preservation of some servants, whom he thinks somewhat hardly torn from him of late. . . . Whether as things now stand the King is not to follow nature, where the conservation of the more general commands and governs the less. . . . Whether, if he could preserve those ministers, they can be of any use to him hereafter? Since no man is served with a greater prejudice than he that employs suspected instruments, or not beloved, though able and deserving in themselves. . . . Whether to preserve them there be any other way than for the King to be first right with his people?'[63] And Davenant concluded his poem to the queen:

> Madam, you that studied Heaven and Times
> Know there is Punishment, and there are Crimes.
> You are become (which doth augment your state)
> The Judges Judge, and Peoples Advocate:
> These are your Triumphs which (perhaps) may be
> (Yet Triumphs have been tax'd for Cruelty)
> Esteem'd both just and mercifully good:
> Though what you gain with Tears, cost others Blood.[64]

The conclusion is irresistible that the concession which Suckling and Davenant regarded as the condition of reconciliation with the people was the sacrifice of Strafford to the justice of parliament.

The intrigues of the aristocratic factions for places seemed to be on the verge of success in the first months of 1641. The first

63 *The Works of Sir John Suckling* pp. 322–5.
64 Sir William Davenant, *op. cit.* pp. 298–9.

instalment of new appointments began on 20 January, when Lyttleton was promoted Lord Keeper, Bankes became Chief Justice of the Common Pleas and Heath was made a judge. Sir Edward Herbert succeeded Bankes as Attorney-General, and the king originally intended to fill Herbert's place as Solicitor-General with Gardiner, the Recorder of London, and to make Oliver St John Recorder of London, but at the last moment he substituted the name of Oliver St John for that of Herbert as Solicitor-General. This was politically significant because St John was the Earl of Bedford's legal adviser and close adherent; and the king's change of mind indicated that pressure had been applied.[65] On 19 February the Earls of Bedford, Essex, Hertford and Bristol, Viscount Saye, and Lords Savile and Mandeville (and a few days later the Earl of Warwick) were appointed privy councillors. They were 'all persons at that time very gracious to the people, or the Scots . . . and had been all in some umbrage at court, and most of them in visible disfavour. . . .' All but two of them had been signatories of the Petition of the Twelve Peers for a parliament in 1640.[66] Sir John Temple's information was that Hamilton had joined with Jermyn to secure the promotion of these eight peers.[67] At the beginning of April Temple still thought that Jermyn's influence was dominant, and that not only was the queen guided by him but also 'a strange interest hath he gotten now in the king'.[68] It may have been through Jermyn that the queen had 'secret interviews with Bedford and Pym' and offered to secure their appointments as Lord Treasurer and Chancellor of the Exchequer.[69] In April Nathaniel Tomkyns told Sir John Lambe that Pym 'has been with the king twice of late'.[70] In this negotiation the king had three aims: first, to obtain from parliament an adequate revenue for the crown in place of the extra-parliamentary taxes of the 1630s which had been condemned by parliament; second, to preserve episcopacy; and third, 'to save the life of the Earl of Strafford'. On the first point Bedford and Pym seem to have satisfied the king of their good

65 *De L'Isle and Dudley Manuscripts* Vol. VI, pp. 366, 367–8, 369; *C.S.P.D.
    1640–1641* p. 439.
66 Clarendon, *History* Vol. I, pp. 258–62; *C.S.P. Venetian 1640–1642* p. 218.
67 *De L'Isle and Dudley Manuscripts* Vol. VI, p. 387.
68 *ibid.* pp. 397–8.
69 Gardiner, *History* Vol. IX, p. 273.
70 *C.S.P.D. 1640–1641* p. 560.

intentions. Pym drew up a memorandum of 'the king's revenue and expenditure' for Bedford's information, and, according to Clarendon, he and Bedford 'engaged to procure the king's revenue to be liberally provided for and honourably increased and settled', and they laid plans for 'many good expedients by which they intended to raise the revenue of the crown'. On the second point they 'would have been willing to have satisfied the king, the rather because they had no reason to think the two Houses, or indeed either of them, could have been induced to have pursued the contrary.' On the third point they also reached agreement with the king, on the basis that Strafford would be made incapable of any public employment and banished or imprisoned for life.[71] But the negotiations were weakening their position in parliament, where the country gentry were suspicious that if the 'great men' got places they would do little to reduce the cost of the court, and would become 'desirous more to pacify the irate prince, and to comply with his desire in keeping up bishops and other things' than to proceed with 'the thorough reformation of Church and State'.[72] They did not feel strong enough to proceed without the support of the Earl of Essex, who vetoed the whole scheme by insisting on nothing less than the death penalty for Strafford, telling Clarendon, who was employed by Bedford in an effort to change his mind: 'Stone-dead hath no fellow.'[73] The king resolved that he would not appoint the opposition leaders to the vital political offices until they had proved that they would and could do him service in parliament by voting him new revenues, preserving the bishops, and saving Strafford's life. Clarendon thought that this would have been 'very reasonable at another time' but was 'very unseasonable' in this crisis; for by advocating the king's views before they were responsible for his policies they would risk undermining their base of power in parliament before they had secured a new base of power in the court, and 'it could not be expected they would desert that side by the power of which they were sure to make themselves considerable without an unquestionable mark of interest in the other, by which they were to keep up their power

71 Clarendon, *History* Vol. I, pp. 279–82; *C.S.P.D. 1640–1641* pp. 565–7.
72 Clarendon, *History* Vol. I, p. 241; Vol. II, pp. 13–14; Robert Baillie, *Letters and Journals* ed. D. Laing (3 vols., Edinburgh, 1841) Vol. I, p. 291.
73 Clarendon, *History* Vol. I, pp. 318–21.

and reputation.'[74] And the opposition leaders in parliament resolved that they could not do any service for the king in parliament in relation to his revenue, the bishops, and Strafford, until they were appointed to the chief offices in the government and so assured that the king had really abandoned past policies and past advisers, and really meant to reform church and state.[75]

The collapse of the negotiations between the king and the leaders of the parliamentary opposition, and the failure of the scheme to bring them into the government on the basis of a programme of moderate reforms of church and state, left the court in an uncertain and divided state of mind. The great lords at court continued to look for a settlement in terms of the appointment of the opposition leaders to the chief offices in the government, but Jermyn and the courtiers who looked to him for a lead faced a crisis. The king had failed to regain the initiative and was being driven reluctantly from one ungracious surrender to another. The question was no longer what concessions the king should make or what reforms he should offer, but whether there were any demands parliament might make, under pressure from the agitations of the puritan clergy and the London mob, that he would be able to resist, unless he could find a base of power for which he could defy parliament. Jermyn turned his eyes towards the army in the north.

The army, which had been raised to fight the Scots in 1640, had been stationed in Yorkshire since the cessation of arms and getting more and more annoyed at the failure of parliament to provide money for its pay. On 6 March 1641 Sir John Hotham reported to the House of Commons that £125,000 was owing to the English army, towards which £50,000 had been allocated, and £50,000 was owing to the Scots army, towards which £15,000 had been allocated, but the Scots Commissioners said that unless their army received £25,000 immediately 'they should be compelled to advance further'. Under this threat the Commons decided to send to the Scots, as well as the £15,000 already allocated to them, a further £10,000 out of the £50,000 earmarked for the English army.[76] Several officers of the army were

---

74 *ibid.* p. 431.
75 *ibid.* pp. 279–82; *De L'Isle and Dudley Manuscripts* Vol. VI, pp. 368–9.
76 *The Journal of Sir Simonds D'Ewes* ed. W. Notestein (New Haven, 1923) pp. 368, 448, 449–50.

members of parliament: Henry Percy, captain of a troop of cuirassiers he had raised at his own charge for the king's body-guard, was member for Northumberland; Henry Wilmot, commissary-general of the horse, was member for Tamworth in Staffordshire; William Ashburnham, a lieutenant-colonel of horse, represented Ludgershall, Wiltshire; and Hugh Pollard, a captain in the army, sat for Beeralston, Devon. They were already angry at the neglect of the Commons to keep up the pay of the army, but now they were 'more scandalized' at this favouritism towards the Scots, and 'Wilmot stood up and told them, if such papers as that of the Scots would procure monies, he doubted not but the officers of the English army might easily do the like.'[77] And indeed on 20 March the officers in Yorkshire sent a letter to the General of the Army, the Earl of Northumberland, complaining of the long neglect of parliament to send their pay and 'that our former petitions have neither found credit nor brought remedy to our sufferings.'[78] Percy invited to his lodgings in Whitehall to discuss the situation those officers who were in London—his fellow MPs Wilmot, Ashburnham and Pollard, and two other officers, who were not MPs, Sir John Berkeley, a lieutenant-colonel in the army, and Daniel O'Neill, major in Sir John Conyer's regiment of horse.

Percy, his brother the Earl of Northumberland having no son, was 'the heir male apparent of one of the greatest families of Christendom'.[79] O'Neill belonged to the old native Irish aristo-cracy and, having been deprived of his inheritance, had left Ireland and made his career at the court in England and with the army in the Netherlands. He seems to have attached himself to the Earl of Northumberland, and to the latter's 'confidant' and 'diligent attender', Viscount Conway.[80] Wilmot was the son and heir of an Englishman who had made a career in the Irish ad-ministration and gained an Irish viscountcy. He owned land in Oxfordshire and owed his seat in parliament to the Earl of Essex,

---

77 *Portland Manuscripts* Vol. I, H.M.C., 13th Report, Appendix, Part I (1891) pp. 15, 18; Edward Husbands, *An Exact Collection* (London, 1642) p. 218.
78 *C.S.P.D. 1640–1641* pp. 507–8.
79 *The Journal of Sir Simonds D'Ewes* ed. W. H. Coates (New Haven, 1942) p. 259.
80 *D.N.B.*; Clarendon, *History* Vol. I, p. 186; Vol. III, pp. 513–14; Warwick, *op. cit.* pp. 28, 145; *De L'Isle and Dudley Manuscripts* Vol. VI, p. 98.

to whom he was devoted.[81] Ashburnham belonged to the still-powerful Villiers connection and had married the widow of the Earl of Marlborough, through whom he had large estates in Wiltshire. He was the younger brother of John Ashburnham, a Groom of the Bedchamber and close friend of the king.[82] Sir Philip Warwick regarded O'Neill, Wilmot and Ashburnham as followers of the Earl of Holland.[83] This pointed to the most obvious fact about the group that gathered at Percy's lodgings: they were courtiers, especially on the queen's side. Percy himself was a courtier and in 1635 Lord Conway had written to Wentworth: 'Mr Percy is a diligent courtier, his chief patron the Duke of Lennox, his addresses are most on the queen's side; but I cannot find that he gains much love anywhere ... I believe he will not make any great profit by the Court, because he begins the Pater Noster with, "Give us this day our daily bread".'[84] Two years before, Wentworth, who strove hard to make friends with the Percies, had appointed him to a captaincy in the Irish army, but had been forced to cancel the appointment because the king had promised the place to Lorenzo Cary, brother of Viscount Falkland.[85] Percy was unsuccessful in his efforts to obtain the place of ambassador to the French court or to become one of the Gentlemen of the King's Bedchamber, and he quarrelled with his brother-in-law the Earl of Carlisle, saying that 'he had rather be damned than receive a courtesy from my Lord of Carlisle', which led to a coolness between him and his sister the Countess of Carlisle. But he managed to gain the queen's favour, by which he obtained the places of Master of Horse to the Prince of Wales and Captain-General of the Island of Jersey, and the Order of the Garter for his brother.[86] Sir John Berkeley was one of the queen's servants and favourites, and the kinsman of Henry Jermyn who 'loved him better than anybody else'. He had been sent as ambassador to Queen Christina of Sweden in 1637 and knighted in 1638.[87] O'Neill 'was very well known in the Court, having spent

81 D.N.B.; Keeler, op. cit. pp. 63, 395; Clarendon, History Vol. III, pp. 388–390; Warwick, op. cit. p. 274.
82 D.N.B.; Keeler, op. cit. pp. 89–90.
83 Warwick, op. cit. pp. 145–6.
84 Knowler, op. cit. Vol. I, p. 393.
85 ibid. Vol. I, pp. 128, 138–40, 142, 144, 205, 209, 228.
86 ibid. Vol. I, p. 363; Brennan, op. cit. Vol. II, pp. 217, 228–9.
87 D.N.B.; Clarendon, History Vol. IV, pp. 232–3, 266–7.

many years between that and the Low Countries, the winter seasons in the one, and the summer always in the army in the other . . . and he had a fair reputation in both climates, having . . . a natural insinuation and address which made him acceptable in the best company. And . . . he had . . . some part in most of the intrigues of the Court. . . .' His focus seems to have been on the queen's side and his ambition was to become a Gentleman of the King's Bedchamber.[88]

These officers and courtiers discussed not only the grievances of the army but also the current political situation. They agreed that the army should petition the king and parliament, not only for its arrears of pay, but also for the 'preserving of bishops' both in their function in the church and their place in the House of Lords, and for the settling of the king's revenue 'to that proportion it was formerly' before the abolition of 'illegal' taxes by the Long Parliament. They resolved that Percy should communicate this to the king and offer him their assistance, providing that he asked them to do nothing dishonourable, nor against their duty to parliament, the liberties of the subject and the laws of the land; he should also tell the king that 'they were most confident that they could engage the whole army thus far.' Finally, they all took a solemn oath on the bible 'to be constant and secret in all this'.[89] It is significant that the two main points on which the officers offered to support the king—over episcopacy and his revenue—were two of the three points on which many at court were hoping for an agreement with Bedford and Pym at this very period, in late March and early April. And on the third point of the negotiations with Bedford and Pym—the fate of Strafford— the views of the officers, though not expressed, were probably closer to those of the parliamentary opposition than to those of the king. Wilmot and O'Neill 'were both very indevoted' to Strafford, who had tried to force Wilmot's father to give up crown lands that he had acquired in Ireland, and who had blocked O'Neill's attempts to succeed to the estates that his father had left in Ireland.[90] Sir Philip Warwick commented that Wilmot, O'Neill and Ashburnham 'were merry lads, and none of them

88 Clarendon, *History* Vol. III, pp. 513–14.
89 Husbands, *op. cit.* pp. 218–19; *Portland Manuscripts* Vol. I, pp. 15–20; 'Verney Papers: Notes of Proceedings in the Long Parliament', *Camden Society* Vol. XXI (1845) pp. 96–7.
90 *D.N.B.*; Clarendon, *History* Vol. I, p. 206.

good willers to Strafford, but more the Lord Holland's dependants, a greater man on the queen's side than his, which made them so froward towards him.'[91] Thus Percy and his friends were still operating within the context of the court and aristocratic schemes to reach a settlement by bringing the leaders of the parliamentary opposition into the government and by sacrificing Strafford to popular hatred.

The letter of 20 March from the officers in Yorkshire to the General of the Army had been brought to London by Captain James Chudleigh, who was the son of a well-to-do Devonshire baronet, Sir George Chudleigh, and 'a young man, and of a stirring spirit, and desirous of a name'.[92] He showed a copy of the letter to Davenant, who said that it 'was a matter of greater consequence' than Chudleigh imagined, and took him to Court to see Suckling and Jermyn. Their minds were working no longer in the direction of agreeing with the opposition, as Percy's friends still were, but of crushing the opposition. They talked of sounding the affections of the army towards the king, of a declaration from the army in support of the king, of the army marching on London to back the king in resisting the demands of parliament and the London mob. The precondition of any such design was that the army should be under the command of generals who were loyal to the king and could be trusted to carry out such a plan. Northumberland's loyalty could not be relied on, and in any case he was anxious to resign from his command as General, and his ally Conway would probably retire from the Lieutenant-Generalcy at the same time. Jermyn and Suckling agreed that the Earl of Newcastle should be General, and that their friend George Goring should be Lieutenant-General. Goring had combined a successful military career in the Netherlands with a flamboyant life as a courtier in England, and he was at present colonel of a brigade in the army in Yorkshire and governor of Portsmouth. Suckling went round to Goring's lodgings in Covent Garden, where he found Goring in bed and fearful that he had come to collect a gambling debt. Suckling explained that Newcastle was to be General of the Army and that Goring could be Lieutenant-General if he wished. Goring agreed to go to Court to 'hear more of this business' and on his way

91 Warwick, *op. cit.* pp. 145-6.
92 Clarendon, *History* Vol. III, p. 74.

along St Martin's Lane met Jermyn, who whispered in his ear that 'he had somewhat to say to him concerning the army . . . and desired him to meet him that evening at the Court, on the Queen's side'. The queen took Goring to see the king. It is hard to believe that Jermyn, Suckling, Davenant, Chudleigh and Goring knew nothing of the proposals of Percy, Wilmot, O'Neill, Ashburnham, Berkeley and Pollard, since both groups were so closely associated with the court and with the queen. But Jermyn and Percy did put their plans to the king independently of each other. The divergence between the two groups probably sprang from this—that Percy and his friends were still thinking in terms of how to *persuade* the aristocratic factions to come to terms with the king, while Jermyn and Suckling were now thinking of how to *force* them to do so. The king urged Jermyn and Goring to meet Percy and his friends. Two meetings took place and revealed differences over whether, and in what circumstances, the army should march on London; and over the command of the army. Wilmot and Ashburnham seem to have opposed a march on London out of hand; Jermyn, Goring and Percy seem to have been ready to consider it seriously. But the differences between the plotters were most clearly seen when they came to discuss the appointment of a general: Jermyn and Goring proposed the Earl of Newcastle, Percy nominated the Earl of Holland, and Wilmot and Pollard favoured the Earl of Essex. The choice of Newcastle, who would have been most acceptable to the king and queen, would have pointed to a military coup against parliament; the choice of Holland, who would not have been entirely acceptable either to the king or to parliament, would have pointed to an effort to avoid a complete breach between the court and parliament; and the choice of Essex, who would have been most acceptable to parliament, would have pointed to a desire to keep the army out of politics.[93] No doubt Wilmot and Pollard were thinking as soldiers rather than as politicians and of the best appointment from the military point of view. But this difference reveals again that Percy's friends were thinking in terms of agreement with parliament, and that Jermyn was not. The king had been considering the appointment of Essex as general, and Essex himself thought that he 'had been in a manner offered it',

93 Husbands, *op. cit.* pp. 215–23; *Portland Manuscripts* Vol. I, pp. 15–23; 'Verney Papers', pp. 94–9.

but in the end, despairing of winning over Essex in the matter of Strafford, the king appointed Holland. He was still pursuing the strategy, which Jermyn had rejected, of winning over the aristo-crats with places.[94] In this the king's overriding aim now was to save Strafford's life, but this did not figure in the plans of either Percy or Jermyn. This may, however, have been the unexpressed aim of Jermyn and Suckling, for the queen had now changed her mind and joined in her husband's struggle to save the earl.[95]

At all events Percy's group and Jermyn's group failed to agree. Chudleigh returned to Yorkshire to sound out the reactions of the officers to Jermyn's designs. The results of this were not very encouraging, and when he returned to London on 5 April he found that Percy and his friends had backed down and that Jermyn and Goring had dropped the whole idea.[96]

The ambivalent attitude of the court and the aristocracy to-wards Strafford dominated his trial and continued until his execution. He was feared and admired; his defence excited sym-pathy and anger; and the popular hatred shown towards him was as distasteful to the aristocrats as it was successful in persuading them to consent to his death.

> Great Strafford, worthy of that name tho' all
> Of thee could be forgotten but thy fall.
> How great thy ruin when no less a weight
> Could serve to crush thee than three kingdoms' hate;
> Yet single they accounted thee (although
> Each had an army) as an equal foe.
> Thy wisdom such, at once it did appear
> Three kingdoms' wonder, and three kingdoms' fear,
> Joined with an eloquence so great to make
> Us hear with greater passion than he spake;
> That we forced him to pity us whilst he
> Seemed more unmov'd and unconcern'd than we.
> And made them wish who had his death decreed
> Him rather than their own discretion freed.
> So powerfully it wrought, at once they grieve

94 Clarendon, *History* Vol. I, pp. 359–60; *C.S.P. Venetian 1640–1642* p. 141.
95 Clarendon, *History* Vol. I, p. 217.
96 Husbands, *op. cit.* pp. 220–7.

That he should die, yet feared to let him live.
Farewell great soul, the glory of thy fall
Outweighs the cause, whom we at once may call
The enemy and martyr of the state,
Our nations glory and our nations hate.[97]

Suckling, perhaps moved by Strafford's defence at his trial, no doubt sickened by the pusillanimity of the lords and of the king himself, and recognizing that if the king were ever to make a stand it should be on this issue, in which his conscience and honour were concerned not to allow a man to die for serving him loyally, resolved upon a gambler's throw to rescue Strafford from the Tower. On Sunday morning, 2 May, a Captain Billingsley presented himself at the Tower with an order from the king to admit him with a hundred men. Suckling was nearby at a tavern in Bread Street with sixty armed men. Sir William Balfour, the Lieutenant of the Tower, suspecting a plot to rescue Strafford, refused to admit Billingsley. Suckling dismissed his men with orders to return the next evening. But the next day mobs beset parliament with demands for the execution of Strafford, and on 5 May Pym informed the Commons that there was a plot to rescue Strafford from the Tower and to bring up the army to overawe parliament. Suckling fled, and so did Jermyn, Percy and Davenant. Suckling and Jermyn got to France; Davenant was arrested in Kent; Percy was almost captured in Sussex and took refuge at Petworth, confessing his part in the plots to his brother, who passed it on to parliament.[98]

The great aristocrats were angered by the influence of 'the young tampering favourites on the queen's side, the two Henrys Percy and Jermyn', and that the king was ready to listen to 'such youths (unsworn councillors), and, as my lord of Essex called them in the House, the new Juntillio'.[99] The power of court favourites and backstairs advisers was seen to be still very great and the influence of the great lords of the reconstituted privy council to be much less than expected:[100] the army plot following

97 *The Poetical Works of Sir John Denham* ed. T. H. Banks (New Haven, 1928) p. 153n., *cf.* pp. 153–4.
98 Husbands, *op. cit.* pp. 232–4; Gardiner, *History* Vol. IX, pp. 348–61.
99 Warwick, *op. cit.* p. 179; *Manuscripts of the Earl of Egmont* Vol. I, H.M.C., 16th Report (1905) Part i, p. 134; H.M.C., 4th Report, p. 295.
100 B. H. G. Wormald, *Clarendon: Politics, History and Religion 1640–1660* (Cambridge, 1951) p. 35.

hard on the heels of the refusal of the king to appoint the parliamentary leaders to the chief offices in the government, it seemed
that Charles preferred rather to take advice of Henry Jermyn
than of the Earl of Bedford. But, having toyed with the idea of
coercing parliament, Charles reverted to the plan of winning over
its leaders with offices. After the execution of Strafford, through
the summer of 1641, the influence of the Marquis of Hamilton,
both in court and in parliament, appeared to be as great as ever
and to form a bridge between the two. 'Marquis Hamilton is (for
ought I can understand) in great esteem both in the House of
Commons and with the Lords of the Upper House', wrote
Edward Nicholas on 15 July: 'He is doubtless a wise and able
man, and exceeding gracious and powerful with the king. . . .'[101]
He kept in close touch 'with Mandeville, Essex and others, and
chiefly with the Lord Saye' in an effort 'to prepare them to a better
correspondence with the king'.[102] Since the death of the Earl of
Bedford in May, Lord Saye aspired to lead Bedford's old faction,
though he did not succeed to either the old earl's 'authority with
his confederates' or 'his credit with the king'.[103] The Bishop of
Lincoln, John Williams, who had been the leader of the opposition within the church hierarchy to Archbishop Laud, appeared
as another bridge between the court and the opposition. He was
the bishop most closely linked with the aristocracy, in whose
house the sons of the Earls of Hertford, Leicester, Pembroke and
Salisbury had been educated; he was also the bishop with the
greatest influence in the House of Lords. Williams urged the king
to resume the policy of appointing the opposition peers to offices
in the government and court. As chairman of the House of Lords
Committee on Religion, in which he was working out a scheme
of moderate reform of the church with a sub-committee of
divines 'of very contrary opinions', anglican and puritan,[104] he
recognized, however, that the opposition peers felt unwilling to
take office without changes in the church.[105]

The policy of promoting leaders of the opposition was continued to some extent. In May the Earl of Newcastle, who had

101 *C.S.P.D. 1641–1643* p. 53.   102 Burnet, *op. cit.* p. 188.
103 Clarendon, *History* Vol. I, p. 334*n*.
104 John Hacket, *Scrinia Reserata* (London, 1693) Part II, pp. 36, 146–7,
    163; H. R. Trevor-Roper, *Religion, the Reformation and Social Change*
    (London, 1967) pp. 255–6, 265–6.
105 Clarendon, *History* Vol. II, pp. 545–8.

been implicated in the army plot, resigned as Governor of the Prince of Wales and was succeeded by the Earl of Hertford, who was promoted to Marquis. He had been hostile to the court and his appointment was 'to the general satisfaction and public joy of the whole kingdom; and to the no little honour and credit of the court, that so important and beloved a person would attach himself to it under such a relation. . . .'[106] His younger brother, Sir Francis Seymour, who 'had been always very popular in the country, where he had always lived, out of the grace of the court', and who had led the resistance to shipmoney in Wiltshire and been elected to the Long Parliament for Marlborough, had been created Lord Seymour of Trowbridge on 19 February, and was appointed a privy councillor on 8 August.[107] Thus the Seymours were attached to the court. The Percy–Sidney connection received some satisfaction from the appointment of the Earl of Leicester as Lord Lieutenant of Ireland. The Earl of Holland was chosen as General of the Army in April, and his half-brother, the Earl of Newport, was made Constable of the Tower in May: both these earls were courtiers who had associated themselves with the discontented peers. Lord Saye, Bedford's heir as leader of the opposition in the House of Lords, was appointed Master of the Court of Wards.[108] On 23 July the Earl of Essex was installed as Lord Chamberlain of the King's Household in place of the Earl of Pembroke. 'Although in the past he has shown himself utterly opposed to the king's interests,' wrote the Venetian Ambassador, 'his Majesty hopes that the stimulus of ambition as well as of profit will suffice to secure his devotion, and if he succeeds in winning over the earl he will have achieved a great gain, since that nobleman possesses the strongest party in parliament.'[109] 'It was thought this extraordinary grace to the most popular person of the kingdom would have had a notable influence upon the whole party. . . .'[110] Essex probably took office with some reluctance, and the king's nephew, the Elector Palatine, understood that the appointment 'was a thing my Lord of Essex did not at all

106 Clarendon, *History* Vol. I, pp. 563–4; Vol. II, pp. 528–9; *C.S.P. Venetian 1640–1642* p. 172
107 Clarendon, *History* Vol. II, pp. 533–4; Keeler, *op. cit.* pp. 337–8.
108 *C.S.P. Venetian 1640–1642* pp. 142, 154; Gardiner, *History* Vol. IX, p. 374; Vol. X, p. 47.
109 *C.S.P. Venetian 1640–1642* p. 195.
110 Clarendon, *History* Vol. I, p. 345.

sue for, and would not have accepted it, but that he saw the king was resolved the other should not keep it, and that if he had refused that also, after so many other things which were put upon him, the world might have thought, that the high hand he carried in parliament, was not so much for to maintain the liberties of the subjects, as out of a spleen to the Court.'[111] He entered the court on his own terms, probably thinking of himself as a mediator between the king and the opposition; and in accepting office 'many men believed that he rather gratified the king than that his majesty had obliged him in conferring it.'[112] During July there were rumours that there would be 'a great change and addition of officers at court', before the king went to visit Scotland, following the conclusion of peace with the Scots. It was thought that Lord Saye would become Lord Treasurer and Pym Chancellor of the Exchequer; that the Earl of Salisbury or Lord Newburgh would be Master of the Court of Wards; that Lord Mandeville, or Denzil Holles, or John Hampden would be Secretary of State; and that the Earl of Bath and Lord Brooke would be added to the privy council.[113] But the king postponed the appointment of a new Lord Treasurer and other officers until his return from Scotland.

There was an uneasy suspicion that the king was about to adopt a new policy. The dismissal of the Earl of Pembroke was soon regarded as more significant of the king's intentions than the appointment of the Earl of Essex. It was thought that his dismissal had been secured by the queen, 'who cherishes oldstanding grudges against' him, and by courtiers that he had offended in the exercise of the office of Lord Chamberlain of the King's Household. It was also felt he had angered the king by supporting the attainder of Strafford and 'countenancing of those tumultuous people that came out of London to Westminster crying for justice when time was against the Earl of Strafford'.[114] Sir John Temple wrote to the Earl of Leicester on 29 July: 'The remove of my Lord of Pembroke from being Lord Chamberlain hath

111 John Forster, *Eminent British Statesmen* (London, 1838) Vol. VI, p. 72.
112 Clarendon, *History* Vol. II, p. 15.
113 *De L'Isle and Dudley Manuscripts* Vol. VI, pp. 405, 406; *C.S.P.D. 1641–1643* pp. 7, 53, 62, 63, 65.
114 Clarendon, *History* Vol. I, p. 345; Vol. II, pp. 539–41; *C.S.P.D. 1641–1643* p. 62; *De L'Isle and Dudley Manuscripts* Vol. VI, p. 405; *C.S.P. Venetian 1640–1642* p. 195.

much dashed that party . . .'; and he concluded that it was now unlikely that Saye would be Lord Treasurer, or Pym Chancellor of the Exchequer, or Salisbury Master of the Court of Wards, or Holles Secretary of State.[115]

Strafford dead was not much less of an obstacle to agreement between the king and the opposition than Strafford living, for Charles could never forgive the men who had forced him to consent to his death. He turned to the men who had opposed the attainder. This it was that brought the Seymours into his favour; and that also reconciled him to the Digbys. The Earl of Bristol, since his quarrel with the Duke of Buckingham over the Spanish match, 'could never recover any admission to the Court, but lived in the country, in ease and plenty in his fortune, and in great reputation with all who had not an implicit reverence for the Court; and before, and in the beginning of, the parliament, appeared in the head of all the discontented party. . . .'[116] His eldest son, Lord Digby, 'had from his youth, by the disobligation his family had undergone from the duke of Buckingham and the great man who succeeded him . . . , which obliged him to a country life, contracted a prejudice and ill-will to the court; and so had in the beginning of the parliament engaged himself with that party which discovered most aversion from it, with a passion and animosity equal to their own. . . .'[117] But as early as December 1640 the Countess of Carlisle had noted that Bristol 'behaves himself very well and that the King is satisfied with him. . . .'[118] At the time when the queen and Hamilton were negotiating to bring the leaders of the opposition into the government, there were rumours that Bristol would be Lord Privy Seal and that Digby would be Secretary of State; and Bristol was made a privy councillor in company with the other opposition peers in February 1641.[119] While Bedford and Essex could not agree with the king to save the life of Strafford, Bristol could; and in the House of Lords, with the help of Lord Savile and the Earl of Clare, he tried to do so. In the House of Commons, Digby passionately opposed the third reading of the bill of attainder.[120] The crowds

115 De L'Isle and Dudley Manuscripts Vol. VI, p. 406.
116 Clarendon, History Vol. II, pp. 531-3.
117 ibid. Vol. I, p. 461.
118 De L'Isle and Dudley Manuscripts Vol. VI, pp. 350-1.
119 ibid. p. 367, 387; C.S.P.D. 1640-1641 p. 439.
120 Baillie, op. cit. Vol. I, pp. 327, 488-9; Clarendon, History Vol. I, p. 462;

that demonstrated against Strafford at Westminster on 3 May were especially hostile towards Bristol, 'an apostate from the cause of Christ, and our mortal enemy', and his 'false son the Lord Digby'.[121] Digby's influence in the Commons collapsed,[122] and at Henry Jermyn's suggestion, the king proposed to send him as ambassador to Paris,[123] which may have been significant in relation to the queen's hopes of help from France. On 8 June he was involved in a row in the House of Commons, when he accused Goring of perjury in his evidence about the army plot, probably infuriated by the fact that Goring had implicated Bristol.[124] The king promptly elevated Digby to the House of Lords, no doubt as a reward for his services in the Commons. Unpopular and suspect, Digby and Bristol turned from parliament to the court. 'The Earl of Bristol, finding his credit much impaired in both Houses', where he was being spoken of as an 'evil counsellor' who 'should be removed from about the king . . .', 'endeavoured much to supply that defect by strengthening himself with friends at court. . . .'[125]

On 8 August, on the eve of his departure for Scotland, the king announced several new promotions: the Duke of Lennox was created Duke of Richmond, the Earl of Bristol was made a Gentleman of the King's Bedchamber, and the Earl of Bath, Lord Seymour and Lord Dunsmore were appointed to the privy council. At the same time Edward Nicholas, Clerk of the Council, was designated Secretary of State to fill the vacancy left by Windebank, and Lord Savile was promised Sir Henry Vane's place as Treasurer of the Household.[126] These appointments do not look highly significant, but were nevertheless regarded as 'an affront to the parliament'.[127] To Sir John Temple, probably reflecting the reaction of the Percy–Sidney connection, they appeared as a political coup of menacing proportions: 'It is admirable to see what an alteration one week hath produced among

Gardiner, *History* Vol. IX, pp. 273, 276, 339–40, 345–7; *The Lord Digby His Last Speech against the Earl of Strafford* (1641) B.M. E.198(1).
121 John Nalson, *An Impartial Collection* (London, 1682) Vol. I, p. 188.
122 Baillie, *op. cit.* Vol. I, p. 348; *C.S.P. Venetian 1640–1642* p. 184.
123 *De L'Isle and Dudley Manuscripts* Vol. VI, pp. 397–8; *C.S.P.D. 1641–1643* p. 53, 81.
124 'Verney Papers', p. 90; Husbands *op. cit.* pp. 215–17.
125 *C.S.P.D. 1641–1643* pp. 46, 81.
126 *ibid.* p. 81.　　127 *C.S.P. Venetian 1640–1642* p. 202.

us,' he told the Earl of Leicester: 'I know not how to make your Lordship either to conceive or believe the same at this distance, it being not safe to write either the ways or the particulars.'[128] The ways were traced to the Earl of Bristol, who 'has endeared himself with the Duke of Lennox,' Thomas Smith told the Earl of Northumberland, 'and, as I am informed, was the promoter of his now being made Duke of Richmond. . . .'[129] The duke 'was of the noblest extraction, being nearest allied to the King's person of any man who was not descended from King James. . . .' The king had married him to the only daughter of his dead favourite the Duke of Buckingham, and had made him Lord Warden of the Cinque Ports and a privy councillor; but he was essentially a courtier and a friend of the king, being 'of small experience in affairs' and 'used to discourse with his Majesty in his bedchamber rather than at the Council-board . . .'. 'He was almost the only man of great quality and consideration about the King who did not in the least stoop or make love' to the opposition.[130] Lord Dunsmore also belonged to the Villiers clan, having married a niece of Buckingham; and Nicholas was another link with the great favourite, having come into the royal service as Buckingham's secretary. It was curious company for the Earl of Bristol, who had been one of Buckingham's bitterest enemies, but now the descendants of the dead Buckingham were united with those who had tried to save the dead Strafford and the king felt that he had been true to himself. Bristol's appointment was crucial and politically significant. He regarded it as the extinction of his former disgrace and the mark of his complete return to royal favour: 'It has pleased the King,' he wrote to Sir Thomas Roe, 'after many years, totally to remove from me the marks of his former displeasure by commanding me to wait on him as a Gentleman in Ordinary of his Bedchamber as I did in times past when he was Prince.' Bristol expected to have great influence, for he offered to assist Roe in the diplomatic negotiations at Ratisbon and 'in his own particular'; and he hoped to have a hand in settling the king's government on a stable base, believing that 'domestic distractions . . . grow near a period.'[131]

128 *De L'Isle and Dudley Manuscripts* Vol. VI, p. 410.
129 *C.S.P.D. 1641–1643* p. 81.
130 Clarendon, *History* Vol. I, pp. 160–1, 207, 361; Vol. II, pp. 527–8; *Life* pp. 93–6.
131 *C.S.P.D. 1641–1643* pp. 106, 130–1.

The appointments of 8 August were a revolution in the king's policy: no longer would he seek to come to terms with the opposition in parliament or seek to buy off his opponents with places. Henceforth he would give offices and favours only to those who had actually done him service in parliament by supporting his views, not merely offered to serve him in the future.[132]

At the same time the discontented court lords, who were trying to keep their power in both the court and the parliament, found their position in parliament endangered by the revelations of the army plot. The Earl of Northumberland, fearing that he might be implicated by his brother's part in it, extracted a confession from him and passed it on to parliament, which 'was the first visible instance of the defection of the earl of Northumberland towards his Majesty's service. . . .'[133] The Earl of Holland had been named as General by some of the conspirators, so when he was actually appointed General he used his position to make inquiries in the army about the plot and to make reports to the House of Lords that were damaging to the king.[134] If these actions caused Northumberland and Holland to gain the confidence of parliament, they also caused them to lose favour at court;[135] and the Earl of Newport also lost favour at court by revealing the information that Goring had given him about the army plot, and by refusing to support schemes for rescuing Strafford from the Tower. Holland especially was balanced on a knife-edge: his favour at court had been declining for some time;[136] moreover his income depended very heavily on royal favour. He made one final effort to discover whether the king still had any regard for him[137] and, being rebuffed, was faced with ruin and the loss of such following as he had. In such circumstances many a courtier before him had taken the path to rebellion.[138]

Now that the king seemed to have reversed the policy of trying to conciliate the discontented lords, and to have turned for

132 C.S.P. Venetian 1640–1642 p. 203.
133 Clarendon, History Vol. I, p. 203.
134 ibid. Vol. I, pp. 387–9, 433–4n, 480n; 'The Nicholas Papers', Camden Society New Series, Vol. XL (1886) p. 16.
135 C.S.P.D. 1641–1642 p. 46.
136 De L'Isle and Dudley Manuscripts Vol. VI, pp. 346, 392.
137 Clarendon, History Vol. I, pp. 433–4n, 379–80, 387–9, 480n.
138 Stone, op. cit. pp. 481–8.

advice to men like Richmond and the Digbys, there was growing fear of his intentions when he returned from Scotland. In September there were many consultations in aristocratic salons. Leading members of the opposition met at Lord Mandeville's house at Chelsea.[139] 'The leaders of the party, who are the Earls of Essex, Warwick and Newport and some others have held long conferences in the house of the Earl of Northumberland,' reported the Venetian ambassador: 'The particulars of these discussions have not transpired, but all agree that they have turned upon the best means of resisting any attempt which the king might make on his return.'[140] Northumberland's sister, the Countess of Leicester, 'drew the principal persons who were most obnoxious to the Court, and to whom the Court was most obnoxious, to a constant conversation at Leicester House . . .', and drew her husband closer to the opposition.[141] The Earl of Holland, after disbanding the army, returned to London 'in great pomp' and withdrew from attendance on the queen and 'wholly betook himself to the conversation and friendship' of the leaders of the opposition. At his house in Kensington he had consultations with the Earl of Essex, the Earl of Newport, Viscount Saye, Lord Mandeville, Lord Dungarvon, John Pym, Nathaniel Fiennes (son of Viscount Saye) and Sir John Clotworthy. The Countess of Carlisle, following the lead of her brother Northumberland and her sister Leicester, and of Holland, who 'always held a strict friendship' with her, 'withdrew herself from her attendance upon the queen'. She and Holland revealed all they knew 'of the natures and dispositions of the king and queen' and of their counsels, of the army plot and of the consultations there had been at Court to save Strafford, and 'many sharp sayings uttered in that time'.[142] The Earl of Essex was 'much less inclined to the king by the infusions the earl of Holland every day instilled in him'.[143] The upshot of these consultations was that in the second session of the Long Parliament the opposition should direct its main attack upon the continuing presence of evil counsellors about the king, and would demand that the great officers of state and privy

139 *Diary and Correspondence of John Evelyn* ed. W. Bray (4 vols., London, 1857) Vol. IV, p. 76.
140 *C.S.P. Venetian 1640–1642*, p. 215.
141 Clarendon, *History* Vol. I, pp. 434–5*n*, 480–1*n*.
142 *ibid.* pp. 387–9, 433–4, 480–1; D'Ewes, *Journal* ed. Coates, p. 353.
143 Clarendon, *History* Vol. I, p. 480*n*.

councillors should be men that the two Houses could trust.[144] Such meetings revealed the dominant role of aristocrats in the leadership of the Long Parliament, and the fact that a number of great court lords had moved into open opposition to the king.

The king was resolved to stand firm in defence of his prerogative to choose his own ministers and advisers; and also in defence of the rights of the bishops.[145] While he was in Scotland, the queen and Nicholas did their best to organize support for him in parliament, but Nicholas was handicapped by not being a member of parliament, and the queen found the leading peers 'too great princes now to receive any direction from me. . . .'[146] In the Commons Lord Falkland, Edward Hyde and Sir John Colepeper took the lead in resisting, though unsuccessfully, the demand for the removal of the king's evil counsellors and the appointment of such as the two Houses approved. In the Lords '. . . the Earl of Bristol and his son the Lord Digby did argue with so much reason and judgement' against it that they got it laid aside; and Nicholas wrote to the king: 'Your Majesty may be pleased to take notice of the singular good service that was in that business done by those two noblemen, and especially by the son, who (I hear) did beyond admiration.'[147] The bill to remove the bishops from the House of Lords and all clergymen from all secular offices, was carried through the Commons, against the opposition of Falkland and Hyde; but it failed to pass the Lords, due especially to the efforts of the Earl of Southampton.[148] When the king returned from Scotland he was encouraged by the support he was gaining in parliament and by the size of the vote in the Commons against the Grand Remonstrance;[149] by the election of the loyal Alderman Gurney as Lord Mayor of London and the welcome he received from the citizens on his entry into the capital;[150] and by reports of popular reaction against parliament, which had done more to please the nobility and gentry

144 Evelyn, *op. cit.* Vol. IV, pp. 76, 80, 81.
145 *ibid.* pp. 80, 83, 96, 99.
146 *ibid.* pp. 4, 5, 11, 13–14, 76, 84, 85, 89, 90–1, 95, 96, 99, 100, 115–16, 117, 121, 124–5, 131.
147 D'Ewes, *Journal* ed. Coates, pp. 44–7, 94–5, 99–101, 104–5; Evelyn, *op. cit.* Vol. IV, pp. 100–1, 120–1.
148 D'Ewes, *Journal* ed. Coates, pp. 21–2, 30–2; Evelyn, *op. cit.* Vol. IV, p. 100.
149 *Manuscripts of the Duke of Buccleuch* Vol. I, H.M.C., 15th Report (1899) p. 286.
150 Evelyn, *op. cit.* Vol. IV, pp. 78, 82, 115, 132; *C.S.P.D. 1641–1643* pp. 132, 177–8, 192; *Manuscripts of the Duke of Buccleuch* Vol. I, p. 266.

than the mass of the people.[151] When he returned the king was thus fully committed to a new policy: not only to appoint to offices the men who did him services in parliament, but also to remove from offices men who opposed him in parliament, and thus by a dual policy of 'the carrot and the stick' to build up a party in the two Houses.

The king 'looks but overly upon the good lords', William Montagu told his father, Lord Montagu of Boughton, on 27 November.[152] The Marquis of Hamilton 'holds not the same greatness with the king as he did before. . . .'[153] 'Lord Holland, they say, has lost himself both with the king and queen . . .', Thomas Wiseman reported on 2 December.[154] So had the Earl of Northumberland, noted Thomas Smith on 10 December.[155] 'My Lord of Essex is not very well looked on . . .,' reported William Montagu.[156] On the other hand, the king was 'often very private with Digby and Bristol. . . .'[157] Bristol's patron, the Duke of Richmond, was made Lord Steward, although parliament asked the king to appoint the Earl of Pembroke.[158] Bristol's ally, Lord Savile, was appointed Treasurer of the Household in place of Sir Henry Vane.[159] It was rumoured that Lord Digby would be Secretary of State, and that the Earl of Bath would be Lord Privy Seal. Although parliament asked the king to make the Earl of Salisbury Lord Treasurer, the talk was that the office would go to Bristol or Sir John Bankes. Gossip also named Bristol for Lord Chamberlain in place of the Earl of Essex, or Groom of the Stole in place of the Earl of Holland; but William Montagu's opinion was that Bristol shunned 'all offices of the Commonwealth' and aimed only to be near the person of the king and to advise him in his bedchamber.[160] The appointment of such men as Bristol, Digby and Savile, who were distrusted by many in

151 *C.S.P. Venetian 1640–1642* pp. 215, 220, 222, 225–6, 250–2.
152 *Manuscripts of the Duke of Buccleuch* Vol. I, p. 286.
153 *C.S.P.D. 1641– 1643* pp. 188–9, 192.
154 *ibid.* pp. 188–9; *Manuscripts of the Duke of Buccleuch* Vol. I, p. 288.
155 *C.S.P.D. 1641–1643* p. 194.
156 *ibid.* pp. 192, 203; *Manuscripts of the Duke of Buccleuch* Vol. I, p. 288.
157 *Manuscripts of the Duke of Buccleuch* Vol. I, p. 286.
158 *ibid.* p. 288; *C.S.P.D. 1641–1643* pp. 188–9, 192.
159 *Manuscripts of the Duke of Buccleuch* Vol. I, p. 288; *C.S.P.D. 1641–1643* pp. 188–9.
160 *Manuscripts of the Duke of Buccleuch* Vol. I, pp. 287, 288; *C.S.P.D. 1641–1643* pp. 188–9, 192, 203, 214.

parliament, and the refusal of the king to appoint men like Pembroke and Salisbury, who were trusted, would have been bad enough. What made the situation critical, however, was the fear that the king was about to purge from the court and government all who had supported the Commons' demands for the appointment, to offices of state and the privy council, of men parliament could trust and for the removal of the bishops from the House of Lords.

During the first two weeks of December there were strong rumours that 'there will be suddenly a great remove at Court of Chief Officers. . . .'[161] 'At the palace they talk freely of changing many of the leading ministers soon, as well as servants of the Court, who in the late disturbances have publicly conspired against the intentions and interests of his Majesty. Those concerned are very uneasy about this and about other steps which may be expected in the future.'[162] Sir Henry Vane was dismissed as Secretary of State, having already lost his place as Treasurer of the Household to Lord Savile.[163] The queen was determined to punish her old friends who had deserted her after she had ceased to work for reconciliation with the opposition. 'The queen doth govern all the king's affairs . . . and this is the cause of Vane's losing his secretary's place,' wrote the king's sister, the Queen of Bohemia.[164] Thomas Smith feared that the same influence would procure the dismissal of the Earl of Northumberland from the office of Lord Admiral.[165] The Earl of Holland was expected to lose his place as Groom of the Stole (the first gentleman of the King's Bedchamber), and the Earl of Newport to be removed from Constable of the Tower.[166] It was thought that the Earl of Essex would not remain as Lord Chamberlain but be sent to command the army in Ireland.[167] Sir Henry Vane the younger was expected to be dismissed from Treasurer of the Navy; Cornelius Holland, protégé of the elder Vane, to lose his place as

161 *C.S.P.D. 1641–2643* pp. 188–9, 192, 201; *Manuscripts of the Duke of Buccleuch* Vol. I, p. 288.
162 *C.S.P. Venetian 1640–1642* p. 262.
163 *C.S.P.D. 1641–1643* pp. 188–9; *Manuscripts of the Duke of Buccleuch* Vol. I, p. 288.
164 *C.S.P.D. 1641–1643* p. 214.
165 *ibid.* p. 194.
166 *ibid.* pp. 192, 201; *Manuscripts of the Duke of Buccleuch* Vol. I, p. 288.
167 *C.S.P.D. 1641–1643* pp. 192, 203, 211; *Manuscripts of the Duke of Buccleuch* Vol. I, p. 288.

Clerk Comptroller to the Prince of Wales; and Sir Henry Mildmay to be removed from the Mastership of the Jewel House. These last three were all Members of Parliament, puritans and prominent in opposition; they all held lucrative offices—Vane's place was worth £800 a year—and so were threatened with serious losses.[168] The writer of a newsletter on 16 December thought that a resolution had been taken to remove all puritans from places about the king, queen and prince of Wales.[169] 'The truth is,' wrote Thomas Smith, 'there are such factions at Court that if some might be hearkened unto the king shall lose all the best friends and servants he hath merely by malicious plots.'[170] '. . . Certainly the good party is tottering,' exclaimed William Montagu.[171] 'In fear of losing their offices and other misgivings,' reported the Venetian Ambassador, 'the parties are seriously perturbed and protest roundly that they are ready to take the most extreme measures to avoid the danger with which the King's anger threatens them.'[172] The king seemed finally to have broken off all attempts to come to terms with the opposition and to be set on a trial of strength. And the court lords and office-holders who did not agree with this or had opposed the king in parliament were driven into complete identification with the opposition, which was the only power potentially strong enough to prevent them losing their places in the court and administration.

Lord Digby, rather than his father, was now the man with the greatest influence over the king, who consulted with him about 'the business of the parliament without reserve'. He entrenched himself in the king's favour with the help of his 'great friendship' with William Murray, a Groom of the King's Bedchamber; and he endeared himself to the queen.[173] He held no public office; he was an adviser in the closet rather than in the council chamber, who rose by courtly virtues and courtly influence. He 'was a man of very extraordinary parts by nature and art, and had surely as good and excellent an education as any man of that age in any

---

168 C.S.P.D. 1641–1643 pp. 192, 201; Manuscripts of Lord Montagu of Beaulieu H.M.C. (1900) p. 135; Keeler, op. cit. pp. 218–19, 274, 371; G. E. Aylmer, The King's Servants (London, 1961) pp. 368–9, 384–5.
169 Manuscripts of Lord Montagu of Beaulieu p. 135.
170 C.S.P.D. 1641–1643 p. 194.
171 Manuscripts of the Duke of Buccleuch Vol. I, p. 288.
172 C.S.P. Venetian 1640–1642 p. 269.
173 Clarendon, Life pp. 44, 85, 93; History Vol. I, p. 484.

country: a graceful and beautiful person; of great eloquence and becomingness in his discourse, (save that sometimes he seemed a little affected), and of so universal a knowledge that he never wanted subject for a discourse.'[174] In the view of Sir John Bramston the king turned away from the great lords of his privy council and took the advice of 'some young gentlemen of the House of Commons [Lord Digby, Lord Falkland, Edward Hyde, Orlando Bridgeman] who had made themselves popular, as they and the king too thought'.[175] The domination of the House of Commons by a small oligarchy of leaders frustrated able and ambitious young men who aspired to play a greater part. They complained 'that everything in the parliament had been guided by the sole arbitrament of a few individuals, who boldly seized the reins of the government and prevented others from stating their own opinions for the common benefit on the matters dealt with. . . .'[176] Since the oligarchy was opposed to the king, these critics of the oligarchy gravitated towards support of the king. Digby, Falkland, Hyde and Bridgeman were all aged between thirty and thirty-two. It is significant that Jermyn, Percy and the 'army plotters' of the earlier 'Juntillio' were all in their early thirties. The domination of parliament by old men opposed to the court meant that the young men seeking to make names and win places for themselves were deflected from an opposition, in whose hierarchy they were unable to rise, to a Court that was anxious to welcome and reward any talents that were placed at its service. This may explain in part the fact that so many of the younger members of parliament supported the king.[177] Digby was 'instrumental in promoting' his friends Hyde, Falkland and Colepeper to the king's favour. Hyde's 'natural parts were very forward and sound; his learning was very good and competent; and he had a felicity both of tongue and pen; which made him willingly hearkened unto, and much approved. . . .' He 'was of a cheerful and agreeable conversation, of an extraordinary industry and activity, and of great confidence: which made him soon at home

174 Clarendon, *History* Vol. I, pp. 461–3.
175 'The Autobiography of Sir John Bramston', *Camden Society* Vol. XXXII (1845) p. 83.
176 *C.S.P. Venetian 1640–1642* p. 222; Clarendon, *History* Vol. I, pp. 241–50, 263*n*.
177 D. Brunton and D. H. Pennington, *Members of the Long Parliament* (London, 1954) p. 188.

at a court.'[178] Although Colepeper 'was of a rough nature', 'warm and positive in debates' and 'might very well be thought a man of no very good breeding, having never sacrificed to the Muses, or conversed in any polite company'—'no man less appeared a courtier'—yet 'he had, with all his uncourtliness . . . and ungracefulness in his mien, and motion, a wonderful insinuation and address into the acceptation, and confidence of the king, and queen . . .'; and 'an entire confidence and friendship with Mr John Ashburnham', a Groom of the King's Bedchamber and close friend of the king.[179] Early in the New Year of 1642 Falkland was appointed Secretary of State, to fill the vacancy left by the dismissal of Vane, and Colepeper was appointed Chancellor of the Exchequer, the office which for so long it had been expected Pym would fill. Hyde was offered the place of Solicitor-General, but declined it, preferring to advise the king in secret and through his friends Falkland and Colepeper. The Earl of Southampton, who married the daughter of Lord Dunsmore, became a Gentleman of the King's Bedchamber, and was admitted to the privy council in company with Falkland and Colepeper.[180] All these appointments were clearly in line with the king's new policy and were rewards for concrete services in parliament. They were achieved by court intrigue and court influence, and power continued to lie with Digby the courtier rather than with any of the holders of public offices.

Digby 'was equal to a very good part in the greatest affair, but the unfittest man alive to conduct it, having an ambition and vanity superior to all his other parts, and a confidence peculiar to himself, which sometimes intoxicated and transported and exposed him.' 'His fatal infirmity is, that he too often thinks difficult things easy; and doth not consider possible consequences when the proposition administers somewhat that is delightful to his fancy, and by pursuing whereof he imagines he shall reap some glory to himself. . . . The king himself was the unfittest person alive to be served by such a counsellor, being too easily inclined to sudden enterprises, and as easily amazed when they are entered upon.'[181] Besides appointing to offices those who

---

178 Warwick, *op. cit.* p. 196.   179 Clarendon, *Life* pp. 48–9.
180 *ibid.* pp. 42, 44–6; Clarendon, *History* Vol. I, pp. 460–3; *C.S.P.D. 1641–1643* pp. 240, 241, 253.
181 Clarendon, *History* Vol. I, pp. 461–3.

served him in parliament, there was another side to the king's new policy, and that was to punish those who opposed him in parliament and to break the opposition. Inherent in this was the idea of a coup. In face of the success of the puritan faction in the elections to the Common Council of London, and the riots of the 'December Days' against bishops,[182] Digby translated the king's policy, which had been to build up a party in parliament to defeat the opposition, to the crushing of the opposition by a coup against its leaders. Without consulting the privy council, or even his friends Falkland, Hyde and Colepeper, Digby persuaded the king to accuse Lord Mandeville, Pym, Hampden, Holles, Haslerig and Strode of treason, and to go in person to arrest them in the parliament house.[183] The failure of this coup and the violent reaction in favour of the accused members, obliged the king to flee from London. His supporters were thrown into complete disarray; the court was shattered; and the administration of the realm fell into the hands of Pym and his friends. The king left Whitehall with Lord Digby and thirty or forty gentlemen, including the faithful Endymion Porter: 'Whither we go, and what we are to do, I know not, for I am none of the Council. My duty and loyalty have taught me to follow my king and master, and by the grace of God nothing shall divert me from it.'[184] But blind loyalty was insufficient to sustain a crown. It was the power and intrigues of Porter and his ilk: the court favourites Jermyn and Digby, that had brought this disaster on Charles, who was king now only in name.

Belatedly and half-heartedly Charles had reacted to the crisis of 1640 by adopting a policy of coming to terms with the opposition in parliament by appointing its leaders to the chief places in the government and making concessions to their demands for reforms in church and state. This policy had been abandoned because the king would not agree to the death of Strafford. The king had toyed with the idea of using the army against the parliament, but when this proved impossible he had tried to win over

182 Valerie Pearl, *London and the Outbreak of the Puritan Revolution* (Oxford, 1961) pp. 132–7, 210–28.
183 Clarendon, *History* Vol. I, pp. 484–5, 505–6, 524–6.
184 *C.S.P.D. 1641–1643* p. 256.

his opponents by appointing them to lucrative or prestigious offices. Still forced to concede demand after demand of the parliament, he had resolved to make no more concessions and to build up a party of his own in parliament to support his stand, by means of a new policy of appointing to offices peers and MPs who had demonstrated concrete support for his views and of dismissing from office peers and MPs who opposed his views. While the king did manage to win over to his side some who had opposed him earlier, he also drove into complete identification with the opposition those court lords and office-holders who did not share his views. The king had shown clearly that he did not rely on the advice of his ministers and privy councillors, but on the advice of his personal friends and court favourites. This caused the final breach between the opposition and the king. He had ignored the party that was appearing for him in parliament and resorted to a coup that failed. Only the threat of civil war and social disorder led a large part of the nobility to rediscover an identification between their interests and those of the crown, and so gave Charles a party with which to fight to recover his power.

3
Religion and Politics: The Godly People

Brian Manning

Preface

The king, in the earlier part of 1642, did not have the power or the means to resist indefinitely the demands of the two Houses of Parliament for the limitation of monarchical power. But many of the nobility and gentry did not wish to see the power of the crown reduced any further and they rallied to the king. Thus one party of the nobility and gentry supported the king and another party of the nobility and gentry supported the two Houses. The issue was primarily constitutional and political, and the conflict was primarily between these two sections of the nobility and gentry—although probably the greater part of the nobility and gentry was unwilling to commit itself to either side. But there was a religious issue as well. The 'godly people' who wanted reforms in the church did not immediately identify the constitutional conflict with the 'cause of god'. Most of them came from the middle ranks of the population and were less concerned about the constitutional conflict than the nobility and gentry. The 'middle sort of people' had not only religious grievances but also secular ones, and their grievances were not just against the government of Charles I but against the nobility and gentry and richer classes in general. They were forced to become parliamentarians by the hostility of the royalists towards the 'godly' and 'middle' sort of people. They became the hard core of the parliamentarian party, and their increasing importance and influence converted the civil war from a constitutional into a religious conflict. Godliness created a selfconsciousness among the middle sort of people, marking them off from both the rich and the poor. They supported parliament for their own reasons and on their own terms. Godliness reflected their 'class-consciousness'; and the civil war changed further— from being a conflict between two sections of the nobility and gentry to becoming a conflict between the nobility and gentry and the middle rank of the people.

BRIAN MANNING

RICHARD BAXTER, the puritan divine, observed that constitutional and religious grievances had become intertwined by 1640, because 'the King had at once imposed the Shipmoney on the Commonwealth, *and* permitted the Bishops to impose upon the Church their displeasing Articles, and bowing towards the Altar, and the Book for dancing on the Lord's day, and the liturgy on Scotland, etc. and to suspend or silence abundance of ministers. . . .' Nevertheless, Baxter made a distinction between the constitutional and the religious opposition to Charles I, and he believed that there were 'two sorts of men' in the Long Parliament: the 'one party made no great matter of these alterations in the Church; but they said, that if Parliaments were once down, and our propriety [i.e. property] gone, and arbitrary government set up, and law subjected to the Prince's will, we were then all slaves, and this they made a thing intolerable; for the remedying of which, they said, every true Englishman could think no price too dear: these the people called Good Commonwealth's Men. The other sort were the more religious men, who were also sensible of all these things, but were much more sensible of the interest of religion, and these most inveighed against the innovations in the Church, the bowing to Altars, the Book for Sports on Sundays, the casting out of ministers, the troubling of the people by the High Commission Court, the pilloring and cutting off men's ears, (Mr Burton's, Mr Prynne's, and Dr Bastwick's) for speaking against the Bishops, the putting down lectures, and afternoon sermons and expositions on the Lord's Day, with such other things, which they thought of greater weight than shipmoney. But because these latter agreed with the former in the vindication of the peoples' propriety and liberties, the former did the easilier concur with them against the proceedings of the Bishops and High Commission Court.'[1]

In Baxter's view this distinction between the 'Good Commonwealth's Men' and 'the more religious men' corresponded to a social division: the nobility and gentry were more concerned about the constitution, the middle rank of the people about religion. The nobility and gentry who 'adhered to the Parliament' in the civil war did so, in Baxter's opinion, chiefly out of concern for 'the Publick Safety and Liberty', that is, for political rather than

1 *Reliquiae Baxterianae* ed. Mathew Sylvester (London, 1696) p. 18.

for religious reasons.[2] They agreed, no doubt, with the reasons given by the Earl of Northumberland in May-June 1642 for supporting parliament: '. . . we believe that those persons who are most powerful with the King do endeavour to bring Parliaments to such a condition that they shall only be made instruments to execute the commands of the King, who were established for his greatest and most supreme council'; '. . . let us but have our laws, liberties and privileges secured unto us. . . .'[3] Sir John Hotham was one of those who adhered to parliament for political rather than religious reasons. He 'was as well affected to the government of the Church of England . . . as any man that had concurred with them . . .',[4] but he 'was a man that loved liberty, which was an occasion to make him join at first with the Puritan party . . .', though '. . . in more than concerned the civil liberty he did not approve their ways'.[5] '. . . He was manly for the defence of the liberty of the subject and privilege of Parliament, but was not at all for their new opinions in Church government.'[6] In this he reflected the views of many of the gentry in his own county who supported parliament in the civil war, for exactly half of the parliamentarian gentry in Yorkshire were not puritans.[7] And in the House of Lords there were thirty-one peers who supported parliament at the outbreak of the civil war, but about half of them showed no signs of puritanism.[8] Thomas May observed that the nobility and gentry thought it much clearer that the king had violated the laws and liberties of the kingdom than that he had favoured popery,[9] and even puritan gentry thought that there was more justification for parliament to go to war in 1642 for 'defence of the just English liberties' than for defence of 'the true protestant religion': John Hutchinson, a Nottinghamshire gentleman and puritan, was 'convinced in conscience of the righteousness of

---

2 *ibid.* p. 31.

3 G. Bankes, *The Story of Corfe Castle* (London, 1853) pp. 122–3, 129–30.

4 Edward, Earl of Clarendon, *The History of the Rebellion* ed. W. D. Macray (6 vols., Oxford, 1888) Vol. II, p. 259.

5 *State Papers Collected by Edward, Earl of Clarendon* (Oxford, 1773) Vol. II, p. 185.

6 *The Diary of Sir Henry Slingsby of Scriven, Bart.* ed. D. Parsons (London, 1836) p. 92.

7 J. T. Cliffe, *The Yorkshire Gentry from the Reformation to the Civil War* (London, 1969) pp. 344–50.

8 G. F. Trevallyn Jones, *Saw-Pit Wharton* (Sydney, 1967) p. 53.

9 Thomas May, *The History of the Parliament of England* (London, 1647) Book I, pp. 113–18.

the parliament's cause in point of civil right; and though he was satisfied of the endeavours to reduce [i.e. bring back] popery and subvert the true protestant religion . . . yet he did not think that so clear a ground for the war as the defence of the just English liberties. . . .'[10] The immediate issue over which the civil war broke out—the Militia Ordinance—was not a religious issue. Oliver Cromwell recalled that '. . . religion was not the thing at the first contested for, but God brought it to that issue at last, and gave it unto us by way of redundancy, and at last it proved to be that which was most dear to us',[11] implying that he himself had at the beginning seen the issue as political, and this no doubt reflected the fact that he was a gentleman as well as a puritan. For the leaders of the parliamentarian party, puritan or not, 'the thing at the first contested for' was the limitation of the king's power;[12] but those that were not puritans tended to desert the party when religion came to obtain 'the most eminent place in the parliament's cause', while those that were puritans, like Hutchinson and Cromwell, remained loyal.[13]

Non-puritan gentlemen supported parliament for political reasons alone, but puritan gentlemen did so for both political and religious reasons. Sir Simonds D'Ewes, a wealthy Suffolk squire, was as concerned as any nobleman or gentleman with constitutional questions, and with the defence of 'the liberty of the subjects of England'; but when in June 1642, like the Earl of Northumberland, he had to make a choice between king and parliament, he referred, unlike the Earl of Northumberland, to religion rather than to politics. His younger brother had joined the king at York and had written to Sir Simonds on 17 June: 'I was in good hopes to have seen you here before the arrival of these will come to your hands: but I should think this or any other pains well awarded, if I could be the happy inducement to bring you hither. I daily understand how you stand affected, and

10 Lucy Hutchinson, *Memoirs of the Life of Colonel Hutchinson* ed. J. Hutchinson and revised C. H. Firth (London, 1906) pp. 78–9.
11 W. C. Abbott, *The Writings and Speeches of Oliver Cromwell* (4 vols., Cambridge, Mass., 1937–47) Vol. III, p. 586.
12 David Underdown, *Pride's Purge: Politics in the Puritan Revolution* (Oxford, 1971) p. 9.
13 John Corbet, 'An Historicall Relation of the Military Government of Gloucester' (London, 1645) in *Bibliotheca Gloucestrensis* ed. J. Washbourn (Gloucester, 1825) Vol. I, p. 17; May, *op. cit.* Book. I, pp. 113–18; Cliffe, *op. cit.* p. 346.

what your opinions are, and out of that sincere affection I bear you, I heartily wish you fortunate in their continuance.' On 21 June Sir Simonds sat down to compose the most important letter of his life, for it was to announce his decision to remain with the two Houses of Parliament rather than to join the king: 'I would be willing to redeem the reunion of his Majesty and the two Houses with my dearest blood; that so religion might be established in that power and purity amongst us, and preaching so settled in those places where atheism, profaneness, and ignorance now reigns, as that all men might know their duty to God and the King. . . .'[14] Although Sir Simonds was an expert 'in the municipal laws and ancient records of this state', and was well qualified to make up his mind about the legal and constitutional issues in 1642, it was not in the end on these grounds that he justified his stand, but on religious grounds. And his religious reasons were more positive than dislike of 'innovations in the Church', or fear of a return to popery, for they were based on a desire for 'reformation' and the rule of godliness in England. Similarly, although Hutchinson studied 'the things then in dispute, and read all the public papers that came forth between the king and parliament, besides many other private treatises, both concerning the present and foregoing times', and became convinced of 'the righteousness of the parliament's cause in point of civil right', this was not sufficient to persuade him to take up arms for parliament, and he was not drawn into the fighting until he found 'a clear call from the Lord'—in other words, a religious justification.[15] D'Ewes and Hutchinson put religion first, but whether gentlemen put religion or politics first in 1642, they were all aware that there were both religious and political issues, and that these, though interrelated and interdependent, could be distinguished from each other.

D'Ewes and Hutchinson felt able to understand and competent to decide the legal and constitutional questions, but others of the gentry, and most people of the middle and lower ranks of society, felt as Richard Baxter, who confessed that he 'was not judicious enough in Politicks and Law to decide this Controversie which so many Lawyers and Wise men differed in'.[16] But Baxter knew

14 *The Autobiography and Correspondence of Sir Simonds D'Ewes*, ed. J. O. Halliwell (2 vols., London, 1845) Vol. II, pp. 290-3.
15 Hutchinson, *op. cit.* pp. 78-9, 94, 98.   16 *Reliquiae Baxterianae* p. 39.

what reforms he wanted to see in the church, and that the only hope of achieving such reforms was through parliament; so when he became convinced that the king intended to crush the parliament by force, he could not but agree that the 'religious men' must take up arms to defend the parliament.[17] Groups of puritans in London and the provinces had placed their hopes for reformation in the parliament and hence their cause was bound up with the success or failure of the parliament. Oliver Heywood always remembered the reaction of his father and godly neighbours in Lancashire to the news of Charles I's attempt to seize the Five Members in January 1642: '. . . yea I remember a whole night wherein he, Dr Bradsha, Adam Ferniside, Thomas Crompton and several more excellent men did pray all night in a parlour at Ralph Whittels, as I remember upon occasion of K. Chas. I demanding the five members of the House of Commons, such a night of prayers, tears, groans as I was never present at in all my life: the case was extraordinary, and the work extraordinary.'[18] But for Baxter and such puritan groups the defence of the parliament was not an end in itself—as it was for the Earl of Northumberland and Sir John Hotham and the 'Good Commonwealth's Men'—but was the means to the reformation of the church.

When the king and the two Houses of Parliament appealed to arms against each other, the 'godly people' did not automatically flock as a body to the defence of the latter. Like most people in 1642, they hesitated, uncertain at first what course to take. John Hutchinson, although he 'was clearly swayed by his own judgment and reason to the parliament', hung back from declaring himself and 'contented himself with praying for peace', 'thinking he had no warrantable call at that time, to do anything more'.[19] Eventually he did take up arms for parliament and became a leading parliamentarian in Nottinghamshire; but his prolonged hesitation was significant because, although judging parliament to be in the right on legal and constitutional grounds, he did not immediately identify the cause of parliament with the cause of religion. Similarly, at the start of the civil war, the first reaction

17 *ibid.* p. 26, 39.
18 *The Autobiography and Diaries of Oliver Heywood* ed. J. H. Turner (Brighouse, 1882) Vol. I, p. 83.
19 Hutchinson, *op. cit.* pp. 78–9, 94, 98.

of the young Lancashire puritan, Adam Martindale, was to 'have been quiet and meddled with no side'.[20]

In October 1642, John Goodwin, puritan minister of St Stephen's, Coleman Street, London, appealed specifically to 'Christians of ordinary ranke and qualitie' to support parliament, in a tract that broke sharply from the exclusively legal and constitutional arguments of the main body of parliamentarian propaganda up to that point, and proclaimed a war for religion. He argued that victory for the royalists would mean greater power for the bishops, the reintroduction of 'Romish error and superstition' into the church, the encouragement of 'loosenesse, wickedness, and prophanenesse', and the persecution of the godly people. He claimed that parliament was defending 'the truth and purity' of the religion that the godly people professed: 'they are they that have . . . shaken the foundation of Popery, Prelacy, and prophannesse in the Land; and that are at worke upon it night and day, to make it a land of righteousness. . . .'[21] And Richard Baxter maintained that it was 'principally the differences about Religious Matters that filled up the Parliament's Armies, and put the Resolution and Valour into their Soldiers . . . Not that the Matter of Bishops or no Bishops was the main thing, (for Thousands that wished for Good Bishops were on the Parliament's side). . . . But the generality of the People through the Land . . . who were then called Puritans, Precisians, Religious Persons, that used to talk of God, and Heaven, and Scripture, and Holiness, and to follow Sermons, and read Books of Devotion, and pray in their Families, and spend the Lord's Day in Religious Exercises, and plead for Mortification, and serious Devotion, and strict Obedience to God, and speak against Swearing, Cursing, Drunkenness, Prophaness, Etc. I say, the main body of this sort of Men, both Preachers and People, adhered to the Parliament.'[22]

Baxter, however, was aware that not all the puritans (as he defined them) supported parliament in the civil war, for after speaking of 'the generality' of puritans, he added in parenthesis 'I say not all', and he noted that 'some few of the stricter sort

20 'The Life of Adam Martindale' *Chetham Society* Vol. IV (1845) pp. 34–5.
21 John Goodwin, 'Anti-Cavalierisme', in *Tracts on Liberty in the Puritan Revolution* ed. William Haller (3 vols., New York, 1933–4) Vol. II, pp. 220, 258–9, 262–4.
22 *Reliquiae Baxterianae*, p. 31.

Neutrality of may

were against them, or not for them (being Neuters). . . .'[23] He instanced that Sir Francis Nethersole in Warwickshire, 'a religious Knight, was against the Parliament's War and Covenant, (though not for the Justness of the War against them). In Gloucestershire, Mr Geree, an old eminent Nonconformist, and Mr Capell, a learned Minister . . . and some others with them were against the lawfulness of the War; so was Mr Lyford of Sherborn in Dorsetshire, and Mr Francis Bampfield, his Successor, and some other Godly Ministers in other Counties: And many resolved to meddle on no side.'[24] Baxter's own father, who was called a puritan because he was 'noted for praying and hearing Sermons', for reading the Scriptures and observing the Sabbath, 'was so far from medling on either side, that he knew not what they were doing, but followed his own business. . . .'[25] While Baxter drew attention to the puritans who 'resolved to meddle on no side', Clarendon claimed that 'very many persons of quality, both of the clergy and laity, who had suffered under the imputation of Puritanism, and did very much dislike the proceedings of the Court and opposed them upon all occasions, were yet so much scandalized at the very approaches to rebellion that they renounced all their old friends, and applied themselves with great resolution, courage, and consistency to the King's service, and continued in it to the end. . . .'[26] One such was Lord Montagu of Boughton in Northamptonshire, who was an opponent of the court before 1640 and 'so severe and regular in his life, that he was by the most reckoned amongst the Puritans . . .', but declared for the king in 1642.[27] In Yorkshire, out of 679 families of gentry, there were 132 puritan families, of which 64 supported parliament, 24 supported the king, 23 were divided or changed sides, and 21 were neutral.[28] The significance of these figures depends on the definition of 'puritan'. Baxter and his contemporaries used the term, as a nickname for godly protestants who were zealous in religious observances and strict in the conduct of their lives, without reference to particular theological doctrines or to particular forms of church government, and in this sense the puritans were not all on one side in the civil war. But Baxter's view that 'the main

what p?

23 *ibid.*   24 *ibid.* pp. 34–5.   25 *ibid.* pp. 44–5.
26 Clarendon, *op. cit.* Vol. II, pp. 370–1.
27 Sir Philip Warwick, *Memoires of the reigne of King Charles I* (London, 1701) pp. 221–6.
28 Cliffe, *op. cit.* p. 344.

body of this sort of Men' adhered to the parliament, receives some support from the fact that almost half of the puritans among the gentry in Yorkshire did support the parliament; and most of the puritans in the House of Lords did likewise.[29]

Why did 'the main body' of puritans support the parliament? It seems likely that the average puritan was influenced by the example of ministers and laymen who were noted for godliness. Adam Martindale, son of a Lancashire yeoman, was drawn into the parliamentarian party because 'all the ministers in our neighbourhood, to a man, except only two tippling boon companions, and all serious Christians generally declared themselves satisfied for the cause of that party among whom I sheltered myself, whose opinion and practice all those that think I should have sleighted them, must grant to be a strong temptation.'[30] Similarly, Baxter confessed that the very fact that godly people declared for parliament led him to do the same, and 'the Consideration of the Quality of the Parties that sided for each Cause, in the Countries, did greatly work with me, and more than it should have done.'[31] 'The devout people' of Nottingham adhered to parliament, and 'the ordinary civil sort of people' followed them.[32] 'Upon my knowledge,' wrote Baxter, 'many that were not wise enough to understand the Truth about the Cause of the King and Parliament, did yet run into the Parliament's Armies, or take their part . . .' only because they saw other religious people do so, 'as Sheep go together for Company . . .'.[33] It was not just the lead given by some puritan preachers, for Baxter emphasized the role of puritan laymen, saying that since a great number of those persons that were accounted most religious fell in with parliament, 'the generality of the stricter diligent sort of Preachers joyned with them . . .', and indeed were acting under pressure from 'the younger unexperienced sort of religious People. . . .'[34]

Besides, the royalist party seemed to be the party of the ungodly: '. . . the Gentry that were not so precise and strict against an Oath, or Gaming, or Plays, or Drinking, nor troubled themselves so much about the Matters of God and the World to come,

29 Jones, *op. cit.* pp. 53–4; Lawrence Stone, *The Crisis of the Aristocracy 1558–1641* (Oxford, 1965) pp. 742–3.
30 Martindale, *op. cit.* pp. 34–5, 36–9, 39–41.
31 *Reliquiae Baxterianae* p. 39.
32 Hutchinson, *op. cit.* p. 105.
33 *Reliquiae Baxterianae* p. 33.   34 *ibid.* pp. 33, 39.

and the Ministers and People that were for the King's Book, for Dancing and Recreations on the Lord's Days; and those that made not so great a matter of every Sin, but went to Church and heard Common Prayer, and were glad to hear a Sermon which lasht the Puritans, and which ordinarily spoke against this strictness and preciseness in Religion, and this strict Observation of the Lord's Day, and following Sermons, and praying Extempore, and talking so much of Scripture and the Matters of Salvation, and those that hated and derided them that take these Courses, the main body of these were against the Parliament.'[35] This was not just the view of a parliamentarian, for the royalist William Chillingworth reproached his own party with 'profaneness', want of piety and lack of zeal for reformation,[36] and Clarendon criticized 'the license, disorder, and impiety' of the king's soldiers.[37] If this were true, it must have confirmed religious people in thinking that the parliamentarian party was the party of religion and reformation. 'And abundance of the ignorant sort of the Country, who were Civil, did flock in to the Parliament, and filled up their Armies afterward, merely because they heard Men swear for the Common Prayer and Bishops, and heard others pray that were against them; and because they heard the King's Soldiers with horrid Oaths abuse the name of God, and saw them live in Debauchery, and the Parliament's Soldiers flock to Sermons, and talking of Religion, and praying and singing Psalms together on their Guards.'[38]

If the example of a few 'godly' preachers and laymen was one factor in bringing the general body of puritans into the parliamentarian party, persecution by the anti-puritan royalists was another, and perhaps more important factor in forcing the mass of puritans into the parliamentarian armies and garrisons. Probably nothing did more to convert puritans into parliamentarians than the assumption of the king's supporters that all puritans were the king's enemies. Puritans, as the label was applied in the seventeenth century, were an obtrusive and identifiable minority, because of their appetite for sermons, their refusal to take part in sports and traditional pastimes on Sundays, their reading the bible

35 *ibid.* p. 31.
36 *The Works of William Chillingworth* (Oxford, 1838) Vol. III, p. 14.
37 Clarendon, *op. cit.* Vol. III, p. 222.
38 *Reliquiae Baxterianae* p. 33.

and praying with their families, and more especially because of the peculiarities of their manners and appearance: 'When puritanism grew into a faction,' wrote a puritan lady, 'the zealots distinguished themselves, both men and women, by several affectations of habit, looks, and words. . . . Among other affected habits, few of the puritans, what degree soever they were of, wore their hair long enough to cover their ears, and the ministers and many others cut it close round their heads, with so many little peaks, as was something ridiculous to behold.'[39] This invited attack.

During the summer of 1642 in Hereford puritans preachers were shouted down as 'Roundheads' and threatened with physical violence.[40] At Ludlow puritans were called 'Roundheads' and encountered so much hostility 'that they durst not leave their homes to come to the fast.'[41] 'There is such an antipathy in the generality of the poor and gentry here, against any one that seems but religious . . .',[42] it was reported from York, that such as 'prayed and read the Scriptures, morning and evening' were denounced as 'Purtians and Roundheads'.[43] 'Insomuch that if a Stranger past in many places that had short Hair and a Civil Habit, the Rabble presently cried, "Down with the Round-heads"; and some they knockt down in the open Streets,' wrote Baxter: 'In this Fury of the Rabble I was advised to withdraw a while from home; whereupon I went to Gloucester: As I past through a corner of the Suburbs of Worcester, they that knew me not, cried, "Down with the Round-heads", and I was glad to spur on and be gone.' After a month he returned to Kidderminster but still 'found the beggarly drunken Rout in a very tumultuating Disposition, and the Superiors that were for the King did animate them, and the People of the Place who were accounted Religious were called Round-heads, and openly reviled, and threatened as the King's Enemies (who had never medled in any Cause against the King:) Every drunken Sot that met any of them in the Streets,

39 Hutchinson, *op. cit.* p. 95; William Lilly, *Monarchy or No Monarchy in England* (London, 1651) pp. 106–7.
40 *Portland Manuscripts*, Vol. III, H.M.C., 14th Report, Appendix, Part II (1894) pp. 87, 88–9; 'Letters of Lady Brilliana Harley', *Camden Society*, First Series, Vol. LVIII (1854) pp. 170–1.
41 'Letters of Lady Brilliana Harley', pp. 166–7, 172.
42 *Weekly Intelligence* B.M. E.121(34).
43 'Some Memoirs Concerning the Family of the Priestleys', in 'Yorkshire Diaries and Autobiographies in the Seventeenth and Eighteenth Centuries', Vol. II, *Surtees Society* Vol. LXXVII (1883) pp. 18–19.

would tell them, "we shall take order with the Puritans ere long". '[44]

As soon as the King's army was set on foot his soldiers took all puritans for their enemies without the need for any other evidence than their puritanism. In Shropshire Baxter's father 'and all his Neighbours that were noted for praying and hearing Sermons, were plundered by the King's Soldiers, so that some of them had almost nothing but Lumber left in their Houses: though my Father was so far from medling on either side, that he knew not what they were doing, but followed his own business. . . .'[45] When the king came to Nottingham to raise his standard in August 1642 his troops ranged over the country: '. . . a troop of cavaliers, under the command of Sir Lewis Dives, came to Stanton, near Owthorpe, and searched Mr Needham's house, who was a noted puritan in those days . . . they found not him, for he hid himself in the gorse, and so escaped them. His house being lightly plundered, they went to Hickling, and plundered another Puritan house there, and were coming to Owthorpe, of which Mr Hutchinson having notice, went away to Leicestershire; but they, though they had orders to seize Mr Hutchinson, came not at that time because the night grew on. But some days after he was gone, another company came and searched for him and for arms and plate, of which finding none, they took nothing else.' He took refuge in Northamptonshire, in 'the house of a substantial honest yeoman', and 'this man and his wife, being godly, gave Mr Hutchinson very kind entertainment. . . .'[46] The 'godly people' of Nottinghamshire were plundered and driven from their homes 'by the rudeness of the King's army' merely 'on account of their godliness'. Henry Ireton, who belonged to the minor gentry and 'had an education in the strictest way of godliness' and was 'a very grave, serious, religious person', formed some of these refugees into a troop of horse which he led into the Earl of Essex's army. But, when the king's army marched out of Nottinghamshire, most of the refugees, including John Hutchinson, returned to their homes, 'desirous to live in peace. . . .' They found 'by experience', however, that 'they could not do so, unless the parliament interest was maintained'; and so they

44 *Reliquiae Baxterianae* pp. 40, 42.
45 *ibid.* pp. 44-5.
46 Hutchinson, *op. cit.* pp. 97-8.

met in Nottingham and consulted 'how to raise some recruits for
the Earl of Essex, to assist in which, Mr Hutchinson had provided
his plate and horses ready to send in'.[47] Puritans found that their
only security against being beaten and plundered by the king's
soldiers was to join the parliament's army or to take refuge in one
of the parliament's garrisons. 'The debauched Rabble through
the Land, emboldened by his Gentry, and seconded by the
Common Soldiers of his Army, took all that were Puritans for
their Enemies: And though some of the King's Gentry and
Superiour Officers were so civil that they would do no such
thing, yet that was no Security to the Country, while the multitude did what they list. So that if any one was noted for a strict
and famous Preacher, or for a Man of a precise and pious Life,
he was either plundered, or abused, and in danger of his Life:
So that if a Man did but pray in his Family, or were heard to
repeat a Sermon, or sing a Psalm, they presently Cried out,
"Rebels, Roundheads", and all their Money and Goods that were
portable proved guilty, how innocent soever they were themselves. . . . But upon my certain knowledge this was it that filled
the Armies and Garrisons of the Parliament with sober, pious
Men. Thousands had no mind to meddle with the Wars, but
greatly desired to live peaceably at home, when the Rage of
Soldiers and Drunkards would not suffer them: some stayed till
they had been imprisoned; some till they had been plundered,
perhaps twice or thrice over, and nothing left them; some were
quite tired out with the abuse of all comers that quartered on
them; and some by the insolency of their Neighbours; but most
were afraid of their Lives; and so they sought refuge in the
Parliament's Garrisons.'[48] Goodwin's warning to 'godly people'
of the fate they would suffer at the hands of 'Cavaliers, Papists,
and Athiests, that have taken the field against you', seemed amply
justified.[49]

Baxter himself fled from the fury of the rabble and the king's
soldiers to the Earl of Essex's army and then to Coventry, where
he found about thirty puritan ministers 'who fled thither for
Safety from Soldiers and Popular Fury, as I had done, though
they never meddled in the Wars. . . .' There he was joined by 'the

47 Hutchinson, *op. cit.* pp. 79, 94, 100.
48 *Reliquiae Baxterianae* p. 44.
49 Goodwin, *op. cit.* pp. 44–5.

Religious part of my Neighbours at Kidderminster that would fain have lived quietly at home' but could not and so came to Coventry, where 'some of them that had any Estates of their own, lived there on their own charge; and the rest were fain to take up Arms, and be Garrison Soldiers to get them bread'. Thus the garrison at Coventry 'consisted half of citizens, and half of Country-men: the Country-men were such as had been forced from their own Dwellings, the most religious Men of the Parts round about, especially from Bremicham, Sutton-Coldfield, Tamworth, Nuneaton, Hinkley, Rugby, Etc. These were Men of great Sobriety and Soundness of Understanding as any Garrison heard of in England.'[50] Similarly, the godly from over a wide area took refuge in the parliamentarian garrison at Manchester;[51] while Henry Martindale 'and many yeomen's sons' in Lancashire fled to the parliamentarian garrison at Bolton to escape being forced to serve in the Earl of Derby's royalist regiments, 'and took up arms there' for the parliament.[52] Adam Martindale was suspected of being a Roundhead because his brother Henry was in arms for parliament at Bolton, though in fact he 'would have been quiet and meddled on no side', but in order to avoid being compelled into the royalist ranks, he went to Liverpool and became clerk to the parliament's forces there.[53] The resistance of such towns to the king reflected not only urban puritanism but rural puritanism as well,[54] which is a warning against underestimating the part played by countrymen in the parliamentarian party.

Led by example and frightened by persecution, puritans became parliamentarians. But the rank and file of the parliament's forces was not recruited from puritans alone, but far more from tenants who merely obeyed their landlords and from poor people who came in for the pay and the plunder.[55] When the parliament's

50 *Reliquiae Baxterianae* pp. 43–5.
51 'Tracts Relating to Military Proceedings in Lancashire during the Great Civil War', *Chetham Society* Vol. II (1844) p. 122; 'The Life of Master John Shaw' in 'Yorkshire Diaries and Autobiographies', *Surtees Society* Vol. LXV (1875) p. 137; 'Some Memoirs Concerning the Family of the Priestleys', pp. 9, 18–19, 26–7.
52 Martindale, *op. cit.* pp. 31–2.
53 *ibid.* pp. 34–9.
54 *ibid.* pp. 31–3; Hutchinson, *op. cit.* pp. 110–11, 112.
55 *Reliquiae Baxterianae* p. 31; Hutchinson, *op. cit.* pp. 110–11; 'Tracts Relating to Military Proceedings in Lancashire during the Great Civil War', pp. 45, 51–2.

army reached Northampton on 7 September 1642 '. . . our regiments being drawn into the field to exercise, many of them discovered their base ends in undertaking this design, and demanded 5s a man, which they say was promised them monthly by the Committee, or they would surrender their arms; whereupon Colonel Hampden and other commanders laboured to appease them, but could not. . . .'[56] A regiment of 450 Bluecoats from London entered Oxford on 22 September and mustered next day in the Parks, 'where they appeared very untractable and undocile in their postures; and besides, they began to mutinie amonge themselves and against their commanders, sayinge that they were promised 5s by the month for every man as a reward besides his daily paye at their first settinge forth, and nowe the moneth was out, and they would have that which was promised them, or else they would doe no more service nor muster. . . .' Lord Saye pacified them for a time and imprisoned some of the mutineers, but the trouble broke out again and Lord Saye threatened to disarm and dismiss them, but they said that they must have their money before they would consent to surrender their arms and be disbanded.[57] This was the first in the whole series of mutinies over pay in the parliament's armies, which eventually came to a climax in 1647.

At Gloucester '. . . many inferiour officers forsook us' for lack of pay, 'and common souldiers ranne to other places that yielded a large and constant entertainment, and required lesse service . . .'[58] Soldiers who served only for the pay were indifferent as to which party they served providing that they were paid. And parliamentarian soldiers who were captured by the royalists were often content to take up arms for the king. When the king captured Banbury Castle in 1642 '. . . half the common soldiers at the least readily took conditions, and put themselves into the King's army. . . .'[59] When the prisoners taken by Prince Rupert at Cirencester were brought to Oxford in 1643, they were viewed by the king and 'some of the properest fellowes of them, after they had taken the newe protestation appointed lately by his majestie, were newe apparrelled and tooke into serve for his

56 *C.S.P.D. 1641–1643* pp. 385–6.
57 *The Life and Times of Anthony Wood* Vol. I, ed. A. Clark, *Oxford Historical Society* Vol. XIX (1819) pp. 64–6.
58 Corbet, *op. cit.* pp. 25–6, 70.
59 Clarendon, *op. cit.* Vol. II, p. 374.

majestie . . . and most of them dispersed up and downe into other regiments, as occasion served.'[60] Similarly, royalist soldiers captured by the parliamentarians took service with their captors, and Baxter asserted that in the New Model Army '. . . the greatest part of the Common Soldiers, especially of the Foot, were ignorant men, of little Religion, abundance of them such as had been taken Prisoners, or turned out of Garrisons under the King, and had been Soldiers in his Army. . . .'[61]

Nehemiah Wharton, a godly London apprentice, who joined the Earl of Essex's army at the outbreak of the civil war, was shocked that many of his fellow soldiers were interested only in pay and the prospect of plunder, and that they did not stop even at robbing their own comrades.[62] Adam Martindale who had become clerk to Colonel Moore at Liverpool, found the Colonel's 'family [i.e. household] . . . was such a pack of arrant thieves, and they so artificial [i.e. skilful] at their trade, that it was scarce possible to save anything out of their hands, except what I could carry about with me, or lodge in some other house. Those that were not thieves (if there were any such) were generally (if not universally) desperately profane and bitter scoffers at piety, and these headed by one that had a mighty influence over the Colonel. . . .'[63] Puritan preachers never tired of inveighing against the swearing, drunkenness, profaneness, immorality of parliament's soldiers, who fought for pay and plunder rather than the cause.[64] After the Lancashire parliamentarians had captured Hoghton Tower sixty of them were killed by an explosion of the powder magazine. According to one account this was the work of two papists, who after surrendering and receiving quarter fired the powder, and was a good example of the treachery and perfidy of papists.[65] But a puritan minister gave a different picture: 'The miscarriages of great and small in the taking of Preston did us

60 Wood, *op. cit.* Vol. I, p. 88.
61 *Reliquiae Baxterianae* p. 53; C. H. Firth, *Cromwell's Army* (reprinted, London, 1962) p. 37.
62 *C.S.P.D. 1641–1643* pp. 385–8, 400.
63 Martindale, *op. cit.* pp. 36–7.
64 John Pigot, *The Sharpness of the Sword: or Abner's Plea for Accommodation* (London, 1643); Thomas Coleman, *The Hearts Ingagement* (London, 1643); Herbert Palmer, *The Glasse of Gods Providence* (London, 1644); Christopher Love, *England's Distemper* (London, 1645).
65 'Tracts Relating to Military Proceedings in Lancashire during the Great Civil War', pp. 80–1.

more mischief than all our enemies from the entrance of our hostility to that time. . . . Our men . . . being burdened with the weight of their swearing, drunkenesse, plundering, and wilful waste at Preston, it dispossessed them by the help of Powder to which their disorders laid a Train fired by their neglected Matches, or by that great Souldiers' Idoll, Tobacco. . . . O that this thundering Alarm might ever sound in the eares of our Swearing, Cursing, Drunken, Tobacco-abusing Commanders and Souldiers unto unfaigned Repentance. . . . "I tell you nay, but except ye repent, ye shall all likewise perish. . . ." '[66]

There was, nevertheless, a godly element in parliament's army, and it became increasingly influential. Nehemiah Wharton thought that he was fighting 'the Lord's battle'.[67] He described the appetite of the Earl of Essex's soldiers for puritan sermons, which 'subdued and satisfied more malignant spirits amongst us than 1,000 armed men could have done', and '. . . wrought wonderfully upon many of us, and doubtless has fitted many of us for death, which we all shortly expect.'[68] When they had to spend a night in the open and in the rain, they sang psalms until morning.[69] They plundered the papists, and broke into churches, destroying the rails round communion tables, smashing stained glass windows and cutting up surplices for handkerchief.[70] In Northamptonshire '. . . our soldiers sallied out about the country and returned in state, clothed in surplice, hood, and cap, representing the Bishop of Canterbury.'[71] At Coventry they seized 'an old base priest . . . and led him ridiculously about the city. . . .'[72] Arriving at Hereford on a Sunday, 'about the time of morning prayer, we went to the Minster, where the pipes played and the puppets sang so sweetly that some of our soldiers could not forbear dancing in the holy quire, whereat the Baalists were sore displeased. The anthem ended, they fell to prayer, and prayed devoutly for the King, the Bishops, Etc; and one of our soldiers with a loud voice said, "what! never a bit for the Parliament" which offended them much more. Not satisfied with this human service we went to divine; and, passing by, found shops open, and men at work, to whom we gave some plain dehortations, and

66 *ibid.* pp. 127–8.
67 *C.S.P.D. 1641–1643*, pp. 380, 397.
68 *ibid.* pp. 372, 382–3, 388, 391, 394, 397, 400.
69 *ibid.* p. 393.   70 *ibid.* pp. 372–3.
71 *ibid.* p. 384.   72 *ibid.* p. 382.

went to hear Mr Sedgwick, who gave us two famous sermons. . . .'[73] At Coventry 'a whore which had followed our camp from London was taken up by the soldiers, and first led about the city, then set in the pillory, after in the cage, then ducked in a river, and at last banished from the city.'[74] Thus Wharton gives a picture of a raw, popular puritanism in the Earl of Essex's army; a picture which embraces the main features of the puritan movement—anti-papist and anti-clerical, seeking to enforce sabbatarianism and a stricter moral discipline, and to remove from the church all relics of popery—communion tables railed in like altars, ministers wearing surplices, images in stained glass windows—and to bring in more preaching and less ceremony.

Although Adam Martindale complained about thieving, profane parliamentarians, who were 'bitter scoffers at piety', nevertheless he '. . . enjoyed sweet communion with the religious officers of the company, which used to meet every night at one another's quarters, by turns, to read scriptures, to confer of good things, and to pray together.'[75] Cromwell, first as a captain, 'had a special care to get religious men into his troop' of horse;[76] then as a colonel he chose 'godly, pretious men' for officers of his regiment of horse,[77] and filled the ranks with 'freeholders and freeholders' sons' who 'upon matter of conscience engaged in this quarrel, and under Cromwell'.[78] '. . . If you looke upon his owne regiment of horse,' exclaimed a critic of Cromwell, 'see what a swarme ther is of thos that call themselves the godly; some of them profess to have sene vissions and had revellations.'[79] An officer in the Earl of Stamford's regiment of horse was shocked to find that '. . . all the officers of no one company were all of the same opinion what Religion they fought for: some loved the book of Common Prayer and Bishops, others were zealous for extempory prayers and Elders, another thought Bishops so many Elders, and Elders so many Bishops, and therefore they fought to set Jesus Christ in his throne (meaning) independency:

73 *ibid.* pp. 399–400.   74 *ibid.* p. 382.
75 Martindale, *op. cit.* pp. 36–7.
76 *Reliquiae Baxterianae* p. 98.
77 'The Quarrel between the Earl of Manchester and Oliver Cromwell', *Camden Society*, New Series, Vol. XII (1875) p. 72.
78 Bulstrode Whitlock, *Memorials of the English Affairs* (4 vols., Oxford, 1853) Vol. I, p. 209.
79 'The Quarrel between the Earl of Manchester and Oliver Cromwell', p. 72.

some liked the Chaplain of the Regiment, another thought his Corporal preached better. . . . And one would think, that every Company had been raised out of the several Congregations of Amsterdam. . . .'[80]

At Nottingham 'all the devout people of the town were very vigorous and ready to offer their lives and families' for parliament,[81] and at Gloucester it was those 'who were held up by the deep sense of religion' that were most determined to resist the king.[82] When the Earl of Derby besieged Manchester in September 1642 '. . . Christians nearer and further off were united in one argument of support; viz. That God had not mustered his precious saints, from all adjacent parts in Manchester, to shut them up into the hands of the enemy, but rather to shew them his salvation.' 'A spirit of Piety and Devotion in Prayers and singing of Psalms rested generally upon Persons and families, yea Taverns and Innes where it might not put in the head formerly.' 'God kept up the Souldiering spirit, by Prayers, and Psalms, mutuall encouragement, and the blast of the Silver Trumpets (the Ministers of God) sounded by a Divine breath when Temptation was at highest, and their spirits at the lowest. . . .' 'Our Souldiers from first to last had prayers and singing of Psalms dayly at the street ends, most of our Souldiers being religious honest men, of a civill and inoffensive conversation, which came out of conscience of their oath and protestation.' When the Earl withdrew and lifted the siege 'the Saints sung the Song of Moses' in the church, while outside the soldiers 'with a loud voice and one consent, clapping their hands apace they reported God fearfull in praises, working wonders.'[83] '. . . Those who are most religious, have stuck most to the Parliament . . .,' claimed Jeremiah Burroughes.[84] Parliamentarians were a minority in Gloucester, less than a quarter of the population in Nottingham, and less than one fifth of the inhabitants of Manchester:[85] it was religion that sustained this minority.

80 *A Copy of a Letter Writ from Sjt. Major Kirle* (1643) B.M. E.246(35).
81 Hutchinson, *op. cit.* p. 105.
82 Corbet, *op. cit.* p. 42.
83 'Tracts Relating to Military Proceedings in Lancashire during the Great Civil War', pp. 56, 120, 122.
84 Jeremiah Burroughes, *The glorious Name of God* (London, 1643) p. 56.
85 Corbet, *op. cit.* p. 42; Hutchinson, *op. cit.* p. 105; 'Tracts Relating to Military Proceedings in Lancashire during the Great Civil War', pp. 50-1, 219-21.

It was a general assumption among puritans that the religious people were to be found chiefly in the middle ranks of the population. 'Freeholders and Tradesmen are the Strength of Religion and Civility in the Land: and Gentlemen and Beggers, and Servile Tenants, are the Strength of Iniquity; (Though among these sorts there are some also that are good and just, as among the other there are many bad).'[86] The rich were subject to too many temptations and to 'the three or four Sins of Sodom, Pride, Fulness of Bread, and Abundance of Idleness, and not considering the Poor and Needy. And their Fulness and Idleness tempt them to further Voluptuousness and Sensuality, to Filthiness, or to Time-wasting needless kinds of Sports.' The rich were worldly, valuing 'Riches and Honours in the World', and wanted a religion 'Consistent with a Worldly Mind; which Outside-formality, Lip-service and Hypocrisie is; but Seriousness, Sincerity and Spirituality is not'. And, most important of all, the nobility and gentry resisted a godly discipline.[87] A godly discipline, which was to be exercised by a minister and lay elders elected by the congregation, was the main aim of the puritans, whether it was to be within the framework of a reformed episcopacy, or of presbyterianism, or of congretational Independency. But the nobility and gentry did not relish being subjected to constant surveillance, and liability to public rebuke, by elders who would be likely to be their social inferiors, '. . . exposing us eternal apprentices to the Arbitrary Jurisdiction of a new Corporation of Apron Elders, Mechanical Artisans . . . ,' protested Sir Thomas Aston.[88] Henry Oxinden of Barham in Kent believed that 'the multitude' aimed at such a government in the church 'wherein themselves . . . may be able to tyrannize over their betters, whom naturally they have ever hated and in their hearts despised.' 'I think it therefore high time for all gentlemen to cast about with themselves, and endeavour rather to maintain episcopal government in its former state, with some diminution in temporalities, than to introduce I know not what presbyterial government; which will upon the matter equalize men of mean condition with the gentry. . . .'[89]

86 *Reliquiae Baxterianae* p. 89.
87 *ibid.* pp. 31, 94; Corbet, *op. cit.* p. 17.
88 Sir Thomas Aston, *A Remonstrance against Presbytery* (1641) B.M. E.163 (1).
89 *The Oxinden and Peyton Letters 1642–1670* ed. D. Gardiner (London, 1937) pp. 36–7.

The poor, on the other hand, did not have either the leisure or the education to form their own opinions on religious questions. '. . . Plowmen, and many others, are so wearied or continually employed, either in the Labours or the Cares of their Callings, that it is a great Impediment to their Salvation . . .': the poorer peasants were ignorant and 'like Bruits'.[90] The poor tenant-farmer was servile and took his religion from his landlord: 'his religion is a part of his copyhold, which he takes from his land-lord and refers it wholly to his discretion'.[91] 'The needy multitude' was opposed to the puritan discipline because of 'their naturall hatred of good order':[92] they resented the efforts of the puritans to suppress their traditional sports, recreations and customs. The anti-puritan mobs at Kidderminster were composed of 'poor Journey-men and Servants' and ignorant 'Beggers at the Town-sends'.[93] They resisted the yoke of the godly middle sort of people. 'The vulgar Rabble of the carnal and prophane, the Fornicators, Drunkards, Swearers, Etc. did every where hate them that reproved their Sin, and condemned them by a holy life. This Difference was universal, and their Enmity implac-able . . . So that every where serious, godly People . . . were spoken against and derided by the Name of Precisians, Zealots, Over-Strict, the holy Brethren, and other Terms of Scorn.'[94] In places where the puritan 'middle sort of people' already had some influence and power before the civil war, the outbreak of that conflict provided the opportunity for the poor—the servants, journeymen, labourers and paupers—to free themselves from the surveillance and oppression of the godly, and 'they were like tyed Mastiffs newly loosed, and fled in the Face of all that was religious, yea, or Civil, which came in their way.'[95]

'The freeholders', however, 'were not enslaved to their Land-lords as the Tenants are', and 'the Tradesmen have a Correspon-dency with London, and so are grown to be a far more Intelligent sort of Men than ignorant Peasants . . .', 'their constant Converse and Traffick with London', promoting 'Civility and Piety'

90 *Reliquiae Baxterianae* pp. 30, 89.
91 *ibid.*; Christopher Hill, *Economic Problems of the Church from Archbishop Whitgift to the Long Parliament* (Oxford, 1956) p. 55.
92 Corbet, *op. cit.* p. 14.
93 *Reliquiae Baxterianae* pp. 40, 85.
94 *ibid.* pp. 31–2.
95 *ibid.* p. 42.

among them.[96] Richard Heywood of Bolton was a yeoman by rank and a clothier by trade, and he went once or twice a year to London, where he went to hear sermons by the chief puritan preachers, such as Edmund Calamy and Thomas Case, and bought 'the best books, the most plain, practical experimental treatises in divinity such as Calvin, Luther in English, Mr Perkins, Dr Preston, Dr Sibbs, wherein he took much pleasure in reading'.[97] The strength of puritanism at Kidderminster lay in the master weavers, who dominated the town before the civil war. They were not rich—'three or four of the Richest thriving Masters of the Trade, got but about £500 or £600 in twenty years, and it may be lose £100 of it at once by an ill Debtor'; and even 'the magistrates of the Town were few of them worth £40 per. An. and most not half so much.' 'The generality of the Master Workmen' got not much more than their 'Food and Raiment' and 'lived but a little better than their Journey-men, (from hand to mouth) but only that they laboured not altogether so hard.' They had some leisure and some education and 'were of such a Trade as allowed them time enough to read or talk of holy Things: . . . and as they stand in their loom they can set a Book before them, or edifie one another. . . .'[98]

The concept of 'godliness' helped to create a selfconscious middle sort of people, for it distinguished them from the 'profane and ignorant rabble' on the one hand, and from the 'worldly and debauched nobility and gentry' on the other; and provided them with a standard other than a material one by which they could feel superior both to those not much poorer than themselves and to those very much richer than themselves. Francis Cheynell complained that in every parish there was 'a prophane and ignorant multitude who are borne with a Pope in their belly, and are not yet redeemed from that grosse superstition and vaine Conversation which they received by Tradition from their Fathers. . . .'[99] They loved their Whitsun-ales and Lords-day sports,[100] and they would 'stand up and make much adoe' to defend the 'ancient Ceremonies, beloved Customes and Traditions

96 *ibid.* pp. 30, 89.
97 Heywood, *op. cit.* Vol. I, p. 84.
98 *Reliquiae Baxterianae* pp. 89, 94.
99 Francis Cheynell, *Sions Memento, and Gods Alarum* (London, 1643) p. 38.
100 William Mewe, *The Robbing and Spoiling of Jacob and Israel* (London, 1643) pp. 26–7.

of our Fathers. . . .'[101] 'Oh Beloved,' cried Stephen Marshall, 'the generality of the people of England, is extremely wicked. . . .'[102] 'The bulk of our people are wicked, and their hearts are not as yet prepared to the yoke of the Lord,' lamented Edmund Calamy: 'They are unreformed themselves; and it is no wonder they are so opposite to a thorough reformation. . . .'[103] 'The maine bent and stream of nations runnes downward to vice and profanenesse: the generall desires and endeavours of men are tending to loosenesse: nor unstained worship in the Church, nor impartial justice in commonwealth, would they have. . . .'[104]

Stephen Marshall asserted 'that many of the nobles, magistrates, knights and gentlemen, and persons of great quality' were '. . . patrons of alehouses and disorders'; and 'in many of their families (not to mention Religion) there is not so much as a face of civility.'[105] The sins which the preachers of godliness most inveighed against were the sins of the nobility and gentry, whose bad examples had corrupted the mass of the people. Drunkenness was one sin that had spread from the upper classes to the lower.[106] Swearing was another, being at one time 'the language onely of great persons, who held it a matter of breeding . . . and an ornament of their speech', it had spread from 'graceless Gentlemen' to the mass of the people, so that 'every base fellow thinkes it is a gracefull kind of speaking, to sweare and to blaspheme, especially in such oathes as are in fashion at Court.'[107] Pride in dress had also spread from the upper classes to the lower.[108] Dress was the foremost symbol of status in this society and the puritan in his plain and sober attire was extending from the church to society at large his protest against a false regard for externals, and rejecting the standards of a hierarchical aristocratic society. 'I more prize a poor, ragged, despised Christian in whom appears anything of Christ,' wrote Oliver Heywood, 'than the most gaudy

---

101 Humphrey Hardwick, *The Difficulty of Sions Deliverance and Reformation* (London, 1644) pp. 9–12.
102 Stephen Marshall, *Reformation and Desolation* (London, 1642) pp. 45–6.
103 Edmund Calamy, *Englands Lookinge-Glasse* (London, 1642) pp. 56–7.
104 Hardwick, *op. cit.* pp. 9–12.
105 Marshall, *op. cit.* pp. 45–6.
106 Samuel Fairecloth, *The Troublers Troubled* (London, 1641) p. 31; Shaw, *op. cit.* pp. 396–7, 411.
107 Peter Smith, *A Sermon Preached before the Honorable House of Commons* (London, 1644) p. 36.
108 *ibid.* pp. 34–5; Martindale, *op. cit.* pp. 6–7, 9.

and glorious gallants in best attire and largest attendants; in my eyes a rich and revelling gentleman is but a vile person compared with a poor praying saint.'[109] Heywood, the son of a Lancashire weaver, exhibited the influence of puritan preaching on the growth of middle-class consciousness: he was at school with 'many great men's sons' and he rejoiced that he was able to resist their bad examples, which 'too sadly verified that dreadful scripture of the paucity of rich men that are saved, and not many noble are called.'[110] 'It is more honour to be a gracious man than a rich man,' wrote Adam Martindale, who was the son of a Lancashire yeoman.[111]

The middle sort of people, being the yeomen and better-off peasant farmers, the master craftsmen and small traders, were characterized by an independence of thought and opinion, which was rooted in their economic independence.[112] They owned their own land, or had sufficient land on a long lease to be independent of landlords; or they had their own businesses, and they were employers of labour. They were the independent small producers and in this period production in both agriculture and industry was largely under their control. They were a distinct economic class: above them stood the class of rentiers (the landlords who lived chiefly off rents) and financiers (the merchants who lived chiefly by the manipulation of money and credit), and below them lay the class of wage-earners (the servants and labourers who lived off wages in money or kind).[113] Suppression of the peasantry and reduction of the independence of the towns were the conditions for the development of monarchical absolutism on the continent of Europe, and prevented the growth of a middle class. But in England the rise of a significant middle class was the main obstacle to the development of monarchical absolutism.[114] Godliness encouraged the middle sort of people to assert their independence and to oppose any trends towards absolutism. According to Corbet it made them 'more knowing' than the rest of

109 Heywood, *op. cit.* Vol. I, p. 141.
110 *ibid.* p. 159.
111 Martindale, *op. cit.* p. 102.
112 Corbet, *op. cit.* pp. 8–10.
113 Christopher Hill, *Economic Problems of the Church* pp. 11–12; *Society and Puritanism in Pre-Revolutionary England* (London, 1964) Ch. IV.
114 J. P. Cooper, 'Differences between English and Continental Governments in the Early Seventeenth Century', *Britain and the Netherlands* ed. J. S. Bromley and E. H. Kossmann (London, 1960) pp. 82–9.

the common people and so more 'apt to contradict and question' and not so easily 'brought to the bent'; and it enabled them to form their own opinions on 'such things as concerne the life of a morall man'. The puritan was responsible for his own salvation: he had to be sure in his own mind and conscience that he was following the truth, for he would not be able to excuse himself from error by saying that he merely took his opinions from another man, nor excuse himself from sin by saying that he merely followed the lead of another man. He had 'a knowledge of things pertaining to divine worship according to the maine principles of the Christian profession. Which religion is not according to the will of man, but grounded upon an unchangeable and eternall truth . . . and it hath . . . in its nature an irreconcileable enmity against arbitrary government. . . .'[115] The bible was god's word, and it contained the law by which human beings were to conduct themselves in all their affairs, ecclesiastical and secular: this law was true and just, unchanging and unchangeable, and to put human will above it, or to put human invention in place of it, was to usurp god's authority. Man was a sinner, his will was self-seeking and a law made by a man would be for his own rather than the general good, and to extend his own power. Slavery lay in obedience to man and his law, liberty lay in obedience to god and his law. A tyrannical and arbitrary ruler was one who obeyed only laws that he made himself, or who put his sinful and self-seeking will above the law and claimed to be able to make or change the law merely as his own discretion. The fundamental laws of the constitution, and the laws which were made by the whole community, which could not be changed at the whim of the ruler or any one individual, were laws which sought the good of all and not just of one.[116] Puritans believed in the rule of law in both religion and politics, and that in obedience of both rulers and ruled to the law lay both religious and political liberty. It is not necessary to suppose that they transferred their concept of liberty from religion to politics, for this concept included both church and state in its inception.

The middle sort of people had secular as well as religious grievances against the government of Charles I. The king and some of the nobility and gentry had tried to cash in on the profits of industry by means of royal monopolies and projects, such as the

Westminster Soap Company, through which it was alleged 'that many Citizens of London were put out of an old Trade, in which they had beene bred all their time, and which was their onely lively-hood, by Knights, Esquires, and Gentlemen, never bred up to the Trade. . . .'[117] This was also resented by many of the nobility and gentry, but in their case because they were excluded from a share in monopolies and projects. The nobility and gentry generally were opposed to shipmoney and so were the middle sort of people, but not on the same grounds. In a tract, written in 1637 but not published until 1641, William Prynne noted that the 'middle rank of the people' objected to shipmoney because of 'the inequalitie of taxing of it': '. . . Ordinary Merchants charged, to pay, ten, twelve, fifteene, yea, twenty five pound, or more; when as diverse of your great Officers, Earles, and Lords, who had fortie times greater Estates and Annuall revenewes, payd but two, three, foure, or five pounds at the most'; in cities and corporations 'the middle and poore sort of people, payd more than the richest; and in the Countrey . . . some Farmers pay more than the richest Knights and Gentlemen. . . .'[118] In 1638 a group of yeomen led the opposition to shipmoney in the parish of Enfield in Middlesex, and their complaint was that the sheriff had altered their assessments 'so as to ease the burden on the wealthy landholders in the county, forcing it to fall more heavily on the yeomen and farmers'.[119] Thus the middle sort of people had grievances not only against the government of Charles I, but also against the nobility and gentry and the rich in general. Though resentment against shipmoney united different social groups in opposition to the Personal Government of Charles I in the 1630s, it also sharpened the antagonism between 'the middle and poore sort of people' and the rich and powerful.

The complaint against shipmoney was part of a general grievance of the middle sort of people against the system of taxation, whether imposed 'unconstitutionally' by the royal prerogative or 'constitutionally' with the consent of parliament, and that was that it fell disproportionately upon them. 'There is reason to believe that in the century after 1523 there was a steady shift of

117 *A Short and True Relation concerning the Soap-busines* (London, 1641).
118 [William Prynne], *An Humble Remonstrance to His Majesty, Against the Tax of Ship-money* (1641) p. 23.
119 Mildred Campbell, *The English Yeoman* (reprinted London, 1960) p. 368.

the burden from the larger to the smaller taxpayers right down the social scale.'[120] The nobility and gentry and the richer classes were not paying their fair share of taxation: they were increasingly successful in passing on the burden to the rest of the population, which meant the middle sort of people, for the poor had nothing with which to pay. Indeed it was one of the aims of shipmoney to reverse this process and to make the rich pay more. Such success as it had in doing this[121]—though Prynne claimed that it had none—was ended when it was abolished by the Long Parliament, and the middle sort of people were left entirely at the mercy of the taxes voted by parliament, which had for a long time fallen more heavily on them than on the rich. This grievance of the middle sort of people found expression in a pamphlet of 1641 which urged on parliament 'the inequality, and unconscionable disproportion of rating of the subsidies. . . .' 'The poorer sort cannot pay the King: the greater sort, as having the law in their own hands, will pay but what they please, but the middle sort, they must and shall pay; and in such a disproportion as is insufferable. . . .' A yeoman of £100 a year was rated at £5, but a landowner of £1,000 a year was rated at only £20, a mere four times as much though his income was ten times greater; and a landowner of £10,000 a year was rated at only £100, a mere twenty times as much though his income was a hundred times greater. This reduced the king's revenue and 'must necessarily begger most of the poore inferiour Yeomandry of the Kingdome' and ruin 'poore Renters and Farmers'. So the pamphlet demanded: '. . . let every mans estate . . . bee made liable to pay proportionally. And as your . . . middle sort of people, are usually rated by the Justices or their appointment, then shall you doe right, both to the King and the middle sort of subjects. Wherefore you can never doe your selves more right, then to redresse this abuse. . . .'[122] The gentry, who dominated the House of Commons, were aware that the subsidies fell more heavily on the middle sort of subjects than on the rich,[123] but a parliament of landowners was not ready to reform a system from which they benefited, and the grievance

120 Stone, *op. cit.* pp. 495–9; Cooper, *op. cit.* p. 89.
121 M. D. Gordon, 'The Collection of Ship-Money in the Reign of Charles I', *Transactions of the Royal Historical Society*, third series, Vol. IV (1910).
122 *Considerations Touching Trade* (1641) pp. 11–14.
123 *The Journal of Sir Simonds D'Ewes* ed. W. H. Coates (New Haven, 1942) p. 121.

of the middle rank of the people remained and was taken up again after the civil war by the Levellers.[124]

As in the state so in the church taxation fell more heavily on the middle and poorer sort of people, and though townsmen generally tended to get off lightly, the burden of tithes fell disproportionately on yeoman and farmers. Furthermore, since many tithes went into the pockets of lay landowners who had impropriated them, this amounted to a tax for support of the nobility and gentry.[125] So there were grounds for the warning in 1641 that freedom from tithes 'is the secret thing which our common Freeholders and Grand-Jury-Men [usually yeomen] doe so much ayme at, if Bishops and their Courts were overthrowne.'[126]

From the 1590s to the 1630s the middle rank of people in the towns—'the small tradesmen and the better-off craftsmen'—was engaged in a struggle to secure or recover a voice and a share in the government of the towns from the oligarchies of wealthy merchants and richer townsmen who monopolized the government and commerce of the towns.[127] They also demanded a vote in the elections to parliament[128] and a voice in the affairs of their local church, especially in relation to the choice of ministers and the establishment of a godly discipline within their own congregation.[129] But the middle rank of people in the countryside—the yeomen and the better-off farmers—had a better established status and a more secure place in the community than the middle rank of the people in the towns: they had a share in the running of their own village, they sat on juries and had a voice in the government

124 Don M. Wolfe, *Leveller Manifestoes* (reprinted London, 1967) pp. 270, 303, 407.
125 Christopher Hill, *Economic Problems of the Church*, Chs. V, VI.
126 *A Certificate from Northamptonshire* (London, 1641) p. 14.
127 Penry Williams, 'Government and Politics in Ludlow, 1590–1642', *Transaction of the Shropshire Archaeological Society* Vol. LVI, Part III (1960) pp. 283–8; Roger Howell, *Newcastle upon Tyne and the Puritan Revolution* (Oxford, 1967) pp. 39–42, 53–61.
128 W. T. MacCaffrey, *Exeter 1540–1640* (Cambridge, Mass., 1958) pp. 222–4; M. R. Frear, 'The Election at Great Marlow in 1640', *Journal of Modern History* Vol. XIV (1942); R. L. Bushman, 'English Franchise Reform in the Seventeenth Century', *Journal of British Studies* Vol. III (1) (1963); J. H. Plumb, 'The Growth of the Electorate in England from 1600 to 1715', *Past and Present* No. 45 (1969).
129 Heywood, *op. cit.* Vol. I, pp. 83–4; 'Some Memoirs Concerning the Family of the Priestleys', p. 17.

of their county, and they usually had a vote in parliamentary elections.[130] This tended to make them less radical than their social counterparts in the towns, though they did want a part in the government of their parish church. The parish church, however, was subject not only to the central control of the bishop and his officials but also to the local control of the nobility and gentry, who appointed the ministers of most churches and provided a considerable proportion of the income of many churches.[131] In order to increase their part in the running of their parish church, men of the middle rank had thus to challenge not only the bishops but the nobility and gentry, and seek to transfer the control of the local church to elders elected by the congregation, who would often be men of the middle rank, especially since they would have to be men of approved godliness. It is this that lies behind the warning that Viscount Conway received from his chaplain in October 1641, that in Somerset '. . . our chiefest farmers have their loins girt with a divinity surcingle, and begin to bristle up for a lay eldership.'[132]

For the middle rank of the people the civil war came at the climax of a struggle for a greater measure of democracy in local affairs, parliamentary elections and ecclesiastical government—a democracy not extending so far as to include the mass of the poor (servants, labourers, paupers), but confined to the better-off farmers and craftsmen. This struggle is well illustrated by a dispute which broke out in the parish of St Saviour's in Southwark—an industrial suburb of London which played a key role in the English Revolution. In 1556 the parishioners at large had been excluded from a voice in electing the churchwardens and in overseeing the expenditure of the parish's revenue by a self-elected vestry of thirty, who chose the six churchwardens out of their own number and the four auditors of the accounts. In the reign of James I some of the parishioners petitioned parliament for the restoration of the right to elect the churchwardens and to oversee their accounts. 'In all ages and countries where civil offices are elective,' they argued, 'the commonpeople and handicraftsmen (though they were never admitted to exercise any public offices) yet they were never denied voices in elections of civil officers,

130 Peter Laslett, *The World We have lost* (London, 1965) Ch. 3.
131 Christopher Hill, *Economic Problems of the Church* pp. 144–5.
132 *C.S.P.D. 1641–1643* p. 144.

sheriffs, bailiffs, and chief officers throughout the whole realm, are chosen by the inhabitants and commonalty assembled, except only in such places where there is power given by their charters to make laws to the contrary. The knights of the shire, and burgesses for Parliament are chosen by the freeholders, which in most places consist of great multitudes.' But they did not advocate a 'popular election' by 'the ruder sort', but rather a restriction of the franchise to those parishioners who were rated £3 or more for the subsidy, who numbered about 200. If parliament thought this number too large and too 'popular', they would agree to raise the qualification to £5.[133] The tradition of democracy was very much alive in 1642 among the middle rank of the people, who tended to believe that ancient rights had been filched from them by the richer people and must be recovered by a struggle. Their views were expressed by a pamphlet of 1642 which justified the Militia Ordinance of the two Houses of Parliament by claiming that according to 'the most ancient practice and custome of this Kingdoms . . . the Lieutenants and supream Commanders of the Militia in every County, were elected . . . by the Common-counsell . . . through every Province, Countrey and County, in a full Folkmoth or County Court by the Freeholders of the County': '. . . The Freeholders in ancient times did thus in every County elect their Lieutenants and Captains of their Militia, to Train and Order them; yea, and the high Sheriffs too, who had the command of the whole power of the County, whom they then likewise elected. . . .'[134]

The democratic movement of the middle sort of people involved both church and state, but it tended from 1640 onwards to find a focus in the campaign for a change in the government of the church, which could not be without the abolition of episcopacy. William Lilly observed that the Londoners who went to Westminster to demonstrate against the bishops 'were most of them men of mean or a middle quality themselves, no aldermen, merchants or common-council men, but set on by some of better quality; and yet most of them were either such as had public spirits, or lived a more religious life than the vulgar, and were

---

133 John Stow, *A Survey of the Cities of London and Westminster* ed. John Strype (London, 1720) Book. IV pp. 9–10.
134 [?William Prynne], *A Soveraign Antidote to Prevent, Appease, and Determine our unnaturall and destructive Civill Warres and dissentions* (London, 1642) p. 9.

usually called Puritans, and had suffered under the tyranny of the Bishops; in the general they were very honest men and well-meaning . . . as men in whose breasts the spirit of liberty had some place; and they were even glad to vent out their sighs and sufferings in this rather tumultuous than civil manner; being assured if ever this Parliament had been dissolved, they must have been wrackt, whipt and stript by the snotty clergy and other extravagant courses. . . .'[135] 'The Bishops and their Courts' had oppressed 'the meaner sort of tradesmen and artificers', impoverishing 'many thousands' of them and forcing 'great numbers' of them to flee during the 1630s, 'some into New England and other parts of America, others into Holland'.[136] The hostility of the middle sort of people to the bishops was not just the result of a difference of view about ecclesiastical government, for it was compounded in large measure of anti-clericalism. This had its roots in resentment against clerical taxes and exactions, dislike of clerical interference in lay affairs, and the feeling of the godly people that they were as competent as the clergy, indeed more competent than most of the clergy to decide theological and moral questions, to live religious lives and to teach the people.[137] But the nobility and gentry were not much less obstacles to the reform of the church than the bishops, and although the middle rank of the people rallied to parliament when they feared that the king intended to dissolve it by force, they did so because without parliament there would be little hope for reform of the church at all. Their support did not spring from any sense of identity of interests with the nobility and gentry, more often the reverse, and was conditional upon parliament carrying out the reform of the church.

The parliamentarians made a deliberate effort to win the support of 'the yeomanry' and the middle rank of the people. Henry Parker, the foremost apologist for parliament's stand against the king, claimed 'that most of the faulty, and decayed Nobility, and Gentry, are of the King's party, and so are the Lees of the people; but almost all of the Yeomanry (which is the most considerable ranke of any Nation) and a very choyse part both of Nobility and

135 Lilly, *op. cit.* pp. 106–7.
136 S. R. Gardiner (ed.) *The Constitutional Documents of the Puritan Revolution* (third edition revised, Oxford, 1947) pp. 214–15.
137 Christopher Hill, *Society and Puritanism* Chs. 8–10.

Gentry at this time side against the King and the Papists'.[138] Corbet said that the nobles and gentleman who sided with the king did so from 'a desire of vast dominion, dignity, revenge, or rapine' and out of 'an hatred of the commons, and a strong disposition to the ends of tyranny', caring not 'to render themselves the slaves of princes, that they also might rule over their neighbours as vassals'.[139] Ludlow held that 'many of the nobility and gentry were contented to serve' the king's 'arbitrary designs, if they might have leave to insult over such as were of a lower order. . . .'[140] In a sermon Jeremiah Burroughes explained 'why so many of the Gentry in most Counties throughout the Kingdome' supported the king: because '. . . many of them had rather inslave themselves and their posterities to those above them, then not to have their wils upon those that are under them: they would faine bring it to be with us as it is in France, that the Gentry should be under the Nobility and Courtiers, and all the country people, the peasants, bee under them as slaves, they live in miserable bondage under the Gentry there, who generally are Cavalliers. There is no Countrey in the world, where countrey men, such as we call the yeomandry, yea, and their Farmers and workmen under them, doe live in that fashion and freedome as they doe in England, in all other places they are slaves in comparison, their lives are so miserable as they are not worth the enjoying, they have no influence at all into the government they are under, nothing to doe in the making of Laws, or any way consenting to them, but must receive them from others, according to their pleasure; but in England every Free-holder hath an influence into the making and consenting every Law he is under, and enjoyes his owne with as true a title as the Nobleman enjoyes whatsoever is his. This freedome many of the proud Gentry are vexed at, and hence it is their hearts rise so against those that are chosen by them, and against their Ordinances. But the Commons begin to discerne this more than they have done, and to be so wise as to hold their own faster then they have.'[141] Another parliamentarian tract alleged that the royalists 'intend in England

---

138 H. Parker, *The Contra-Replicant, His Complaint to His Majesty* (1643) B.M. E.87(5).

139 Corbet, *op. cit.* pp. 8–9, 16–17.

140 *The Memoirs of Edmund Ludlow*, ed. C. H. Firth (2 vols., Oxford, 1894) Vol. I, p. 96.

141 Jeremiah Burroughes, *The glorious Name of God* (London, 1643) pp. 50–1.

a government at discretion, and all made in all probability, or after the French fashion . . .'; but, the author claimed that 'the middle sort of people of England, and Yeomanry' 'will especially oppose the change as whereby they from being in the happiest condition of any of their rank perhaps in Europe, nay in the world (who here live like men, and are wont to fight, or die like men in honour or defence of their country) might well be reduced to the terms of the peasants of France, of villeinage, and slavery. . . .'[142] When the Earl of Derby was repulsed from Manchester, the defenders appealed: '. . . O England's Yeomen and husbandmen look to yourselves, for if you stand not to it, as we of Manchester do, but be overcome, look for ever to be slaves. . . .'[143]

The parliamentarians played upon the fear of the middle rank of the people that, if the royalists won the war, not only their desire for a greater share in the affairs of the community would be frustrated, but also their existing share would be taken from them. They represented the royalist cause as being directed specifically against them and exploited any evidence of royalist disregard for them. The fears of the yeomen were confirmed when in the summer of 1642 royalist gentry tried, often successfully, to exclude yeomen from the grand jury, 'the representative body of the county';[144] and when the king had a meeting with the gentry of Yorkshire, the freeholders of the county protested at being excluded, '. . . conceiving our selves according to the proportions of our estates, equally interested in the common good of the countie. . . .'[145] When the king took the arms of the trained bands the two Houses of Parliament accused him of practising one of 'the most mischievous principles of tyranny . . . that ever were invented, that is to disarm the middle sort of people, who are the body of the Kingdome. . . .'[146] A parliamentarian pamphleteer claimed this as proof that the royalists 'intend in England a government at discretion, and all made in all probability, or after the French fashion', for 'the middle sort of people of England,

---

142 *A Soveraigne Salve to Cure the Blind* (1643) B.M. E.99(23).
143 *Weekly Intelligence* (1642) B.M. E.121(34).
144 *Advertisements from York and Beverly* (1642) B.M. E.107(30); 'Sir Roger Twysden's Journal', *Archaeologia Cantiana* Vol. I (1858) pp. 200–3; Alan Everitt, *The Community of Kent and the Great Rebellion 1640–60* (Leicester, 1966) pp. 95–6.
145 *A Letter from the Rt. Hon. Ferdinando Lord Fairfax* (1642) B.M. E.148(4).
146 Edward Husbands, *An Exact Collection* (London, 1642) p. 575.

and Yeomanry' were the chief obstacle to such a change, and since
they composed the main part of the trained bands, 'then by policy,
or even plain force' the trained bands must be disarmed.[147] The
parliamentarians also played upon the fear of the middle rank of
the people that their wealth which they had gained by their hard
work and their status which distinguished them from the mass
of the people were threatened by the royalists. The 'yeomen,
farmers, petty-freeholders, and such as use manufacture that en-
rich the country,' wrote Corbet, were 'a generation of men truely
laborious, jealous of their properties', and their enemies were
'powerfull gentry' who, 'detesting a close, hardy, and industrious
way of living, doe eate their bread in the sweat of other men.
. . .'[148] An effective piece of parliamentarian propaganda was
based on the allegation that the royalist Lord Poulett had said
'that it was not fit for any yeoman to have allowed him from his
own labours, any more than the poor mite of ten pounds a year,
and withall manifested to this purpose, though not perhaps in
these words, that when the power should be totally on their side,
they shall be compelled to live at that low allowance, notwithstanding their estates are gotten with a great deal of labour and
industry. . . .' 'Heaven grant that neither he nor his faction have
either will or power to do this. . . .' 'If the yeoman's estate were
his offence, therefore for that crime he must be limited a petty
proportion of 10 pounds a year, the tradesmen and merchants
were rich, and by this consequence being guilty of the same crime
receive the same punishment, and have such a limitation or less
(as the Yeomen). . . .'[149] The royalist leaders testified to the success of this propaganda in winning the support of the middle
rank of the people for parliament.[150]

At the outbreak of the civil war there seems to have been a great
deal of support for parliament among the middle sort of people.
In Yorkshire the freeholders were expected to support parliament;[151] in Shropshire they were said to be firm to parliament;[152]

147 *A Soveraigne Salve to Cure the Blind* (1643) B.M. E.99(23).
148 Corbet, *op.cit.* p. 9.
149 *A Memento for Yeomen, Merchants, Citizens, and all the Commons in England*
(1642) B.M. E.113(13).
150 *A Declaration Made by the Lord Marquis of Hertford* (1642) B.M. E.118(31);
Clarendon, *op. cit.* Vol. II, pp. 295–6.
151 *Advertisements from York and Beverly* (1642) B.M. E.107(30).
152 *Special Passages* (1642) B.M. E.114(36).

and from Warwickshire it was reported that 'the yeomen of our country stands out very well . . .' for parliament.[153] 'The county of Derby, full of nobility and gentry, was much swayed, even from the beginning of these distractions, against the Parliament; for scarce did any Gentleman in all that county, but Sir John Gell, appear for it at the first. He, with his brother, and some of his kindred, by the help of those freeholders and yeomen that inclined that way, made a party to resist those great ones. . . .'[154] In the eastern and south-eastern counties 'the freeholders and yeomen in general adhered to the Parliament',[155] and 'though many of the chief gentry of those counties were for paying obedience to his Majesty's Commission of Array, yet the freeholders and yeomen being generally of the other side, as oft as they attempted to show themselves, they were crushed, and their endeavours defeated'.[156] In Nottinghamshire, related Mrs Hutchinson, '. . . most of the middle sort, the able substantial freeholders, and the other commons, who had not their dependence upon the malignant nobility and gentry, adhered to the parliament'.[157] In Gloucestershire, according to Corbet, besides a few of the gentry, 'the yeomen, farmers, clothiers, and the whole middle ranke of the people were the only active' supporters of parliament.[158] 'On the Parliament's side,' claimed Baxter, 'were . . . the greatest part of the Tradesmen, and Freeholders, and the middle sort of Men; especially in those Corporations and Countries which depend on Cloathing and such Manufactures.'[159] And the royalist Clarendon agreed that 'the common people, especially in the clothing parts of Somersetshire, were generally too much inclined to' parliament,[160] while in the West Riding of Yorkshire 'Leeds, Halifax, and Bradford, three very populous and rich towns, (which depending wholly upon clothiers naturally maligned the gentry)' were for parliament.[161] At Bristol '. . . the king's cause and party were favoured by the two extreames in that city; the one the wealthy and powerfull men, the other of the basest and lowest

153 *The Proceedings at Banbury* (1642) B.M. E.111(11).
154 May, *op. cit.* Book III, p. 84.
155 *ibid.* Book II, p. 108; Book III, p. 78.
156 John Rushworth, *Historical Collections* (London, 1721) Vol. IV, p. 680.
157 Hutchinson, *op. cit.* p. 80.
158 Corbet, *op. cit.* pp. 9, 16; Clarendon, *op. cit.* Vol. III, p. 130.
159 *Reliquiae Baxterianae* p. 30.
160 Clarendon, *op. cit.* Vol. III, p. 80.
161 *ibid.* Vol. II, p. 464.

sort, but disgusted by the middle ranke, the true and best citizens.'[162] At Worcester the supporters of parliament 'were but of the middle rank of people, and none of any great power or eminence there to take their parts . . .';[163] and from Chichester a parliamentarian reported that 'the strength of our parts consists mainly in honest tradesmen, the gentry are nought . . . and the country people are for the most part blinded and misled by their malevolent hedge-priests, there being not above 6 or 7 honest ministers hereabouts. . . .'[164]

When parliament first raised its army under the command of the Earl of Essex, the citizens of London 'listed themselves plentifully for soldiers . . .',[165] and among the first volunteers were 71 dyers, 88 butchers, 186 weavers, 157 tailors, 124 shoemakers, 88 brokers and 49 sadlers.[166] After the first engagement of the civil war, near Worcester, Lord Falkland reported that the royalists had taken 50–60 prisoners—'most of them were men of mean quality, and so raw soldiers that they understood not the word quarter, but cried for mercy; being demanded of what condition they were; some saith, they were Tailors, some Embroiderers and the like.'[167] But it was the apprentices of London who were most forward in the cause of parliament and it was claimed that 8,000 of them enlisted under the Earl of Essex. By origin and vocation they belonged to the middle rank of the population. They insisted that they were not 'of the base and mechanick scum of the people' but 'have trades and callings, the most of them young men of good parentage; whose friends live honestly and thriftily in the country'; and that they 'are servants to honest and sufficient men, and by their own honest laborious endeavours can be both serviceable and profitable to their masters, and be very beneficial to them, in working at their trades.'[168] But London, important as it is, must not be allowed to overshadow the fact that parliament necessarily recruited most of its soldiers from rural areas.

162 Corbet, *op. cit.* p. 14.
163 *Special Passages* (1642) B.M. E.239(22).
164 *An Exact Relation of 14 days Passages from Portsmouth* (1642) B.M. E.112 (34).
165 Lilly, *op. cit.* p. 112.
166 *The Earl of Essex His Desires to the Parliament* (1642) B.M. E.112(7).
167 *A Letter Sent from the Lord Falkland* (1642) B.M. E.121(22).
168 *A Declaration of The Valiant Resolutions of the Famous Prentices of London* (1642) B.M. E.109(5); Louis B. Wright, *Middle-Class Culture in Elizabethan England* (reprinted, New York, 1958) pp. 23–30.

The trained bands of the capital played a crucial role,[169] but so did Oliver Cromwell's regiment, who were 'most of them free-holders and freeholders' sons'.[170]

Parliament's support, of course, was not confined to 'the godly' nor to 'the middle rank of the people', and at the outset in some parts of the country support was very widespread, but this broad popular enthusiasm soon evaporated. At first in Gloucestershire 'the full streame of the country' ran for parliament, but after Prince Rupert took Cirencester '. . . the country-men in generall were taken off, who in their jocund beginnings still concluded on the victory, but never prepared for a blow, that the whole busi-nesse was dashed at one clap. . . .'[171] The yeomen and farmers in the west country who in the beginning rose for parliament, faded away during the siege of Sherborne Castle: 'If a bullet come over their heads, they fall flat upon their bellies, and some 4 or 5 being slain hath made about half of them run away and we are confident half of those that are left will follow; so that of 4 and 20 hundred that came with us out of Somersetshire and 900 that came out of Dorsetshire and Devonshire, we have not 1200 left, and God knows how many may slip away this night. . . . The short of all is we have no army, nor can possibly with these men do this work.'[172] Parliamentarian supporters had expected a quick victory and underestimated the strength of the royalists,[173] and '. . . such spirits as wanted greatnesse of minde or strong fidelity to persevere, did greedily comply' with the royalists.[174] Unarmed and untrained masses did not make an army and parlia-ment turned to professional soldiers and conscripts who would serve for the pay, but serving only for the pay (and plunder), and lacking belief in the righteousness of the cause, they did not have the morale to surmount defeats and win victories. Lord Brooke urged parliament to 'employ men who will fight merely for the cause sake, and bear their own charges, than those who expect rewards and salaries': 'I shall therefore freely speak my

---

169 Clarendon, *op. cit.* Vol. III, pp. 174–5.
170 Whitelock, *op. cit.* Vol. I, p. 209; C. H. Firth, 'The Raising of the Ironsides', *Transactions of the Royal Historical Society*, New Series Vol. XIII (1899).
171 Corbet, *op. cit.* p. 25.
172 *Braye Manuscripts*, H.M.C., 10th Report (1887) pp. 147–8.
173 Ludlow, *op. cit.* Vol. I, p. 96.
174 Corbet, *op. cit.* p. 25.

conscience, I had rather have a thousand or two thousand honest citizens that can only handle their arms, whose hearts go with their hands, than two thousand of mercenary soldiers, that boast of their foreign experience.'[175] Cromwell told Hampden: 'You must get men of a spirit . . . of a spirit that is like to go on as far as a gentleman will go, or else I am sure you will be beaten still. . . .'[176] He found this spirit in godly freeholders. 'I have heard him often-times say that it must not be souldiers nor Scots that must doe this worke, but it must be the godly to this purpose. . . .'[177] He recruited his regiment from among 'freeholders and freeholders' sons, . . . who upon matter of conscience engaged in this quarrel, and under Cromwell. And thus being well armed within, by the satisfaction of their own consciences, and without, by good iron arms, they would as one man stand firmly and charge desper-ately'.[178] '. . . At his first entrance into the wars, being but a captain of horse, he had a special care to get religious men into his troop. These men were of greater understanding than common soldiers, and therefore were more apprehensive of the importance and consequence of the war; and making not money but that which they took for the publick felicity to be their end, they were the more engaged to be valiant; for he that maketh money his end doth esteem his life above his pay, and therefore is like enough to save it by flight when danger comes, if possibly he can; but he that maketh the felicity of Church and State his end esteemeth it above his life, and therefore will the sooner lay down his life for it. And men of parts and understanding know how to manage their business, and know that flying is the surest way to death, and that standing to it is the likeliest way to escape, there being many usually that fall in flight for one that falls in valiant fight. These things it's probable Cromwell understood, and that none would be such engaged valiant men as the religious.' And besides, they would avoid 'those disorders, mutinies, plunderings, and grievances of the country which deboist [i.e. debauched] men in armies are commonly guilty of'.[179] It was the godly people,

---

175 *A worthy speech made by the Right Honourable the Lord Brooke* (1643) B.M. E.90(27).
176 Abbott, *op. cit.* Vol. IV, p. 471.
177 'The Quarrel between the Earl of Manchester and Oliver Cromwell', p. 72.
178 Whitelock, *op. cit.* Vol. I, p. 209.
179 *Reliquiae Baxterianae* p. 98.

mostly of the middle rank of the nation, who stood firm, while those who were not inspired by religion fell into defeatism, or neutrality, or deserted to the king.[180]

This converted the conflict from a constitutional one into a religious one. This change was generally noted to take place during 1643. 'I must confess,' wrote John Greene in his diary at the beginning of 1643, 'I see little hopes of any accommodation, least of a final victory on either side yet. . . . God grant I never see it made a war merely for religion. . . .' But at the beginning of 1644 he wrote: '. . . Our trouble still menaces, the war being fiercer than ever and may probably hold a long time, for now 'tis made a war almost merely for religion, which I feared.'[181] The assumption of the early parliamentarian pamphleteers that the issues were constitutional and political were challenged, and the ground of the quarrel was said to be not 'whether the town of Hull shall be the King's: but whether this Kingdom shall be the Lord's.'[182] '. . . To what end should we waste time about a discourse of Hull, and the Militia? Come speak to the point. If a King of the Protestant Profession should give his strength and power to his Queene a Papist, and she give it to the Jesuits, to the Beast, it is neither Rebellion nor Treason to fight for the King, to recover his power out of the hand of the Beast; I say, *for* the King, that the power regained may be settled upon the Kings Royall person, and posterity; and then it is to be hoped that the King and they will take warning and beware how they trust out their power another time. We are engaged to fight against the Anti-Christian faction by our very Baptisme' but we must 'fight from Scripture motives, not from Politique considerations.'[183] Purtian preachers admitted that they had been misled at first into thinking that the issue was only constitutional: '. . . at the first, the enemy did so disguise their enterprises, that nothing cleerly appeared, but only that you were compelled to take up Armes for the defence of your Liberties, and to bring Rebells and Traytors to condigne punishment, but now they have ingaged

---

180 Corbet, *op. cit.* p. 42; Jeremiah Burroughes, *The glorious Name of God* (London, 1643) p. 56; *Reliquiae Baxterianae* p. 47.
181 'The Diary of John Greene 1635–59', ed. E. M. Symonds, *English Historical Review* Vol. XLIII (1928) pp. 391, 598.
182 *A Sudden Answer to a Sudden Moderatour* (London, 1643) B.M. E.93(16).
183 Francis Cheynell, *Sions Memento, and Gods Alarum* (London, 1643) pp. 9–10.

all the Antichristian world so farre, that all Christendome, except the Malignants in England, doe now see, that the question in England is, whether Christ or Antichrist shall be Lord or King. . . .'[184]

Baxter dated the change in the character of the parliamentarian cause from the publication of a pamphlet called *Plaine English* at the beginning of 1643.[185] Its author insisted that the only peace settlement acceptable to the supporters of parliament would be 'such an one as may extirpate Popery and superstition, lay the grounds of a pious painfull Ministry, and to that end cast out those scandalous seditious person, who have now showed themselves as ill affected to the state as formerly to the church. . . . Such an one as may purge our doctrine, . . . reforme our Discipline and make it more conducible to the end of all Discipline, the preservation of a Church from corruption in Doctrine and manners. And let it be weighed whether that can be done without the supplanting . . . the Bishops. . . .' But the tract also linked religion and politics, saying that the issue of the war was 'liberty or tyranny, Popery or true piety', and demonstrated that the emphasis on religious issues was accompanied by a greater radicalism in politics: the tract threatened parliament that if it did not perform what the people desired, if 'the representative body cannot, or will not, discharge their trust to the satisfaction not of fancy, but of reason in the people; they may resume (if ever yet they parted with a power to their manifest undoing) and use their power so farre as conduces to their safety. . . .'[186] Gentlemen who had supported parliament on constitutional grounds alone were alarmed by the social consequences of the abolition of episcopacy, but they were even more alarmed by the assertion that the people were the judge of whether parliament performed its trust and could revoke the mandate of their representatives.[187] This association of religious radicalism with political radicalism was precisely what Baxter found among some of the horse regiments of the New Model Army: '. . . they were resolved to take down, not only Bishops, and Liturgy, and Ceremonies, but all that did withstand their way. They were far from thinking of a

184 Stephen Marshall, *A Sacred Panegyrick* (London, 1644) p. 21.
185 *Reliquiae Baxterianae* p. 49.
186 *Plaine English* (1643) pp. 10–11, 19–20, 22, 25–6.
187 *A Plain Fault in Plain-English* (London, 1643) pp. 3–6; *An Answer to a Seditious Pamphlet Entitled, Plain English* (Oxford, 1643).

moderate Episcopacy, or of any healing way between the Episcopal and the Presbyterians. . . .' They talked 'sometimes for State Democracy and sometimes for Church Democracy'. 'I perceived that they took the King for a Tyrant and an Enemy, and really intended absolutely to master him, or to ruine him . . . They said, What were the Lords of England but William the Conquerour's Colonels? or the Barons but his Majors? or the Knights but his Captains?'[188] Not only religious and political radicalism but social radicalism as well: thus the change in the character of the parliamentarian cause was not just a change from a constitutional cause to a religious cause, but to a greater radicalism in politics and society as well as in religion; and this sprang from the fact that the change was caused by the growing importance in the parliamentarian party not just of the godly but of the godly middle sort of people.

There was a growing tension between the leaders of the parliamentarian party, who were drawn from the gentry, and the rank-and-file, who were drawn from the middle sort of people. Colonel Hutchinson, as governor of Nottingham, found 'the townsmen, being such as had lived free and plentifully by themselves, could not subject themselves to government; but were so saucy, so negligent, and so mutinous, that the most honourable person in the world, could expect nothing but scandal, reproach, and ingratitude, for the payment of his greatest merit. . . .'[189] Parliamentarian soldiers would follow only officers of whom they approved,[190] and obey only orders with which they agreed: 'Although the horse would not obey Sir Thomas Fairfax, it was not out of cowardice, for the men were very stout and cheerful in the service, but only had the general fault of all the parliament party, that they were not very obedient to commands, except they knew and approved their employment.'[191] This sprang from puritanism, for Corbet had observed that those who had had the benefit of 'a practicall ministry' were 'apt to contradict and question, and will not easily be brought to the bent'.[192] 'The most religious and the best people were so pragmatical,' confessed Mrs Hutchinson, herself a puritan but also a gentlewoman, 'that

188 *Reliquiae Baxterianae* pp. 50–4.
189 Hutchinson, *op. cit.* p. 156.
190 *C.S.P.D. 1641–1643* pp. 372–3, 379, 391, 392.
191 Hutchinson, *op. cit.* p. 164.
192 Corbet, *op. cit.* p. 10.

no act, nor scarcely word, could pass without being strictly arraigned and judged at the bar of every common soldiers' discretion, and thereafter censured and exclaimed at.'[193] Soldiers in the Earl of Essex's army objected to being commanded by 'profane wretches' and 'ungodly' officers or by a 'God-dam blade, and doubtless hatched in hell', and secured their dismissal.[194] But this sprang not just from godliness: the fundamental source of the rank-and-file's suspicions of their leaders lay in difference of class. Robert Kyrle, a major of horse in the Earl of Essex's army, complained that parliaments' soldiers 'wanted not Scripture for every mutiny, who plunder and call it God's providence, who if they cannot prove any of quality to be a Papist, yet as he is a Gentleman he shall want grace; and that is title enough to possess the estates of all that are more richer than themselves. . . .'[195] Up to a point godliness could unite the puritan gentry and the godly middle sort of people, but it could not overcome the difference of class. The puritan Colonel Hutchinson had 'his experience not only of the ungodly and ill-affected, but even of the godly themselves, who thought it scarcely possible for any one to continue a gentleman, and firm to a godly interest, and therefore repaid all his vigilancy and labours for them with a very unjust jealousy'.[196] This shows that what underlay the godliness of the godly middle sort of people was class feeling. They were conscious that their aims were not always the same as those of the parliamentarian nobility and gentry, and that their grievances were as often as not grievances against the nobility and the gentry and the richer sort of people as such.

193 Hutchinson, *op. cit.* p. 156.
194 *C.S.P.D. 1641–1643* pp. 372–3, 379, 391, 392.
195 *A Copy of a Letter Writ from Sjt. Major Kirle* (1643) B.M. E.246(35).
196 Hutchinson, *op. cit.* pp. 133–4.

4

The Part Played by the Catholics

Keith Lindley

Preface

The Catholics formed yet one more discontented element in English society before 1640. They shared with the protestants the political and constitutional grievances of the 1630s, but in addition they had grievances of their own as Catholics. Fines for recusancy were certainly not reduced by Charles I, but were probably increased, and like the other financial exactions of the period of the Personal Rule, they fell more heavily upon the lesser than upon the greater men. As a persecuted community, the Catholics had little cause to hope for toleration from the regime of Charles I, Laud and Strafford. When it came to the civil war, Catholics, like most other Englishmen, tried to continue to live in peace. But as Catholics they had additional reasons for remaining neutral. They could not support a parliament that was embarking on a crusade against popery and papists, but by keeping quiet and not supporting the king they might hope to avert the wrath of the anti-Catholic parliamentarians. But some Catholics were forced into royalism by the hostility of the parliamentarians. As the royalists tended to assume that all puritans were parliamentarians, so the parliamentarians tended to assume that all Catholics were royalists; and just as the first assumption did more than anything else to convert puritans into parliamentarians, so the second assumption did more than anything else to convert Catholics into royalists. Just as puritans were attacked by anti-puritan mobs and by the king's soldiers, and were forced to take refuge in parliament's garrisons and armies, so Catholics were attacked by anti-popery mobs and by parliament's soldiers, and were forced to find shelter in the king's garrisons and armies. Thus the outbreak of the civil war placed both Catholics and puritans in much the same position, and the responses of both to the situation were similar: the first reaction of both Catholics and puritans was to be neutral, and many maintained this neutrality throughout the civil war, but others were forced by attacks from one side to align themselves with the other in self-defence. At the same time royalist sympathizers, both Catholics and protestants, in districts dominated by the parliamentarians, were cowed into neutrality, as were parliamentarian sympathizers in districts dominated by the king. Nevertheless Catholics did form an important element in the royalist party, as puritans did in the parliamentarian party. The Catholics who became royalists did not do so because they were Catholics, but for the same reasons as the protestants who became royalists. But, whereas the puritan support for parliament drew its impetus from the middle rank of the people, the Catholic support for the king drew its impetus from the nobility and gentry, who

EVER since the first shots were fired, the part played by the Catholics in the civil war has been a highly controversial subject. This controversy still seems very much alive, and a number of modern works give conflicting accounts. Gardiner, Magee and Hill all subscribe to the thesis that the Catholics were ardent royalists[1] (Hill, for instance, goes so far as to describe the Catholics as having been 'solidly royalist' in the civil war); Aylmer, Roots and Hardacre dissent, in varying degrees, from this view. Aylmer suggests that many Catholics would have preferred to remain neutral had they been free to do so, but that parliament's anti-popery forced them to join with the king,[2] while Roots argues further that among those men up and down the country who 'laid low' were a number of Catholics, and that some Catholics 'in appropriate circumstances' adhered to the parliament.[3] Only Hardacre has attempted to make an estimate of precisely what proportion of the Catholics chose to remain neutral. Basing his estimate upon the papers of the Committee for Compounding, where a distinction is drawn between Catholics sequestered for their recusancy only and Catholics who were sequestered for both recusancy and royalism, Hardacre concludes that probably a seventh or an eighth of all sequestered Catholics supported the king in some way, while the majority of Catholics were sequestered merely as recusants, and, furthermore, that among those Catholics

1 S. R. Gardiner, *History of the Great Civil War, 1642–1649* (London, 1901) Vol. I, p. 35; Brian Magee, *The English Recusants* (London, 1938) p. 163; Christopher Hill, *The Century of Revolution, 1603–1714* (Edinburgh, 1961) p. 60.
2 G. E. Aylmer, *The Struggle for the Constitution* (London, 1965) p. 118.
3 I. Roots, *The Great Rebellion, 1642–1660* (London, 1966) pp. 63, 66.

brought in their dependents. These Catholic nobility and gentry adhered to the king for the same reasons as protestant nobility and gentry: they were worried about the consequences of any further reduction of the power of the crown, and they feared that social revolution might follow in the wake of parliament's rebellion against the king. Lower-class Catholics, in so far as they escaped the domination of royalist landlords, did not readily identify their interests with those of the king's party, but, repelled from the parliamentarian party by its hostility towards their religion, they took refuge in neutrality.

BRIAN MANNING

who supported the king there were some whose royalism was simply a reaction to the parliament's violent anti-popery.[4]

The royalist historian, Edward Hyde, Earl of Clarendon, considered the labelling of the royalist party as 'popish', a propaganda move by leading parliamentarians. The Catholics, he claimed, were by no means all ardent royalists; on the contrary, most Catholics chose to drag their feet or to 'sit unconcerned' throughout the war.[5] Clarendon even asserts that parliament 'entertained all of that religion that they could get' and that 'very many' Catholics joined their forces.[6]

Clarendon's observations comprise only a small but valuable contribution in the post-Restoration period to a violent controversy over the part played by Catholics in the civil war. The debate centred principally upon the *Humble Apologie of the English Catholicks*[7] written by Roger Palmer, Earl of Castlemaine, which was an attack on the generally held opinion that English Catholics were, *ipso facto*, traitors. As a Catholic and a loyalist, Palmer was particularly sensitive to any aspersions cast upon the loyalty of his co-religionists to their king, and, consequently, he insisted that the Catholics had been loyal to the royalists, and he compiled 'A Catalogue of those Catholicks that Died and Suffered for their Loyalty' as final proof of that fidelity.[8]

The *Apologie* was published on the 11 November 1666, and the reply of William Lloyd, the fanatical anti-papist Bishop of St Asaph, appeared in the following year.[9] Lloyd was most fortunate in being able to make effective use of William Birchley's *Christian Moderator*,[10] a plea for toleration for Catholics intended for the eyes of the Independents. The anti-apologist contended that Catholics supported the king for one of three reasons. Firstly, 'some came in voluntarily to assist him'.[11] This was indisputable.

4 Paul H. Hardacre, *The Royalists during the Puritan Revolution* (The Hague, 1956) pp. 8, 60.
5 Clarendon, *History of the Great Rebellion* ed. W. D. Macray (Oxford, 1888) Vol. II, pp. 276–7.
6 *ibid.* p. 348.
7 R. Palmer (Earl of Castlemaine), *The Catholique Apology with a Reply to the Answer* (3rd edn., London, 1674).
8 *ibid.* pp. 574–80.
9 W. Lloyd, *The Late Apology In behalf of the Papists Re-printed And Answered, In behalf of the Royallists* (London, 1667).
10 W. Birchley, *The Christian Moderator, in two Parts. Or Persecution for Religion condemned* (4th edn., London, 1652).
11 W. Lloyd, *op. cit.* p. 14.

Secondly, 'many more' Catholics 'were "hunted into his Garrisons", by them that knew you would bring him little help and much hatred', and many of these Catholics gave the king no assistance while they sheltered in royalist garrisons.[12] Finally, there were those Catholics who were fair-weather friends, 'those that fought for him, as long as his Fortune stood; when that once declined, a great part, even of them, fell from him.'[13]

Lloyd's vicious attack upon the *Apologie* prompted Palmer to write a *Reply to the Answer*[14] in which he tried to meet Lloyd's accusations by making incredible claims for the Catholics. The defence is largely a reiteration of exaggerated claims of past and present Catholic loyalty.[15] However, Palmer's *Reply to the Answer* is a feeble retort to a formidable onslaught. Exaggerated claims of Catholic loyalty were not enough, and he significantly failed to explain away the statements of his fellow apologist, William Birchley.

'William Birchley' was the pseudonym of John Austin, a convert to Catholicism, who appears to have remained neutral during the civil war.[16] Birchley pleaded for toleration for the Catholics in 1651 and 1652 in *The Christian Moderator in two Parts. Or Persecution for Religion condemned*.[17] He argued most convincingly, that not all Catholics had opposed the parliament; there were, in fact, gradations of Catholic royalism; and there were Catholics whose only offence had been their Catholicism. Birchley claimed to have gathered his information about the Catholics by having 'sometimes purposely attended at Haberdashers hall to hear their Cases pleaded',[18] and a large part of the *Second Moderator* is concerned with 'Passages observed upon Cases depending at Haberdashers-Hall'.[19] The distinction he drew between active Catholic royalists, passive Catholic royalists and neutral Catholics, would appear to have been based largely upon his observation of cases coming before the Committee for Compounding.

Some Catholics, Birchley admitted, had been guilty of royalism, but this was understandable in view of their great dependence upon Charles I.[20] Yet not all Catholic delinquents, he stressed, had been active royalists; on the contrary, he was convinced that 'a

12 *ibid*. pp. 14, 44.
13 *ibid*. p. 14.
14 R. Palmer, *op. cit.*
15 *ibid*. pp. 17, 98, 283.
16 *D.N.B.*
17 W. Birchley, *op. cit.*
18 *ibid*. p. 58.
19 *ibid*. p. 77.
20 *ibid*. p. 17.

great part of those papists, who are sequestered as absolute delinquents, were never in actuall arms against the Parliament, but onely fled to the enemies Garrisons for shelter'; and this was quite reasonable: 'Since whoever did observe the fury and rage of most of our common souldiers (at the begining of the late troubles) against many of that party, will easily conclude the Papists had reason to distrust their own personall security amongst them.'[21] If not every Catholic delinquent was an active royalist, not every Catholic was a delinquent, and Birchley claimed, quite clearly, that the offence of the majority of Catholic petitioners to the Committee for Compounding was only their religion.[22] If these were baseless generalizations, the government of the Interregnum would be only too aware of it. Birchley was appealing to men who had the records of the Committee for Compounding at their disposal to check and, if necessary, refute his claims.

The problem of placating successive hostile governments, is the background against which the claims of successive Catholic apologists must be viewed. While changes of government explain why conflicting claims were made, they do not resolve the problem of which claims were true and which false. This information can only be obtained by examining the evidence on both sides, and by scrutinizing the sources on which that evidence is based.

It is the object of this study to attempt an assessment of the part played by Catholics in the civil war on the basis of a number of county studies. The local study has a number of real advantages over a broad national study: it allows one to make a reasonably reliable statistical assessment; it makes it possible to measure Catholic royalism and Catholic neutrality through a detailed study of individuals; and it enables one to see this action or inaction in its local, social and economic contexts. Moreover, if the local studies are a reasonable sample of the country as a whole in both extent and variety, then it is possible ultimately to move towards a national picture.

The investigation undertaken in this study is based upon London and eight counties. London, as the centre of the kingdom, is an obvious choice, while the counties have been selected with the object of incorporating as much variety in the sample as possible. The sample takes in varieties in the state of Catholicism in the country (from counties with a large Catholic element to counties

21 W. Birchley, *op. cit.* p. 81.   22 *ibid.* p. 78.

with a tiny Catholic minority) and varieties in the state of the parties (from leading royalist counties to leading parliamentarian counties). Different geographical regions are also represented, starting with London at the centre, and including the home counties with Buckinghamshire, the midlands with Northamptonshire, the south coast with Hampshire, the east with Suffolk, the west with Somerset, the border of Wales with Monmouthshire and the north with Lancashire and Yorkshire.

Shortly after the outbreak of the civil war, parliament ordered the seizure of all royalist and Catholic estates as they fell into parliamentarian hands. With the conclusion of hostilities, royalists and, at a later date, Catholics also, were allowed to resume possession of their estates upon payment of a fine, provided they were not Catholic royalists or other notorious delinquents. The records of these proceedings have survived in the papers of the Committee for Compounding and its predecessor, the Committee for Advance of Money.[23] These papers are not a complete record of all royalists but merely of those who took steps to compound or who were noted as being under sequestration in county returns. However, they do form the largest surviving record of royalists and, if used in conjunction with the recusant rolls, are also the fullest account of Catholics in the period.

Not only do the composition papers record cases of Catholics who had appeared earlier on recusant rolls, they also reveal Catholics who had previously managed to escape conviction as recusants. The oath of abjuration, which contained an outright denial of papal supremacy and the doctrine of transubstantiation, was administered by the commissioners to all compounders who were suspected of Catholic sympathies. The oath, therefore, exposed the church-papist and other ingenious Catholics who had previously evaded conviction. In Monmouthshire, for example, William Jones of Hardwick, gentleman, was 'suspected a recusant, although never yett convicted'[24] until the committee exposed him. The Committee for Compounding was also greatly aided in

23 For a full account of the papers of the Committee for Compounding see M. A. E. Green (ed.), *C.C.C.* (London, 1889–92) Part I, pp. v–xxvi; Part V, pp. v–xliii; *Lancashire and Cheshire Record Society* Vol. XXIV, Introduction, pp. v–xiv; Vol. XCV, pp. 1–42.
24 P.R.O. *S.P.D.* 23/95, f. 232.

its detection of Catholics by the fact that it had at its disposal the recusant rolls and other records dealing with recusants. In these circumstances, the chances of a compounding Catholic, who had previously been convicted of recusancy, successfully concealing his Catholicism from the committee were slight.

In the exposure of former royalists, or 'delinquents' as they were commonly called, the committee relied heavily on informations or discoveries, and most of this information occurs in the records of the Committee for Advance of Money. The records of all informations and proceedings in a particular case were carefully noted down by both the central committee and the local committees and were consulted when the need arose. A careful scrutiny of these records could result in cases being dismissed or charges extended. Furthermore, the work of the committee in uncovering Catholics and former royalists was made easier by the vigilance of 'Discoverers'. Persons revealing Catholics or delinquents who had previously managed to conceal their offence from the authorities were, theoretically, to be suitably rewarded out of the offender's estate.[25] However, the information given by discoverers had to be substantiated, for the commissioners did not accept allegations blindly.

When charges of royalism or Catholicism were denied by a compounder, the commissioners entered into a meticulous examination of the case in question, calling upon the local commissioners and their own officers to scrutinize the records at their disposal and to take depositions from witnesses both for and against the compounder. Furthermore, if the central committee erred, the local committee was always ready to correct mistaken judgements. In April 1650, for example, the central committee congratulated the Lancashire committee on its vigilance in uncovering a Catholic royalist who had previously been fined as a royalist only.[26]

The Committee for Compounding recognized various degrees of royalism, from being actively in arms to merely being present in a particular place when it was a royalist garrison. It is possible, therefore, in a number of cases, to establish the nature of the delinquency committed by Catholic royalists. Where the lowest degree of delinquency is concerned, however, there is usually some doubt since it was in the petitioner's own interest to understate

25 *Lancashire and Cheshire Record Society* Vol. XXIV, p. 175.
26 P.R.O., *S.P.D.* 23/8, f. 15.

his delinquency, and the witnesses produced by him to support his claims were sometimes close relatives, servants or dependents. Yet although the testimony given by interested parties, or by witnesses produced by those parties, has to be treated with caution, the Committee for Compounding was by no means blind to the need for such caution, and there is ample evidence to suggest that such limitations were borne in mind by the commissioners before they reached their final judgement.

Any analysis based upon the papers of the Committee for Compounding must make allowance for a number of other important limitations of this source. The findings of the commissioners may, for example, have been rendered inaccurate in some cases because of corrupt officials or clever evasion by some delinquents. There were undoubtedly some corrupt dealings within both the central and local committees. Edward, Lord Howard of Escrick, for instance, who was a member of the Haberdashers' Hall committee which assessed fifths and twentieths, was later known to have accepted gifts from royalists for reducing their fines;[27] and Captain Benjamin Mason, one of the commissioners for sequestrations in Somerset, was accused of having shown favour to papists and delinquents in the course of his administration.[28] However, although the central and local committee were open to bribery and influence at times, there is nothing to suggest that they were notoriously corrupt. It might even be argued that, by seventeenth-century standards, they were remarkably objective in their dealings, as the scrupulous way in which they examined one charge of corruption, levelled at the Buckinghamshire Committee, might suggest.[29] A number of delinquents may also have attempted to evade charges against them by ingenious practices. Sir Charles Somerset KB, of Troy in Monmouthshire, for instance, seems to have deliberately caused confusion in the minds of the commissioners by petitioning them under different titles.[30]

The volume of business could also sometimes outrun the resources of the local committees and any diminution in their efficiency might result in inaccurate or incomplete returns being made to the central committee. The local committee in Yorkshire,

27 Hardacre, *op. cit.* pp. 30, 31, 73.
28 P.R.O., *S.P.D.* 23/102, f. 311; 251, f. 149.
29 *ibid.* 121, f. 211; 27, ff. 91, 104; 77, ff. 501, 520.
30 *ibid.* 33, f. 423.

for example, had a vast task as they were quick to point out in February 1651 when they failed to complete their instructions.[31] Partly as a result of the magnitude of the task, local committees tended, on the whole, to concentrate their attention on the more substantial delinquents and Catholics in their counties. This is quite evident when one consults the Yorkshire, Northampton-shire and Buckinghamshire statistics (see tables 4.3 and 4.4).[32] As a general observation, it may be said that the findings of the Committee for Compounding are most accurate statistically at the top of the social scale, and least accurate at the bottom, with the attention paid to lesser folk varying from county to county.

Finally, it must also be remembered that neither the central committee's nor the local committee's job was made any easier by the fact that years of war and destruction must have thrown records into confusion. Both the Monmouthshire and Hampshire county committees complained to the central committee of diffi-culties resulting from war-time destruction of some important records.[33]

None of the above-mentioned limitations of the papers of the Committee for Compounding, however, destroys the value of the statistical analysis based on this source which is attempted below. The statistics (tables 4.1–4.6) are derived from the papers of the Committee for Advance of Money and the Committee for Com-pounding; most are based upon actual cases presented to the central committee, but they have also been supplemented by two lists of 1656—the first of 'Popish Recusants' who were still under sequestration[34] and the second of delinquents who also remained sequestered.[35] An earlier list entitled 'Papists: And: Delinquents In the yeare: End: 25th of March 1650 1651'[36] has also been used in the case of London (table 4.2) and three counties where it is available (Monmouthshire, Northamptonshire and Buckingham-shire, see tables 4.3 and 4.4). The 1656 county lists of recusants and delinquents were returned by the local committees in response to an order of the Treasury commissioners of the 14 September 1655,[37] and were, perhaps, the result of efforts to re-establish

31 P.R.O., *S.P.D.* 23/254, f. 41.
32 Below pp. 141, 148.
33 *C.C.C.* Part I, p. 364; P.R.O., *S.P.D.* 23/167, f. 285.
34 P.R.O., *S.P.D.* 23/261, ff. 1–186, recusants.
35 *ibid.* 261, ff. 187–233, delinquents.
36 *ibid.* 254, f. 101. 37 *C.C.C.* Part I, pp. 741–2.

Exchequer control.[38] These returns were entered in volume 261, the first half of which comprised the lists of recusants arranged by counties and the second the lists of delinquents also arranged by counties. By checking off these lists against each other, it is possible to distinguish three groups: royalists, Catholic royalists and neutral Catholics.

The statistics of Catholic neutrality, which are the most striking feature of the tables printed below, are based upon three main kinds of evidence (see table 4.1). The first, and most reliable, basis for classification is the decision of the county committee or the

table 4.1 Catholic neutrality

County	Type of evidence		
	1 Decision of the county committee, central committee or both	2 Petitioner's own plea or that of an interested party	3 1656 lists, 1651 lists or both
Buckinghamshire	15	2	4
Hampshire	14	18	46
Lancashire	9	188	563
London	35	8	6
Monmouthshire	8	17	39
Northamptonshire	13	1	4
Somersetshire	7	11	8
Suffolk	25	18	24
Yorkshire	49	46	58
Total	175	309	752

central committee or both, and, as the table of Catholic neutrality shows, one hundred and seventy-five Catholic neutrals have been classified on this evidence.

The second type of evidence is less sound because the neutrality of the Catholic concerned is based upon his own plea or that of an interested party, and, if that were the only evidence for neutrality, then the classification of the three hundred and nine Catholics as neutrals on this basis would be open to serious question. However, in one hundred and seventy-five of these cases there is some confirmation from the fact that their names also appear upon either the 1656 list or the 1651 list, or both, as recusants but without suggestion of a delinquency charge. It must also be remembered

38 C. H. Firth and R. S. Rait (eds.) *Acts and Ordinances of the Interregnum* (London, 1911) Vol. II, pp. 918–21, 1016–19.

that the commissioners, both central and local, were in a position to examine any case in which they felt they had cause for suspicion and to contradict any claims which they considered false, and yet in not one single case is the petitioner's word questioned or contradicted.

The 1656 lists, with the 1651 lists where they are available, form the third and final basis for classification of Catholic neutrals, and seven hundred and fifty-two Catholics have been identified as neutrals on this evidence. In none of the cases based upon this evidence is there any mention of a charge of delinquency.

1 *London*

London, as the centre of events, claims an indispensable place in this study. Table 4.2 reveals that only about five per cent of London royalists were Catholics, and of the total body of Catholics less than twenty-five per cent were royalists. Only one out of four Catholic knights supported the king, and just over fifteen per cent

table 4.2 London

Protestant royalists		Catholic royalists		Neutral Catholics	
Knights and above	34	Knights and above	1	Knights and above	3
Esquires	45	Esquires	2	Esquires	11
Gentlemen	110	Gentlemen	10	Gentlemen	9
Clergy	8				
Royal servants and office-holders	17				
Below gentry status	62	Below gentry status	2	Below gentry status	3
Women	4			Women	21
Status not known	9	Status not known	1	Status not known	2
Total	289	*Total*	16	*Total*	49

of Catholic esquires; but fifty-three per cent of Catholic gentlemen helped the king in some way. Finally, two Catholics of below gentry status were guilty of delinquency, while the status of the remaining 'papist delinquent' is not known. Although none of the Catholic women was guilty of delinquency, their husbands or fathers may have been.

Delinquency varied in degree from being actively in arms for the king to merely being present in the king's quarters or sending him material support. Both John Larrance (or Lawrence) of

Chiswick, in Middlesex, gentleman,[39] and John Weston of South-wark, esquire,[40] belong to the first category as Catholics who had been in arms for the king. One other Catholic, Thomas Arpe of the Middle Temple, esquire, was returned as a royalist and yet his delinquency probably involved nothing more than his being present in royalist quarters.[41]

In the early days of the Long Parliament, Sir Basil Brook was one of those Catholics singled out for attack. He was rumoured to be planning a popish coup in the year 1641–2, and his name was joined with that of the Earl of Worcester as a threat to the city.[42] On the 6 January 1644, he was committed a close prisoner to the Tower by the House of Commons and was declared a 'convicted papist and delinquent' by the Committee for Advance of Money in the following December.[43] Yet, throughout this attack on Sir Basil, little is said of the precise nature of his delinquency.

There is no conclusive proof of delinquency in seven of the sixteen cases of Catholic royalists, evidence of delinquency being found only in informations exhibited against the persons concerned, without proofs of the accusation and without a final judgement by the central committee or returns from the local committees. However, although some doubt must surround the actual delinquency of nearly one half of the Catholic royalist category, the evidence quoted points more to delinquency than to neutrality and hence their inclusion in that category.

The great majority of London Catholics referred to in the papers of the Committee for Compounding appear to have remained neutral during the hostilities, and the classification of Catholic neutrals in London in the overwhelming majority of cases is based upon the most reliable kind of evidence to be found in these papers.[44] In three cases, for instance, former charges of delinquency are dismissed by the committee. James Clarke of White-friars, surgeon, who was originally sequestered as both a Catholic and a delinquent, denied the charge of delinquency in 1652 and alleged that he was 'about his Lawfull occasions beyond the Sea'

---

39 P.R.O., *S.P.D.* 23/220, f. 582; 15, f. 241; 261, f. 46.
40 *ibid.* 116, f. 321; 169, f. 319.   41 *ibid.* 33, f. 274; 169, ff. 368–9.
42 *Portland Manuscripts*, H.M.C., 14th Report, Appendix, Part II, p. 67; *A new Plot against the Parliament. A discovery of the treacherous practises of Papists in this citie. Likewise the reason of the guard placed at the Earle of Worcesters, Sir Basil Brooks and my Lord Peters house* (London, 1641).
43 *D.N.B.*; P.R.O., *S.P.D.* 19/4, f. 363.   44 Above pp. 131–6.

when the charge was made or he would have cleared himself earlier.[45] Clarke backed up his own testimony with a number of depositions made by witnesses that he was in Flanders at the time the charge was made,[46] and the Committee for Compounding appear to have finally accepted his testimony for in April 1655 they ordered that that portion of his estate which had been seized for delinquency be discharged.[47] Similarly, James Ravenscroft of Islington, gentleman,[48] and Valentine Saunders of Charing Cross, esquire,[49] were cleared of delinquency charges brought against them.

There is a large measure of certainty about the neutrality of seven other Catholics in the neutral Catholic category for their neutrality had been established by the local committee or the Committee for Compounding. For example, Frances Quintin and her father, Joseph Quintin of Clerkenwell, gentleman, were cleared of any imputation of delinquency in a return of the Middlesex committee dated the 21 June 1649.[50]

The cases cited above are not the only signs of a large body of Catholic neutrals in London during the civil war. On the 23 September 1645, George Geldorpe, a foreign merchant and a self-acknowledged Catholic, petitioned the House of Lords claiming that he had neither been in the king's quarters nor in communication with the royalist party, but had lived peaceably within the cities of London and Westminster for the past twenty-two years.[51] John Appleton, 'Doctor of Phisick', was committed to New Prison in April 1646 for being a Catholic, refusing the oath of allegiance, and continuing within the lines of communication in defiance of parliament. No mention was made of delinquency and on the 16 November 1648, Appleton petitioned the House of Lords requesting that he might be freed to practise his profession.[52] Finally, William Davies, who was imprisoned in Windsor Castle on the information that he was a popish priest, petitioned the Lord Protector for his release on the 20 January 1659, claiming that he was not a priest (although he admitted to being a Catholic) and

45 P.R.O., *S.P.D.* 23/74, ff. 842, 897.
46 *ibid.* 74, ff. 845–6.   47 *ibid.* 23, ff. 1674, 1682.
48 *ibid.* 19/22, f. 23; 9, f. 89; 11, f. 259.
49 *ibid.* 23/136, ff. 673, 675.   50 *ibid.* 216, f. 617.
51 House of Lords Archives, 23 September 1645. Petition of George Geldorpe.
52 *ibid.* 16 November 1648. Petition of John Appleton, and annexed papers.

that he had lived 'in and about London duringe the time of the late warres, demeaninge himselfe peaceably and quietly following his vocation being a Student and practitioner at Law'.[53] The Protector appears to have accepted his testimony for there is an order in council for his release.[54]

2 Monmouthshire, Lancashire and Yorkshire

If there had been some special relationship between royalism and Catholicism, one would expect to find this evident in Monmouthshire, Lancashire and Yorkshire, which were three of the leading royalist counties and where there were substantial numbers of Catholics.

Recent research on the Catholics in the civil war period conducted by Cliffe[55] and Aveling[56] has, on the whole, concluded that there were in fact a high proportion of Yorkshire Catholic gentry families within the royalist army in that county. However, in his most recent study, Aveling estimates that of one hundred and ten gentry families in the North Riding affected by Catholicism in 1642, only forty-five were accounted delinquents.[57] None of the secondary authorities on the civil war in Monmouthshire postulates a special connection between Catholicism and royalism. They all appear to agree on the importance to attach to personal loyalty rather than loyalty to ideals in determining party alignment in Monmouthshire,[58] while Dodd casts further doubt on Catholic loyalty to the royalists in Monmouthshire when he writes of 'the legend' of a 'Welsh Popish Army'.[59] Finally, though the civil war in Lancashire is seen by Broxap, Walker and Tupling

---

53 P.R.O., *S.P.D.*, 18/200, ff. 46, 461, 46(ii).
54 *C.S.P.D. 1658–9*, p. 259.
55 J. T. Cliffe, *The Yorkshire Gentry on the Eve of the Civil War* Ph.D. thesis University of London (1960) pp. 421–5, 448.
56 H. Aveling, *Post-Reformation Catholicism in East Yorkshire, 1558–1790* (York, 1960) pp. 43–4; *The Catholic Recusants of the West Riding of Yorkshire, 1558–1790* (Leeds, 1963) pp. 233–4.
57 H. Aveling, *Northern Catholics: the Catholic Recusants of the North Riding of Yorkshire, 1558–1790* (London, 1966) p. 306.
58 J. Webb, *Memorials of the Civil War . . . as It Affected Herefordshire and the adjacent counties* (London, 1879) Vol. I, p. 98; J. F. Rees, *Studies in Welsh History* (Cardiff, 1947) p. 94; D. Williams, *Modern Wales* (London, 1950) p. 97; A. Clark, *Raglan Castle and the Civil War in Monmouthshire* (Chepstow, 1953) p. 16.
59 A. H. Dodd, 'Wales in the Parliaments of Charles I', *Transactions of the Honourable Society of Cymmrodorian* (1946) p. 60.

as a conflict between papists and puritans, they show little or no appreciation of the position of the Catholics before and during the war or the reasons for their assumed allegiance to the king;[60] Roots, in his recent book on the civil war, states on the other hand that 'At no time was popish support for Charles absolute' in Lancashire and that some Catholics remained neutral.[61]

The statistics in table 4.3 clearly show that only in Monmouthshire was the percentage of royalists who were Catholics (i.e. forty per cent) anywhere near large enough to merit the label 'popish' for the royalist party in that county: in Lancashire only twenty-six per cent of the royalists were Catholics, and in Yorkshire they formed a very small part of the royalist party at nine and one third per cent. However, the relative strength of Catholicism in these counties has to be recalled in order to obtain an accurate picture of the attitude of Catholics to the royalists; and, when Catholic royalism is related to Catholicism in general, Yorkshire Catholics appear to have been most inclined towards royalism, for twenty-seven per cent of that county's Catholics were royalists, while Monmouthshire follows second with twenty-three per cent and Lancashire third with under seventeen per cent.

Analysis by status reveals that Catholic royalism, in all three counties, becomes more pronounced as one moves up the social scale. In Monmouthshire, four out of five Catholics of knightly status and above were royalists, fifty per cent of Catholic esquires, and under twenty-five per cent of Catholic gentlemen. There are only four Catholics of below gentry status recorded for Monmouthshire and none of these appears to have been guilty of delinquency. A similar picture of the relationship between status and royalism emerges in Lancashire, where four out of six Catholics of knightly status and above, seventy-five per cent of Catholic esquires, just over fifty-two per cent of Catholic gentlemen, under twenty per cent of Catholic commoners and one out of fifteen Catholic craftsmen and tradesmen supported the royalists. In Yorkshire ten out of thirteen Catholics of knightly status and above were royalists, compared with forty-eight per cent of

60 E. Broxap, *The Great Civil War in Lancashire* (Manchester, 1910) p. 23; F. Walker, 'Historical Geography of South West Lancashire', *Chetham Society* Vol. CIII, pp. 87, 94; G. H. Tupling, 'Causes of the Civil War in Lancashire', *Transactions of the Lancashire and Cheshire Antiquarian Society* Vol. LXV, p. 31.
61 I. Roots, *op. cit.* p. 63.

table 4.3 Monmouthshire, Lancashire and Yorkshire

	Protestant royalists			Catholic royalists			Neutral Catholics		
	Monmouth-shire	Lanca-shire	York-shire	Monmouth-shire	Lanca-shire	York-shire	Monmouth-shire	Lanca-shire	York-shire
Knights and above	7	14	60	4	4	10	1	2	3
Esquires	8	48	90	2	26	26	2	9	28
Gentlemen	10	88	246	10	45	15	34	40	31
Clergy		33	10						
Merchants, clothiers, and lawyers			21						
Below gentry status		247	100	1	75	3	4	521	46
Women	2		3	2	1	3	8	188	41
Status not known			24				15		4
Totals	27	430	554	19	151	57	64	760	153

Catholic esquires, nearly thirty-three per cent of Catholic gentle-men, and three out of forty-nine Catholics of below gentry status. A number of Catholic women also appear to have supported the king, although they were a very small minority, numbering one out of nine in Monmouthshire, one out of one hundred and eighty-nine in Lancashire, and three out of forty-four in Yorkshire.

Fortunately, in the case of Monmouthshire and Yorkshire, the degree of delinquency committed by Catholic royalists can be ascertained in the majority of cases. However, in the great majority of Lancashire cases the nature of the delinquency is not revealed, although this can occasionally be ascertained from other sources.

The common form of Catholic delinquency (where the nature of the delinquency is known) was that of taking up arms for the king. In six out of ten Monmouthshire cases where the degree of delinquency is ascertainable, the persons concerned had been actively in arms for the royalists. They included all of the Catholic royalists of knightly status and above, as well as one esquire, John Morgan of Pentrebach, and one person whose status is not known, John George of Llanvihangel. The most outstanding figures in this category, not only in Monmouthshire, but in the country at large, were the Earl of Worcester and Edward, Lord Herbert, and they were accompanied in their active royalism by their relatives, Sir Charles Somerset and Henry Somerset (the oldest son of Lord Herbert).[62]

Among Lancashire Catholic royalists there were also a number of men who appear to have been most active in the king's service. The Catholic Sir Thomas Tyldesley was an outstanding royalist whose enthusiasm for the king's cause was, according to one con-temporary, greater than the Earl of Derby's.[63] Thomas Clifton of Lytham, esquire (one of the Catholics who petitioned the king to be allowed to arm themselves) was also a most active royalist and brought all his children into the king's service.[64] Similarly, Wil-liam Blundell of Crosby, esquire, Charles Townley of Townley, esquire and Hugh Anderton of Euxton, gentleman, all distin-guished themselves in the king's service.[65]

62 *C.C.C.* Part III, pp. 1705–15.
63 *Chetham Society* Old Series, Vol. XII, p. 19.
64 R. Cunliffe Shaw (ed.), *Clifton papers* (Preston, 1935), p. 23.
65 T. E. Gibson (ed.), *Crosby Records: a Cavalier's Notebook* (London, 1880) p. 25; *Lancashire and Cheshire Record Society* Vol. XCV, p. 204; P.R.O., *S.P.D.* 23/161, f. 469.

At least twenty-nine of Yorkshire's fifty-seven Catholic royalists are classified as having been actively in arms for the king. Seven of these 'papists in armes' died fighting for the king: Henry, 1st Viscount Dunbar, died of wounds received at the seige of Scarborough Castle; Sir Thomas Metham and John Plumpton of Plumpton, esquire, died at Marston Moor; Henry Lawson of Brough, esquire, was killed at Melton Mowbray in 1644, Thomas Markham of Skelton in Cleveland, esquire, at Gainsborough, in Lincolnshire, and Ralph Pudsey of Bolton in Bolland, esquire, at Drogheda, in Ireland; and, finally, Thomas Dolman of Duncoats, gentleman, was slain in the second civil war.[66]

On the other hand there is considerable evidence to suggest that the delinquency of a number of other Catholic royalists was not entirely of a voluntary nature, and may have involved merely residing in a particular place when it was garrisoned by the royalists in order to avoid the violent anti-popery of the parliament's army.

John Jones of Dingestow, in Monmouthshire, esquire, claimed that he had not been in arms, but had been 'constrayned often to repair unto Ragland Castle being two miles from his habitation to avoyde the soldiers but never was engaged against the Parliament.'[67] He further claimed that he had been forced to go to Raglan, 'the violence of the Comon Souldiere being great against Recusants'.[68] John Jones was not the only Monmouthshire Catholic to make this claim; so also did William Floyer of Llantillio Pertholey, Anthony Morgan of Marshfield and William Jones of Hardwick, all Catholic gentlemen.[69] In the case of Floyer, there is no accusation of having borne arms for the king, and the county committee defined his delinquency as 'being taken in the Garrison of Hereford in the yeare 1646 when the same was taken by the parliament forces.'[70]

A number of Lancashire Catholics also appear to be guilty merely of being present in a particular place when it was garrisoned for the king. Sir William Gerard of Bryn, baronet, was not

66 P.R.O., *S.P.D.*, 23/82, f. 42; J. W. Clay, 'The Gentry of Yorkshire at the Time of the Civil War', *Yorkshire Archaeological Journal* Vol. XXIII, pp. 367, 371; P.R.O. *S.P.D.*, 23/99, f. 243; 112, f. 154; 85, ff. 809, 811; P.R.O., *S.P.D.*, 19/22, f. 274.
67 P.R.O., *S.P.D.* 23/11, f. 75.   68 *ibid*. 95, f. 178.
69 *ibid*. 86, f. 532; 103, f. 533; 95, ff. 291, 295, 299.
70 *ibid*. 163, f. 47.

accused of bearing arms but of having 'in the beginning of these unhappie warrs' left his home and 'resided in the Garrisons held against the parliament': he had been in Denbigh Castle when it surrendered to parliament.[71] Similarly, Christopher Anderton of Lostock, esquire, appears to have been present in Wigan and Liverpool when they were royalist garrisons and, far from being accused of having borne arms, witnesses were in fact produced to testify that Anderton was unarmed.[72]

Similar examples of this passive form of Catholic delinquency are also evident in Yorkshire, where two of the county's leading Catholics were classified as delinquents on this basis. Sir Philip Constable of Everingham maintained that he had only gone into the royalist garrison of Newark for security in the latter part of the war, after Everingham Hall had been looted and occupied by the parliamentarians.[73] Sir Andrew Young of Bourn, who claimed that he was not 'conscious to himselfe of having done anything to the disservice of the Parliament', was also classed as a delinquent merely for having lived in Oxford while it was garrisoned for the king.[74] The same apparently involuntary royalism is also to be observed among the lesser Yorkshire Catholics. Thomas Empson of Goole, yeoman, claimed in March 1652 that he had been sequestered for recusancy and delinquency since 1645, 'he being very aged and inferme and never in Armes or in any service against the Parliament though for the preservacion of his life he was forced to fly to a Garrison of the Enemies to Avoyd the fury of the Souldiers that at the same time killed a neighbour, of the petitioners at his owne doores.'[75]

Despite the presence of a large royalist party in Monmouthshire, Lancashire and Yorkshire, the great majority of Catholics in these three counties remained neutral in the conflict. In a handful of cases, neutrality can be explained in terms of the physical or mental incapacity of the persons concerned, but in the vast majority neutrality appears to have been a positive step or even a clear

71 P.R.O., *S.P.D.* 23/89, f. 323.
72 *ibid.* 63, ff. 461–6.
73 P. Roebuck, 'The Constables of Everingham: the Fortunes of a Catholic Royalist Family during the Civil War and Interregnum', *Recusant History* Vol. IX, p. 75; H. Aveling, *Post-Reformation Catholicism in East Yorkshire, 1558–1790* p. 43.
74 P.R.O., *S.P.D.* 23/135, f. 91; 239, f. 62.
75 *ibid.* 83, f. 710.

disassociation from the royalist party. The real strength of Catholic neutralism in these counties can be observed in a number of notable cases where the Catholic concerned, including some of the most prominent men in the counties, clearly and quite voluntarily remained aloof from the royalist party. Furthermore, the neutrality of these Catholics is not based upon negative evidence, the mere absence of a delinquency charge, but upon positive evidence, the dismissing by the Committee for Compounding of delinquency charges laid against them after careful investigation.

Sir Edward Morgan, a Catholic baronet of Llantarnam, in Monmouthshire, was informed against in January 1652 as having been an active delinquent.[76] The charge did not go unchallenged and Sir Edward's son took steps to have the delinquency charge dismissed by claiming before the Committee for Compounding that his father was sequestered for recusancy only.[77] After detailed investigations, the Committee for Compounding finally judged in May 1655 that Sir Edward was not a delinquent but a recusant only.[78]

Sir Edward Morgan of Llantarnam was only one of a number of prominent Catholics who appear to have remained neutral during the hostilities. Sir Thomas Fleetwood of Newton in Lancashire, a Catholic baronet, was alleged to have fortified his house against the parliament and yet Sir Thomas claimed that he 'did it onelie to secure his house against theeves.'[79] The deposition taken against Sir Thomas was tainted for the deponent bore a private grudge against him, and Sir Thomas was finally discharged by the commissioners of the delinquency charge.[80] Similarly, a Yorkshire Catholic baronet, Sir Thomas Gascoigne of Barnbow, was discharged of delinquency after a careful examination of his case.[81]

Lesser Catholics also had delinquency charges dismissed after their cases had been heard by the Committee for Compounding. William Langdale of Langthorpe in Yorkshire, esquire, his son, Philip, and his grandson, William, were all charged with delinquency as well as recusancy and, after further examination, were

76 P.R.O., *S.P.D.* 19/23, f. 43.
77 P.R.O., *S.P.D.* 23/103, ff. 285, 376.
78 *ibid.* 27, f. 407.
79 *ibid.* 85, f. 1147.
80 *ibid.* 85, ff. 1135, 1169–71.
81 *ibid.* 88, ff. 1074, 1126; 17, f. 541.

discharged of the former.[82] Similarly, John Wytham of Cliff, esquire, John Thwaites of Long Marston, esquire, Edward Barton of Towthorpe, senior, and his son, Edward, gentlemen, John Metcalf of Taunton, gentleman, and Lady Elizabeth Ireland of Crofton Hall, were all cleared of delinquency charges and judged guilty of recusancy only.[83]

At least one Catholic may have been hostile to the royalist party. Christopher Anderton of Lostock, in Lancashire, esquire, was, as has been noted, found guilty of delinquency for having spent some time in royalist garrisons.[84] One of the witnesses in the case, a servant to Anderton, claimed that he had been detained at Chester by the king's forces early in 1643 while carrying a letter for his master in which Anderton offered 'to make his peace with the Roundheads'.[85] A further witness claimed that Anderton had told him that 'he wold leave the Kingdome' rather than furnish the Earl of Derby with men and arms; and another testified to having overheard Anderton exclaim that 'he wold rather ly and rott in prison then to act any thinge for the kings partie', and reported that Anderton had gone first to Wales and then to France so as to avoid cooperating with the royalists.[86] As these witnesses were produced by Anderton to testify on his behalf, their depositions are accordingly suspect. However, the committee's reception of these depositions, far from being hostile, showed that they were prepared to believe that there might be some truth in them,[87] and although Anderton was finally judged a delinquent, the nature of that delinquency was only the fact that he had been for a time in two royalist garrisons.

Despite parliamentarian allegations to the contrary, the Catholics of Monmouthshire, Lancashire and Yorkshire did not rally round the king to a man, and the striking impression gained from a statistical analysis of the papers of the Committee for Compounding is not how enthusiastic the Catholics of these counties were for the royalist cause but how reluctant many of them were to take up arms for the king.

82 P.R.O., *S.P.D.* 23/140, ff. 594–9; 28, f. 4; 16, f. 616; 99, ff. 289, 309.

83 *ibid.* 131, f. 275; 172, f. 120; 19, f. 1111; 107, f. 7; 89, ff. 778, 781, 784; 17, ff. 186, 665; 32, f. 195; 94, f. 629; 143, f. 421; 23, f. 1638; 223, f. 733; 95, f. 546.

84 Above p. 144.

85 P.R.O., *S.P.D.* 23/63, f. 469.

86 *ibid.* 63, f. 471.   87 *ibid.* 63, f. 452.

3 Suffolk, Buckinghamshire and Northamptonshire

A study of the behaviour of Catholics in counties which were generally inclined towards the parliament is an appropriate sequel to the study above. Suffolk was one of the leading parliamentarian counties and was associated with the adjacent counties in the staunchly parliamentarian Eastern Association. The royalist party in Suffolk collapsed immediately after the outbreak of the war and those who had aligned themselves with that party fled the county.[88] Although Buckinghamshire was divided in its loyalties, it would appear that the county generally inclined towards the parliament, and from November 1644, it was part of the parliamentary territory.[89] According to Isham and Grenville, the gentry of Northamptonshire were fairly evenly divided between the parties in the civil war.[90] However, two contemporary historians from rival camps (Clarendon and Vicars) regarded Northamptonshire as mostly parliamentarian.[91] Nevertheless, in spite of the general inclination of the county towards the parliament, there appears to have been a fairly substantial royalist party in the county, as the Northamptonshire table would suggest.

Catholic support for the royalists in Suffolk and Buckinghamshire was, as table 4.4 shows, minimal: in Suffolk, three Catholics, and in Buckinghamshire, only one Catholic, supported the royalists. The percentage of Suffolk royalists who were Catholics was under six per cent, while only about four per cent of the total of Suffolk Catholics were royalists. In Northamptonshire, the least parliamentarian of the three counties, the Catholics appear to have been more inclined to join the king's party. Although only about eight and a half per cent of the county's royalists were Catholics, the paucity of Catholicism in the county has to be taken into

88 A. M. Everitt, *Suffolk and the Great Rebellion, 1640–60* (Ipswich, 1960) pp. 14–5.
89 *L. J.* Vol. V, p. 82; Clarendon, *op. cit.* Vol. II, p. 181; *V.C.H., Buckinghamshire* Vol. IV, p. 536; *A most true Relation of the Battell fought by Capt. Hotham against the Earl of New-Castle, neer Tollerton in Yorkshire* (London, 1642).
90 G. Isham (ed.), 'The Correspondence of Bishop Brian Duppa and Sir Justinian Isham, 1650–60', *Northamptonshire Record Society* Vol. XVII, Introduction, p. xxxix; G. N. Grenville (Lord Nugent), *Some memorials of John Hampden, his party, and his times* (London, 1832) ii, p. 216.
91 Clarendon, *op. cit.* Vol. IV, p. 212; J. Vicars, *Magnalia Dei Anglicana. Or, Englands Parliamentary Chronicle* (London, 1646) Vol. III, p. 138.

table 4.4 Suffolk, Buckinghamshire and Northamptonshire

	Protestant royalists			Catholic royalists			Neutral Catholics		
	Suffolk	Buckingham-shire	Northampton-shire	Suffolk	Buckingham-shire	Northampton-shire	Suffolk	Buckingham-shire	Northampton-shire
Knights and above	10	11	17	1	1	1	4	4	5
Esquires	8	8	16			3	8	8	7
Gentlemen	23	19	21	2		2	34	2	3
Clergy	3	2	4						
Below gentry status	2	2	1				4	3	
Women			3				16	4	3
Status not known	2	1	2				1		
Totals	48	43	64	3	1	6	67	21	18

consideration: twenty-five per cent of Northamptonshire Catholics were royalists.

Analysis by status among the three royalist counties reveals that Catholic royalism increased up the social scale. However, for the three parliamentarian counties no such observation can be made, and in the case of Northamptonshire, Catholic royalism increases down the social scale. Only one out of six Northamptonshire Catholics of knightly status and above was a royalist, whereas thirty per cent of the county's Catholic esquires, and forty per cent of its Catholic gentlemen were royalists. The picture in Suffolk bears some similarity, with one out of five Catholics of knightly status and above and two out of thirty-six Catholic gentlemen classified as delinquents, while all the Catholic esquires appear to have remained neutral. In Buckinghamshire, the only Catholic who appears to have supported the king was a knight; the Catholics in the remaining status groups remained neutral. None of the Catholics of below gentry status nor any of the Catholic women recorded on table 4.4 appear to have been guilty of delinquency. However, in Northamptonshire and Buckingham-shire, the number of Catholics in each status group below esquire is small and there is some doubt consequently about the statistics below the esquire level.

In Suffolk, Buckinghamshire and Northamptonshire, a total of only ten cases of Catholic royalism can be ascertained from the papers of the Committee for Compounding. Six took up arms for the king. Sir Anthony Morgan of Heyford, in Northamptonshire, fought for the king at Edgehill,[92] and his half-brother, Thomas Morgan of Heyford, esquire, a colonel in the king's army, was killed fighting with the royalists at Newbury in 1643.[93] The only Buckinghamshire Catholic who supported the king, Sir Richard Minshull of Bourton, was judged by the Committee for Compounding to have 'adhered to the enemy and bin in Armes against the Parliament',[94] and yet Sir Richard appears to have conformed on the eve of the civil war, for he attended the parish church of Buckingham and received communion there in October 1641.[95] Little is known of the precise nature of the delinquency of Sir

92 D.N.B.; P.R.O., S.P.D. 23/103, f. 559.
93 D.N.B.; P.R.O., S.P.D. 23/25, f. 228.
94 P.R.O., S.P.D. 23/4, f. 27.
95 ibid. 194, ff. 62, 67; 104, f. 763.

Henry Torlingham, a Suffolk Catholic royalist. All that remains of the case is an information, dated the 13 November 1648, claiming that Sir Henry had been in arms against the parliament.[96]

In two Catholic royalist cases, the delinquency was of a less active nature. The delinquency of Francis Stockley of Adthorp, gentleman, in Northamptonshire, consisted of sending money to Oxford for the king's service;[97] William Bawde of Walgrave, in the same county, esquire, seems to have been guilty merely of being present in royalist garrisons, without any allegations that he was actively in arms.[98]

The overwhelming majority of Catholics in Suffolk, Buckinghamshire and Northamptonshire appear to have seen neutrality as the safest course. It is true that a few may have had no option owing to advanced years or other infirmities, but there is ample evidence to show that in many cases neutrality was a definite choice.

One of the most notable facts about Northamptonshire is the neutrality of all but one of the county's leading Catholics, and of particular significance is the neutrality of Edward, Lord Vaux, of Harrowden, and Thomas, Lord Brudenell of Deene. Lord Vaux's innocence of any act of delinquency was established by the Committee for Advance of Money, and he subsequently appears in committee records as sequestered for recusancy only.[99] The part played by Lord Brudenell in the civil war has been the subject of controversy: throughout the Commonwealth and Interregnum he consistently, and successfully, denied any royalism; then at the Restoration he claimed that he had loyally assisted the late king. Joan Wake, in her study of *The Brudenells of Deene*, tends to accept Lord Brudenell as a royalist,[100] yet she admits that if Lord Brudenell did raise a troop of horse for the king's service and put it under the command of his brother, as he claimed at the Restoration, then it must have been done with the greatest secrecy for the local committees not to have become aware of it later.[101] Furthermore, the House of Lords in July 1647, having heard testimony on his behalf, proposed that Lord Brudenell be classified as a recusant

96 P.R.O., *S.P.D.* 19/21, f. 124.
97 *ibid.* 22, f. 343.
98 *ibid.* 23/66, ff. 269, 271; 163, f. 369.
99 *ibid.* 19/10, ff. 41, 94; 23/254, f. 101; 261, f. 123.
100 J. Wake, *The Brudenells of Deene* (London, 1954) p. 125.
101 *ibid.* p. 130.

only,[102] and, later, the Committee for Compounding, after a full hearing, acquitted him of the charge of delinquency.[103] The bulk of evidence seems, therefore, to point to Lord Brudenell's inactivity during the hostilities. Other leading Northamptonshire Catholics joined these lords in their neutrality. Sir William Andrews and his son, Sir John, both of Denton, were judged sequestered for their recusancy only,[104] and Sir William Tresham of Lyfden also appears to have remained neutral during the short period of the war he lived through (he died in July 1643).[105]

The neutrality of four out of five Catholic knights in Suffolk is equally striking. Not only did Sir Thomas Timperley of Hintlesham remain neutral in the war, but so too, it seems, did his son, Michael, and his grandson, Thomas.[106] Similarly, Sir Edward Sulyard, Sir Roger Martin and Sir Francis Mannock, baronet, all appear to have been free from a delinquency charge.[107] The extent of Catholic neutrality in Suffolk is particularly notable because this county witnessed some of the most spectacular anti-popery riots. Sir Francis Mannock's house at Stoke-by-Nayland was, for instance, wrecked along with Lady Rivers' Suffolk seat at Long Melford.[108] One might have expected Suffolk Catholics to flee to royalist garrisons for protection; in fact most of them remained at home and stayed neutral.

Neutrality appears to have been the rule for Buckinghamshire Catholics with one exception, Sir Richard Minshull, who opted for the king: his four fellow Catholic knights appear to have remained steadfast in their neutrality. Both Sir Thomas Ashfield of Chesham and Sir John Fortescue of Salden, junior, were originally sequestered for delinquency as well as recusancy until,

---

102 House of Lords Archives, 23 December 1645. Petition of Robert Brudenell and annexed papers; 3 August 1647. Annexed papers; 5 July, 1647. List of persons . . . etc.

103 P.R.O., S.P.D. 23/70, f. 327; 163, f. 447; 157, f. 459; 70, ff. 311–14, 317, 334, 357.

104 ibid. 219, f. 615.

105 ibid. 247, f. 46; M. E. Finch, The Wealth of Five Northamptonshire families, 1540–1640 (Oxford, 1956) p. 99.

106 G. H. Ryan and L. J. Redstone, Timperley of Hintlesham: a study of a Suffolk family (London, 1931) p. 64; P.R.O., S.P.D. 23/131, f. 475; 155, f. 449; 169, f. 211; 123, f. 551.

107 P.R.O., S.P.D. 23/203, ff. 691, 697, 699; 34, f. 99; 261, f. 135; 23, f. 1647; 237, f. 66.

108 'Diary of John Rous', Camden Society Old Series, Vol. LXVI, p. 122; F. Peck, Desiderata Curiosa (London, 1732) Vol. II, Lib. XII, pp. 23–4.

on appeal, the former charge was dismissed.[109] Sir John Fortescue, senior, and Sir Robert Throckmorton of Weston Underwood, both baronets, were free from any charge of delinquency and were returned as sequestered for recusancy only.[110]

With neutralism so strongly entrenched among some of the most prominent Catholic families of Suffolk, Buckinghamshire and Northamptonshire, it is no suprise to learn that many lesser Catholics also appear to have remained strictly uncommitted in the war. The Bedingfields of Gislingham, in Suffolk, for instance, provide a notable example of a neutral Catholic gentry family; no charge of delinquency was ever sustained against Henry Bedingfield, esquire or his sons, John and Henry, gentlemen.[111]

The dominant trend among the Catholics of these parliamentarian counties would appear to have been towards political quietism. In Northamptonshire, the one county of the three least inclined towards the parliament, the percentage of Catholics who were royalists equalled that of London and exceeded that of Monmouthshire and Lancashire, yet three-quarters of Northamptonshire Catholics chose to remain neutral. As we have seen, in the more staunchly parliamentarian counties of Suffolk and Buckinghamshire, Catholic support for the royalists was negligible.

4 Somerset

On the outbreak of the civil war, the gentry of Somerset were generally more sympathetic to the royalist than the parliamentarian party, while the numerous commercial element of the county probably supported the parliamentarians. However, by the end of July 1643, the county was wholly in the possession of the royalist party. Somerset is of considerable interest, therefore, as a study of the behaviour of a very small Catholic minority in a county which was secured by the royalists at an early stage in the war.[112]

Table 4.5 shows quite clearly just how few Somerset Catholics there were among the royalists of that county: only about three and one third per cent of the royalists were Catholics. However,

109 P.R.O., S.P.D. 23/254, f. 101; 64, f. 103–4; 25, f. 285; 260, f. 14(i); 246, f. 631; 87, ff. 152, 156; 147, f. 223.
110 ibid. 246, f. 63(i); 14, ff. 32, 41; 115, ff. 221, 223; 171, f. 549.
111 ibid. 169, ff. 192, 231, 251; 119, f. 545; 227, f. 99.
112 V.C.H., Somerset Vol. II, p. 204; Clarendon, op. cit. Vol. II, p. 294; Vol. III, pp. 112–13.

it must be remembered that the Catholics formed only a very small minority in the county, and so when Catholic royalism is related to Catholicism in general about twenty-seven and two-thirds per cent of Somerset Catholics were royalists. Somerset Catholics were, therefore, the most royalist in inclination of all the counties studied in this survey. The only Catholic knight on the Somerset table supported the king, while the degree of royalism diminishes as one moves down the social scale. Whereas sixty-two and a half per cent of Catholic esquires were royalists, less than twenty-two

table 4.5 Somerset

Protestant royalists		*Catholic royalists*		*Neutral Catholics*	
Knights and above	14	Knights and above	1		
Esquires	39	Esquires	5	Esquires	3
Gentlemen	144	Gentlemen	4	Gentlemen	14
Clergy	7				
Merchants and lawyers	9				
Below gentry status	65				
Women	3			Women	6
Status not known	10			Status not known	3
Total	291	*Total*	10	*Total*	26

and a quarter per cent of Catholic gentlemen opted for that party. Unfortunately, there are no statistics for Catholics of below gentry status for Somerset.

In half of the Catholic royalist cases, royalism involved being actively engaged in arms for the king. Sir Robert Brett of Whit-Staunton, for instance, bore arms for the king and was in the royalist garrison at Exeter on its surrender to the parliament.[113] The behaviour of the Prater family of Nunney Castle is of particular interest. When Nunney Castle was made a royalist garrison by the king in June 1643, Richard Prater, esquire, its Catholic owner, became the governor. There were, however, limits to Prater's loyalty to the royalists for, according to Green, when faced with the probable destruction of his property by the besieging parliamentarians, Prater offered to surrender the castle, change his allegiance, and hold the garrison for the parliament.[114] Richard

113 P.R.O., *S.P.D.* 23/33, f. 386; 83, f. 9.
114 E. Green, 'On the Parish and Castle of Nunney', *Proceedings of the Somersetshire Archaeological and Natural History Society* New Series, Vol. II, Part II, pp. 94–5; P.R.O., *S.P.D.* 23/111, f. 657.

Prater's son, George, was also judged a delinquent, yet he claimed that his delinquency consisted of his having remained in Nunney Castle, 'haveing noe other abode', after it had been made a garrison by the king, and that he had not been engaged for the king.[115]

Most of the cases of Somerset neutral Catholics unfortunately lack detail, but the strength of Catholic neutralism in the county occasionally finds some testimony. Edward Cotton of Whit-Staunton, esquire, was, for instance, originally accused of having been in the garrison of Chester when it was held against the parliament, but he was finally judged sequestered for recusancy only;[116] and another Somerset Catholic, Edward Keynes of Compton Pauncefoot, esquire, remained neutral while his son, Alexander Keynes of Radipole, in Dorsetshire, was in arms for the king.[117]

Although the royalists had, therefore, a relatively large and influential party in Somerset, drawing support, as the Somerset table would suggest, from a large section of the upper ranks of society, most Somerset Catholics appear to have resisted the pull towards royalism and to have taken up a neutral stand.

5 Hampshire

The relative position of the parties in Hampshire on the outbreak of the civil war was by no means clear, and at first it would have been hard to predict what part the county would take in the conflict.[118] However, in the course of events, the sentiment of the county proved more favourable to the royalist than to the parliamentary party.[119]

Hampshire royalists do not appear to have received much support from local Catholics (see Table 4.6). Of the total body of royalists, the Catholics numbered under thirteen and a half per cent, while only thirteen and a third per cent of the total body of Catholics were royalists. Analysis by status once again reveals a

115 P.R.O., *S.P.D.* 23/111, f. 657.
116 *ibid.* 32, f. 219; 241, f. 14.
117 *ibid.* 152, f. 507; 234, f. 49A; 96, f. 477.
118 *V.C.H.*, *Hampshire* Vol. V, p. 338.
119 *A Letter sent from one Mr. Parker at Upper Wallop wherein is related a Battell fought between the Inhabitants of the County and the Cavaliers about the settlement of the Militia* (London, 1642); Clarendon, *op. cit.* Vol. III, p. 239.

decrease in royalism among Catholics as one moves down the
social scale: fifty per cent of those Catholics of knightly status and
above, about forty-four and a half per cent of Catholic esquires,
and about twenty and two thirds per cent of Catholic gentlemen
supported the royalists. The royalists received no support whatever from Catholics below gentry status or from Catholic women.

John Paulet, Marquis of Winchester, became the leading royalist
in Hampshire and his country seat, Basing House, became a royalist
garrison under his command.[120] However, Winchester's commit-
ment to the king in the early stages of the conflict was by no means

table 4.6 Hampshire

Protestant royalists		Catholic royalists		Neutral Catholics	
Knights and above	14	Knights and above	2	Knights and above	2
Esquires	12	Esquires	4	Esquires	5
Gentlemen	35	Gentlemen	6	Gentlemen	23
Clergy	4				
Below gentry status	9			Below gentry status	23
Women	1			Women	24
Status not known	2			Status not known	1
Total	77	*Total*	12	*Total*	78

certain, and there is some evidence to suggest that he was at first
inclined towards neutrality.[121]

A number of other notable Hampshire Catholics bore arms for
the king. Sir William Courtenay of Brambridge, baronet, was, for
example, actively engaged with the royalists and was present in
Oxford at its surrender to the parliament;[122] and Henry Philpott
of Thruxton, esquire, confessed that he had fought for the king
at Edgehill, and he was also informed against as having borne
arms against the parliament at Winchester and elsewhere.[123] In
addition five other Hampshire Catholics are also known to have
been in arms for the king. The delinquency of Nicholas Steward
of Hartley Mawditt, esquire, was of a different nature: if Steward's
testimony is to be believed, the only grounds for delinquency raised

120 *D.N.B.*
121 G. N. Godwin, *The Civil War in Hampshire, 1642-45* (London, 1904) p. 8;
  *A Description of the Seige of Basing Castle, kept by the Lord Marquisse of
  Winchester, for the service of His Majesty, against the forces of the Rebells
  under command of Colonell Norton* (Oxford, 1644).
122 P.R.O., *S.P.D.* 23/5, f. 86; 143, ff. 188-9.
123 *ibid.* 178, f. 191.

against him were his absence from his dwelling place for some time and his presence in royalist quarters, during which time he was never guilty of any active delinquency.[124]

In spite of the presence of a fairly substantial royalist party in the county, the overwhelming majority of Hampshire Catholics chose a neutral course. The most outstanding Catholic neutral was Cecil Calvert, Baron Baltimore. Although Baltimore was among those leading Catholics whom the House of Commons desired to be secured in 1641, parliament's hostility does not appear to have pushed him into the arms of the royalists.[125] In a number of cases the Catholic's neutrality is certified in local returns. William Englefield of Catherington, gentleman, is one such case. On the 10 April 1646, the local committee returned him as sequestered for recusancy only, adding that, as far as they knew, he had never been in arms.[126]

The initial uncertainty as to the relative state of the parties in Hampshire at the beginning of the conflict may thus have been due to a strong neutralist sentiment in the county with which the vast majority of Catholics identified themselves. However, Catholic neutralism was not a temporary phenomenon but persisted throughout the hostilities in spite of the support that a few Hampshire Catholics gave to the royalist party.

The county surveys reveal a number of interesting facts about the behaviour of Catholics in the civil war. Tales of popish armies forming around the royal standard have been shown to be mere propaganda: in no county described above did the Catholics form anything more than a minority of the royalist party. Furthermore, when Catholic royalism is related to Catholicism generally in the counties, it is apparent that the royalists managed to rouse only a very limited support from the Catholics: in no county did anything approaching a majority of the Catholics support the royalist cause. Among those Catholics who supported the king there were many who distinguished themselves in that service, and in the majority of cases where the nature of the delinquency is known

124 P.R.O., *S.P.D.* 23/177, f. 310.
125 *L.J.* Vol. IV, p. 449; G. E. Cokagne, *The Complete Peerage* (London, 1910) Vol. I, p. 393; P.R.O., *S.P.D.* 23/247, f. 7; 33, f. 417.
126 P.R.O., *S.P.D.* 23/204, f. 11.

that delinquency was of the most active kind, the Catholics concerned having been openly in arms for the king. Yet even within the Catholic royalist category there are a number of significant cases where that delinquency does not appear to have been of an entirely voluntary nature, and a number of Catholics were sequestered as delinquents merely for having dwelt in a particular place when it was garrisoned for the king. The most striking fact that emerges from this survey is the extent of Catholic neutralism during the hostilities: in every county studied the great majority of Catholics was neutral throughout the war. Moreover, the neutral Catholics recorded in the papers of the Committee for Advance of Money and the Committee for Compounding may only have formed the nucleus of a more general Catholic neutralism. The recusant rolls bear the names not only of Catholics who appear in the committee papers but of many more Catholics whose names do not appear in the papers. There were, for example, two esquires and thirty-three gentlemen of Monmouthshire on the 1655 recusant roll and only one of the esquires and fourteen of the gentlemen appear in the papers of the Committee for Compounding.[127] The remainder were presumably Catholics who had either played no part in the war or whose degree of delinquency was so small as to escape detection. Finally, although in most counties Catholic neutrality increases as one moves down the social scale, it is far from being true that all Catholic neutrals were social nonentities; among the Catholic neutrals were some of the most prominent Catholics, whose importance was acknowledged not only within their particular county but in the kingdom as a whole.

English Catholics were by no means a unified group in the first half of the seventeenth century. For two generations there was no recognized ecclesiastical leader, and the activities of Catholic missionary priests were regarded by many lay Catholics with trepidation, if not hostility, as inviting further oppression by the government. English Catholics, far from being a unified body, were in fact divided like the rest of the country by status and interest, and only if this fact is appreciated can one understand the division into Catholic royalist and Catholic neutral which has been shown above.

127 P.R.O., *Exchequer* 377/61.

Despite parliamentary reports and rumours to the contrary, the Catholics in the first half of the seventeenth century were not seeking to subvert the government and re-establish Catholicism by force. Bossy has shown that, by the beginning of the century, the Catholics were, on the whole, a loyal group.[128] In general, therefore, the Catholics appear to have felt a natural obedience to monarchy and the ardent royalism of a number of Catholics can be viewed in this context.

Moving from the national to the local scene, Catholic royalism may in part be viewed in terms of the royalism of dominant local figures; the personal following and the example set by local magnates like the Earls of Worcester, of Derby and of Newcastle, to mention but a few.

One of the most striking features of the civil war in Monmouthshire was the lead given by the Catholic and energetically royalist House of Raglan. Worcester's own household, which included many gentlemen's sons, helped furnish the royalist armies with soldiers. Henry Manning, for instance, 'a proper young gentleman, bred a Catholic in the family of the Marquis of Worcester, whose page he had been', fought for the king at the battle of Alresford.[129] Loyalty to Worcester, and hence to the royalist cause, was not confined to the earl's household: his tenants, many of whom must have been Catholics, also appear to have been loyal. Sir William Waller observed in April 1643 that 'the stream of the people . . . were at the devotion of the Earl of Worcester, almost an universall land-lord in that county', and Monmouth was retaken by the royalists in 1644, according to one observer, largely because some of Lord Herbert's tenants kept him informed of the movements of the parliamentarian garrison.[130]

The power and influence of the House of Stanley was of considerable importance in ensuring the king support in the north and west of Lancashire. Derby was the head of the most powerful landowning family in Lancashire, and his deputies and friends

---

128 John Bossy, 'The Character of Elizabethan Catholicism', *Past and Present* No. 21, p. 57.
129 A. Clark, *Raglan Castle and the Civil War in Monmouthshire* (Chepstow, 1953) p. 7; Clarendon, *op. cit.* Vol. V, p. 383.
130 J. Corbet, 'An Historical Relation of the Military Government of Gloucester', *Somers' Tracts* Vol. V, p. 315; J. R. Phillips, *Memorials of the Civil War in Wales and the marches, 1642–49* (London, 1874) Vol. II, p. 217.

were all substantial landowners,[131] and the allegiance of Sir Thomas Tyldesley may be explained by the fact that his ancestors had been connected with the estates of the Derby family for over a century. On the outbreak of the civil war, Tyldesley received a commission from Derby.[132] This process was repeated further down the social scale, for Tyldesley, in turn, gave a commission to a fellow Catholic, William Blundell, to raise a company of a hundred dragoons.[133]

The importance of powerful leadership in drawing men into royalism may also be observed in Yorkshire, where according to Clarendon the Earl of Newcastle 'had a greater reputation and interest . . . than at that present any other man had'; in Northamptonshire, where the creation of the royalist party owed a great deal to the influence of the Earl of Northampton; and in Hampshire, where the Catholic Marquis of Winchester, after a period of hesitation, garrisoned his seat for the king and thereby provided local royalists with a rallying place.[134]

Lower down the social scale, this allegiance to social superiors might be manifest in the allegiance of tenant to landlord, or servant to master. Corbet, a contemporary observer, recorded that the common people who were 'addicted to the king's service' came out of 'blinde Wales, and other dark corners of the land' where the tenant-farmer lived 'by the breath of his great land-lord'. Recent research confirms the view that the Welsh royalist gentry were followed by their tenants into royalism.[135] Most of the people of south-west Lancashire were also dependent upon a small group of landowners of which Tyldesley and Blundell are examples. According to one parliamentarian contemporary, Tyldesley being 'a man much esteemed in the Country, most were willing to comply with him'; he was thus able to raise several companies from among the Catholics of Amounderness. In Sefton, Blundell's parish, the Catholic esquires and gentlemen declared for the king.[136]

131 G. H. Tupling, 'Causes of the Civil War in Lancashire', *Transactions of the Lancashire and Cheshire Antiquarian Society* Vol. LXV, p. 30.
132 'The Stanley Papers', *Chetham Society* Old Series, Vols. LXVI, CLXXI.
133 T. E. Gibson, *op. cit.* p. 23.
134 Clarendon, *op. cit.* Vol. III, p. 382; G. N. Grenville (Lord Nugent), *op. cit.* Vol. II, pp. 216–17; *The Souldiers Report concerning Sir William Wallers fight against Basing-house* (London, 1643).
135 J. Corbet, *op. cit.* pp. 303–4; D. Williams, *op. cit.* p. 97; A. Clark, *The story of Monmouthshire* (Llandybie, 1962) p. 179.
136 F. Walker, *op. cit.* p. 50; *Chetham Society* Old Series, Vol. LXII, p. 19.

Similarly, the allegiance of servant to master or mistress led two London Catholics, Richard Foster, cupbearer to Queen Henrietta Maria, and George Gifford of High Holborn, servant to the Lady Marchioness of Winchester, into the royalist camp.[137]

Family ties, as well as social and economic may likewise have helped draw Catholics into royalism. This might, for instance, partly explain the royalism of the family of Sir Ingleby Daniell of Beswick in Yorkshire, who was followed into the royalist camp by his sons George and Thomas Daniell.[138] There were, however, important exceptions to this family solidarity: while Henry, 1st Viscount Dunbar gave his life for the king, his son and heir, John, 2nd Viscount Dunbar, remained neutral; and while Thomas Appleby of Linton-on-Ouse in Yorkshire, esquire, was a Catholic royalist, his son and heir, Thomas, was sequestered for his recusancy only.[139] Moreover, in Somerset, ties of kinship do not appear to have bound together Catholics in either royalism or neutrality. Division within families may sometimes have resulted from a concern to provide insurance against an uncertain outcome.

It has been seen that in those counties which boasted a substantial royalist party, Catholic royalism increased as one ascended the social scale. Catholic like protestant participation in the war was most marked at the top of the social scale and least marked at the bottom. It was easier for a yeoman, Catholic or protestant, to avoid committing himself than it was for a knight or esquire. Moreover, political consciousness was largely confined to the upper ranks of seventeenth-century society.

Absence of serious economic hardships might also have helped in the raising of royalist troops in a particular county or area of a county. The concentration of Catholic royalism in south-west Lancashire, for example, might be accounted for by the fact that there were no serious agricultural hardships in that area of the county which could have created tension between tenant and landlord.[140] In the absence of such grievances, it was easier for

---

137 P.R.O., *S.P.D.* 19/118, f. 13; House of Lords Archives, 26 June 1648: Report of the Westminster Committee for the Militia.

138 P.R.O., *S.P.D.* 23/172, f. 253; 79, f. 240.

139 G. E. Cokagne, *The Complete Peerage* (London, 1910) Vol. IV, p. 513; P.R.O., *S.P.D.* 23/23, f. 1692; 145, f. 553; 19, f. 1074.

140 F. Walker, *op. cit.* p. 62; B. G. Blackwood, *Social and Religious Aspects of the History of Lancashire, 1635-55*, B.Litt. thesis, University of Oxford (1956) pp. 85-92.

landlords, like William Blundell, to raise companies from among their tenants, whereas in areas like Rossendale, which had strong economic grievances, the enemies of royalism found strong support.[141]

Political allegiance may, in some cases, have been determined by the facts of power; the dominance in a particular region of either party with the consequent pressures exerted in the direction of cooperation with the dominant power. By July 1643, all Yorkshire, with the exception of Hull, had fallen to the royalists and, consequently, Yorkshiremen, Catholic or protestant, must have felt some pressure to join that party. The royalists set up a county committee and extracted money from suspected parliamentarians, and from Catholics, especially neutral Catholics.[142] A number of Yorkshire Catholics may, therefore, have been drawn reluctantly into royalism, and at least three Catholics subsequently pleaded before the Committee for Compounding that they had been forced to cooperate with the royalists. This was argued, for instance, in the case of George Metham of Metham, esquire, who claimed that he had been forced by a royalist contingent to join with them.[143] Furthermore, in Yorkshire there are some significant differences in the distribution of Catholic royalists between the Ridings. West Riding Catholics, in common with the gentry in general in this riding,[144] appear to have been most sympathetic towards the king (forty-four per cent). East Riding Catholics rank second (nearly thirty-eight per cent), while in the North Riding only about twenty-seven per cent of the Catholics were royalists. This distribution might be partly a result of the concentration of action in the early stages of the war in the East and West Ridings where the activities of opposing armies may have forced Catholics to take sides.

All the above reasons for royalism might be applied to protestant as well as Catholic royalists. But the Catholics were in a special position at the time of the civil war: parliament was ostensibly fighting a crusade against popery and, as such, it was the natural ally of violent and fanatical anti-papists. Yet, while the parliament gave almost full rein to anti-popery, the king, at the

141 G. H. Tupling, *The Economic History of Rossendale* (Manchester, 1927) pp. 127–60.
142 H. Aveling, *Northern Catholics* p. 302.
143 P.R.O., *S.P.D.* 23/236, f. 41.
144 J. T. Cliffe, *op. cit.* pp. 409–10.

beginning of the hostilities, offered the Catholics accommodation and protection.[145] At the start, therefore, the immediate threat to Catholicism clearly came from the parliament rather than from the king. Anti-popery violence during the early stages of the war was rife in both London and the counties. According to Clarendon, 'the Papists' houses in all places' were, in 1642, being 'plundered or pulled down, with all circumstances of rage, by the parliament-soldiers', and these soldiers 'in their march took the goods of all Catholics and eminent malignants as lawful prize'.[146] One of the most spectacular outbursts of this anti-popery violence involved attacks upon the Countess Rivers in both Essex and Suffolk.[147] Faced with such hostility and violence some Catholics quite naturally sought protection in the king's quarters, and instances of Catholics who claimed before the Committee for Compounding that they had been forced to seek refuge with the royalists can be found in all the counties studied in this survey. In Monmouthshire, for instance, John Jones of Dingestow, esquire, complained to the central committee after the war that he had been constrained to enter Raglan Castle for his personal safety, 'the violence of the Comon Souldiere being great against Recusants', and that he had never actively opposed the parliament.[148] Furthermore, Meredith's recent study of the Eyres of Hassop in Derbyshire, supports this reason for royalism: the royalism of Rowland Eyre is partly explained by the Earl of Newcastle's victorious advance through Yorkshire and into Derbyshire, and partly by the violence of the parliamentarian Gell against papists and suspected 'malignants' which threw Eyre into the arms of Newcastle.[149] However, it has already been noted that in Suffolk, where the most violent anti-popery riots took place, most Catholics did not in fact flee but managed to remain at home as neutrals:[150] this seems to weaken the theory that Catholics were driven into royalism by parliament's violent anti-popery. Yet it must be remembered that there were no royalist garrisons close

145 *Chetham Society* Old Series, Vol. LXII, pp. 13–14.
146 Clarendon *op. cit.* Vol. II, pp. 276, 318.
147 A. Kingston, *East Anglia and the Great Civil War* (London, 1897) pp. 64–6; F. Peck, *op. cit.* Vol. II, Lib. XII, pp. 23–4.
148 P.R.O., *S.P.D.* 23/95, ff. 178, 188.
149 R. Meredith, 'A Derbyshire Family in the Seventeenth Century: the Eyres of Hassop and their Forfeited Estates', *Recusant History* Vol. VIII, p. 18.
150 Above pp. 147–52.

at hand for Suffolk Catholics to retire into and, consequently, fleeing to the royalists for protection involved the total abandonment of their county and their estates: in these circumstances, most chose to remain at home and attempt to weather the storm.

A Lancashire parliamentarian, Major Edward Robinson, remarked of the Catholics that 'they had a good ground to have been newter in this war had not their spirits and malice against the Protestant religion provoked them to it.'[151] Unfortunately, Robinson never explained what that 'good ground' was. The fact remains, however, that the great majority of Catholics in the counties surveyed remained neutral in the war and that neutrality must be accounted for.

Catholic royalism may be partly accounted for in terms of the lead given by the dominent figures in the counties, and so too might Catholic neutrality. The steadfast neutrality of leading Hampshire Catholics, like Baron Baltimore and Sir Benjamin Titchborne, for instance, may have encouraged lesser folk to remain uncommitted; and in Northamptonshire, the neutrality of Lord Vaux and Lord Brudenell may have acted as a similar encouragement to lesser Catholics to sit still. Similarly, Sir Edward Morgan of Llantarnam appears to have given a lead to neutralism in his neighbourhood, for there was a distinct concentration of Catholic neutrals in the vicinity of Llantarnam.

Family allegiance could also help confirm a Catholic in his neutrality; the Meynells of North Kilvington, in Yorkshire, for example, were solidly neutral,[152] as too were William Langdale of Langthorpe, esquire, his son, Philip, and his grandson, William.[153] However, as was noted earlier, Catholic families, like their protestant counterparts, were not uncommonly divided in the civil war.

In counties which were generally inclined towards the king it is quite clear that the degree of Catholic neutrality increases as one moves down the social scale. Central to an explanation of this phenomenon is the fact that only a small proportion of commoners actually took sides in the war. A tract of September 1642, for instance, commenting upon the situation in Yorkshire, claimed

151 *Chetham Society* Old Series, Vol. LXII, pp. 14–15.
152 H. Aveling (ed.), 'The Recusancy Papers of the Meynell family', *Catholic Record Society* Vol. LVI, Introduction p. xxxvi; P.R.O., *S.P.D.* 23/124, ff. 673, 679.
153 Above pp. 145–6.

that 'the communalty' were 'generally loath to obey one side or other', and this claim has found confirmation in recent research.[154] It would appear, therefore, that the behaviour of Yorkshire Catholics closely resembled that of protestants.

The possession of former monastic property might possibly explain the neutrality of some Catholics who would not welcome an attempt by the church to recover these lands, and who could, perhaps, have seen the possibility of this danger in an outright royalist victory. The ruined abbey of Furness and a considerable part of the lands of Cartmell priory in north Lancashire belonged to the Catholic Preston family who according to Halley 'wished well to the King, but seemed to have been content with good wishes, probably unwilling to strengthen the Catholics, who had not abandoned the hope of recovering the monastic property.'[155] Similarly, in Monmouthshire, the neutrality of Sir Edward Morgan of Llantarnam might be partly explained in these terms, most of his family estate consisting of tithes and monastic property gained during the dissolution of the monasteries.[156] The concentration of Catholic neutrals in Llantarnam and its neighbourhood might also be partly explained by the possible ownership of some former monastic property. However, the holding of former monastic property did not invariably lead to neutrality and it can only be seen as a contributory factor towards Catholic neutrality.

Presence in a parliamentarian region or county, or proximity to a parliamentarian stronghold might also influence a Catholic's choice in favour of neutrality. The large body of Catholic neutrals in London, for instance, could perhaps be explained by the fact that parliament quickly gained control of the City, and so attempts to form a royalist party in London proved abortive.[157] Similarly, in Suffolk some Catholics were driven to leave the county on the advent of war and the popular fury against Catholics. According to Everitt, those who remained saw that 'their only hope

154 J. T. Cliffe, op. cit. p. 406; Certaine Intelligence from Yorke, concerning the meeting of that county for the settling the peace (London, 1642).

155 R. Halley, Lancashire: Its Puritanism and Nonconformity (Manchester, 1872) p. 169.

156 H. Foley, Records of the English Province of the Society of Jesus (London, 1882) Vol. IV, p. 334; D. Williams, op. cit. p. 82.

157 V. Pearl, London and the Outbreak of the Puritan Revolution (Oxford, 1961) p. 235.

of survival lay in strict political quietism.'[158] Even in counties which were largely royalist, like Lancashire, Catholic neutrality could in some instances be partly explained in terms of proximity to parliamentarian strongholds or by actual presence in parliamentarian quarters. Richard Martinscrofte of Manchester, a Catholic joiner, probably had no option but to remain neutral. However, close proximity to a parliamentarian stronghold did not necessarily result in neutrality; in the face of parliamentarian violence, a neutral stand may not have always been possible for Catholics who lived near parliament's quarters.

Catholic neutrality must also be seen in a wider context; it must be viewed against the background of neutralist sentiment in general in the country as a whole, and in some counties in particular.[159] In at least three of the counties studied in this survey (Yorkshire, Somerset and Lancashire) there appears to have been a general desire to neutralize the county during the early stages of the war. Neutralist sentiment in Yorkshire, for instance, led directly to the drawing up of articles of neutrality which were subscribed by the leaders of both parties and would have effectively neutralized the county had not parliament intervened and condemned the whole proceedings.[160] The Catholics of Yorkshire, even more than their protestant counterparts, would not welcome roving armies which threatened their very existence. Many Catholics may have opted for neutrality, therefore, out of a desire to prevent as much conflict as possible, for they would be among the chief sufferers in such conflict. However, although Catholic neutrality might be partly explained in these terms at the beginning of the war, their continued neutrality, after the collapse of treaty negotiations, demands further explanation.

On the outbreak of the civil war the Catholics were faced with an extremely difficult and dangerous situation. The choice was between royalism and neutrality and one of the strongest factors influencing that choice was whether or not they would gain by a royalist victory. If the king were successful, they might expect a return to the type of treatment experienced during the Personal

158 A. M. Everitt, op. cit. p. 14; P.R.O., S.P.D. 23/260, f. 10.
159 Brian Manning, Neutrals and Neutralism in the English Civil War 1642–1646 D.Phil. thesis, University of Oxford (1957), Chs. 1 and 2.
160 Clarendon, op. cit. Vol. II, pp. 286, 461–3; The Declaration and Votes of Parliament concerning the Late Treaty of Peace in York-shire, wherein they renounce the said agreement (London, 1642).

Rule, and if he were defeated outright, they might expect the parliament to put all its threats against them into practice. There was also a third alternative; the Catholics might perhaps benefit from a negotiated peace between the king and parliament with a return to regular government. However, even this alternative was fraught with danger as a negotiated peace might involve agreement on a severe repression of the Catholics. In such a situation, the treatment Catholics had received at the hands of Charles I and his government is of great importance, and there is evidence to suggest that the Catholics were becoming increasingly alienated from the king during the Personal Rule and that that alienation had a decided influence upon their choice of a course of action in 1642.

The king's Catholic subjects were more sensitive to the financial demands of the period of the Personal Rule because they were already burdened with compositions under the recusancy laws. In financial terms, the Catholics were probably in a worse position during the Personal Rule than they had been previously when the king governed with his parliament, and, although it cannot be said that the financial burden was crushing, it can be argued that it was sufficient to alienate many Catholics from their sovereign. Lancashire Catholics, for instance, were not without a voice in condemning the financial exactions and military oppression of the Personal Rule. In 1639 and 1640, impressment for the war against the Scots provoked a great deal of agitation, and Catholic commoners were just as resentful of being dragged away from their homes to fight for the king as their protestant counterparts.[161]

Shipmoney provoked an outcry from all sections of society because it was a form of taxation which hit everybody.[162] In spite of a determined effort to raise the 1640 assessment in Lancashire, the sheriff was forced to report that 'two of the largest hundreds, Amounderness and Lonsdale, altogether stand out and will neither assess nor pay',[163] and there is some significance in the fact that Amounderness and Lonsdale were notoriously Catholic hundreds. One leading Liverpool Catholic, John Cross, was proceeded against for his opposition to shipmoney. After refusing to pay his 1636 assessment, Cross was arrested and sent a prisoner to Lancaster, the mayor and aldermen complaining to the council of the

161 G. H. Tupling, 'Causes of the Civil War in Lancashire', pp. 16, 29, 30.
162 *ibid*. p. 25.   163 *ibid*. p. 28.

'trouble Cross had given on former assessments, he being an obstinate convicted recusant and powerful within the town, and so giving a very evil example, to the hindrance of the service.'[164] John Cross died in 1640,[165] but had he lived, he might not have been an ardent royalist.

Other financial exactions hit exclusively at the gentry, and among these were fines for distraint of knighthood. Among those who refused the obligations of knighthood in June 1631, and consequently incurred fines, were two Lancashire Catholics, Ralph Standish and Roger Bradshaigh, and, according to S. J. Hawkes, this measure was partly responsible for their subsequent inactivity in the civil war.[166] There were other grievances which might have helped to alienate Catholics from the crown besides shipmoney, distraint of knighthood and military burdens. The financial exactions of the forest laws, for example, may also have contributed to that estrangement. According to Joan Wake, the expedient of the forest laws put a considerable strain on Lord Brudenell's loyalty.[167]

Although Catholics were divided by status and interest and were not united in any real sense, they all bore one grievance in common, the financial exactions of the recusancy laws. Charles I's government, especially during the Personal Rule, has been described as being generally lenient in its treatment of Catholics.[168] There are, however, two dissenting voices: while both Havran and Aylmer accept this view as largely true when applied to the upper classes and London Catholics, they do not believe that it holds when applied to the generality of Catholics in the counties.[169]

It is an undisputable fact that Charles I sent fewer Catholics to the scaffold than his two royal predecessors,[170] and in this sense his

---

164 *C.S.P.D. 1636-7* p. 207.
165 *V.C.H., Lancashire* Vol. VI, p. 141.
166 S. J. Hawkes, 'Wigan's Part in the Civil War', *Transactions of the Lancashire and Cheshire Antiquarian Society* Vol. XLVII, p. 89.
167 J. Wake, *op. cit.* p. 123.
168 Brian Magee, *op. cit.* p. 161; W. K. Jordan, *The Development of Religious Toleration in England* (London, 1932-4) Vol. II, pp. 182-5; A. C. F. Beales, *Education under Penalty: English Catholic Education from the Reformation to the Fall of James II, 1547-1689* (London, 1963), p. 97.
169 M. J. Havran, *The Catholics in Caroline England* (London, 1962) pp. vii, 91; Aylmer, *op. cit.* p. 89.
170 M. J. Havran, *op. cit.* p. 111.

government was a moderate one. Yet what price did Catholics have to pay for this clemency? One of the most pressing problems facing Charles I was that of finance, and during the Personal Rule it became a key problem. Faced with the urgent need to increase his revenue, Charles I investigated increasing that part of the revenue which came from recusancy fines, and this source of revenue had the additional attraction of being strictly 'legal', unlike the notorious shipmoney levies.[171] The existing system of recusant fining brought little financial benefit to the king while it helped fill the pockets of numerous officials.[172] A new system was clearly needed if the king was to increase his revenue from recusants, and, after considering a number of expedients, a commission system was adopted in 1626-7. Two commissions were set up to receive recusant revenues, one commission dealing with recusants whose estates lay south, and the other with recusants whose estates lay north, of the Trent. Fining was to become a much more simplified process and as a result, it was hoped, more revenue would reach the king, and, in addition, more recusants were to be brought into the net.[173]

It is difficult to judge whether the new system eased or increased the financial burden on recusants, mainly because of the impossibility of estimating the total financial burdens (including bribes and other extortions as well as open exactions) which the previous system placed upon recusants. However, a description of the state of the Catholic church in England, sent to Rome in 1636 by an anonymous Catholic agent, reached the conclusion that the 'poorer sort' of Catholic was the most hard hit under the new system, and that the main object of the commissioners was to extract as much money as possible out of recusants so as to increase the king's revenue.[174]

The three principal figures involved in the execution of the recusancy laws, Weston, Wentworth and Laud, could hardly be described as being unduly lenient. Until his death in 1635, Lord Treasurer Weston appears to have pressed more money out of the

171 M. J. Havran, pp. 92-3.
172 H. Aveling (ed.), 'Documents Relating to the Northern Commission for Compounding with Recusants, 1627-42', *Catholic Record Society* Vol. LIII, p. 293.
173 *ibid.* pp. 295-303.
174 Westminster Archives, Archbishop's House. *MSS. Archivi Westmonasteriensis* Vol. XXVIII (1635-6), p. 411.

Catholics than ever before,[175] and Wentworth, as receiver general of recusant revenues in the north, was far from lenient in his compositions with recusants.[176] Similarly, Archbishop Laud was as strongly opposed to Catholicism as he was to puritanism and, according to Havran, most of the proclamations of the privy council against recusancy can be traced directly to Laud's influence.[177] Charles himself did not believe in harrying Catholics solely for their religious opinions, and yet, at the same time, unlike his father he had no real interest in granting them toleration and little interest in their welfare.[178] On the whole, Charles showed a remarkable lack of scruple in his dealings with the Catholics. When faced with a parliament, the king was prepared to repudiate any past guarantees he had given the Catholics and to commence a fresh wave of persecution.[179] Neither the king, therefore, nor the leading figures in his government who were concerned with the Catholics, were inclined towards tolerating them, and it was finance that largely determined the policy pursued towards them.

The Catholics had little cause to be grateful to Charles I and his government. There is small reason to suppose that they paid less for their recusancy under Charles I than they had under Elizabeth or James I, and there are indications that they may in fact have paid more. The 'Queen's contribution' provided a real test of the affection of Catholics for Charles I and his government prior to the outbreak of the civil war. However, the amount raised was only £14,000. A few Catholics, like the Marquis of Worcester, gave generously, but most Catholics must have contributed little or nothing.[180] By the time of the northern expedition, therefore, the king appears to have alienated a large section of the Catholic population to such an extent that they failed to respond to the queen's special pleading.

The declared accounts of the king's commissioners for recusant

175 F. C. Dietz, *English public finance 1485–1641* (London, 1964) Vol. II, pp. 251–2; Clarendon, *op. cit.* Vol. I, p. 63.

176 M. J. Havran, *op. cit.* pp. 95, 97; J. Rushworth, *Historical Collections* (London, 1692) Vol. II, p. 247.

177 M. J. Havran, *op. cit.* pp. 148–9; W. Knowler (ed.), *The Earl of Strafford's Letters and Dispatches* (London, 1739) Vol. II, p. 74.

178 W. K. Jordan, *op. cit.* Vol. II, p. 172; M. J. Havran, *op. cit.* p. 70.

179 W. K. Jordan, *op. cit.* Vol. II, p. 172; M. J. Havran, *op. cit.* p. 62.

180 M. J. Havran, *op. cit.* pp. 152–3, 155–6; G. Albion, *Charles I and the Court of Rome* (Louvain, 1935) p. 335.

revenues bear the names of Catholics who had compounded and contributed regularly to that revenue.[181] The names of Catholics who make up the county statistics have been checked alongside these accounts with a number of interesting results. The most significant fact that emerged was that in London and four counties (Hampshire, Buckinghamshire, Northamptonshire and Monmouthshire) there is not one Catholic royalist whose name appears on the declared accounts, and all the Catholics who can be traced on these accounts remained neutral in the war. In the remaining four counties, there are instances of Catholic royalists appearing on the declared accounts, but they are a minority. In Suffolk, eight of the nine Catholics whose names appear in both the papers of the Committee for Compounding and the declared accounts were neutrals. These eight neutrals comprised four knights and four gentlemen, while the only Catholic royalist in the accounts was a gentleman. In Somerset, four out of six Catholics who appear in both the papers and the accounts were neutrals (one esquire, and three gentlemen), while the two Catholic royalists comprised one knight and one esquire. Similarly, in Yorkshire the majority of Catholics who appear in both the papers and the accounts (thirty-seven out of fifty-six) remained neutral in the war while the rest were royalist. Breaking down these Yorkshire figures according to status, four Catholics of knightly status and above, eight esquires, six gentlemen, and one Catholic of below gentry status supported the king in the civil war, in spite of the fact that fines had been regularly extracted from them during the Personal Rule. However, one Catholic knight, twelve esquires, twelve gentlemen and twelve Catholics of below gentry status remained neutral in the war. Finally, in Lancashire, forty-two out of sixty-seven Catholics who appear in both the papers and the accounts were neutrals. The majority of these neutrals were, however, of below gentry status (thirty-two out of forty-two), and the rest were of gentleman status, while the Catholic royalists comprised one Catholic knight, eight esquires, ten gentlemen and six Catholics of below gentry status. There are also numerous instances in all of the county studies of Catholics whose names appear in the accounts only and so were presumably, in the absence of any evidence to the contrary, free from any charge of delin-

181 P.R.O., *Exchequer* 351/415-25 for the south; *ibid.* 426-31 for the north.

quency. It would appear, therefore, that the financial hardships suffered by the Catholics during the Personal Rule, and the resulting alienation of those Catholics from the king, tended to make the majority of them neutral in the civil war, and there are a number of notable cases where the possible relationship between the continuous payment of fines in the 1630s and subsequent neutrality in the war can be demonstrated.

The neutrality of two Suffolk knights, Sir Edward Sulyard of Haughley Park and Sir Roger Martin of Long Melford, may be seen in this light. Sir Edward Sulyard compounded in 1634 at the rate of £110 a year for a lease of his lands and the arrears of his fines, and within the period 1634 to 1638, Sir Edward paid £495 in fines;[182] while Sir Roger Martin compounded in 1633 at £200 a year (just £60 less than the full fine of £20 a month) and paid his fine until 1638, the whole amount totalling £1,100.[183] Similarly, Sir Edward Morgan of Llantarnam, in Monmouthshire, baronet, who was one of the most notable Catholic neutrals in the country, paid the maximum fine under the law of £260 a year for five consecutive years, 1628 to 1632.[184] Although it is not known how he fared during the rest of the Personal Rule, except that he paid his fine for a half year in 1635,[185] the total fine of £1,420 was probably severe enough to alienate Sir Edward from the king and to render him inactive in the civil war.

The two most notable cases of Northamptonshire Catholics who were constantly persecuted prior to the civil war and remained neutral when the war broke out, are those of John Poulton and his son, George, both esquires. John Poulton compounded for two-thirds of his manor of Desborough in 1627 at £40 a year and he paid this amount regularly for four years.[186] His son, George, compounded for two parts of his lands in Desborough in 1627 at £5 a year and he also made regular payments for four years.[187] In 1631, father and son compounded jointly for two parts of the manor Desborough at £66–13s.–4d. and they paid this until 1633 when they also compounded for their arrears of £20 a month at £3–6s.–8d.[188] Thus, from 1633 until 1638 they paid £70 a year in fines.[189]

182 *ibid*. 421–5.   183 *ibid*.
184 *ibid*. 415–19.   185 *ibid*. 422.
186 *ibid*. 416–18.   187 *ibid*.
188 *ibid*. 419–20.   189 *ibid*. 421–5.

The impact of recusancy fines upon the Meynells of North Kilvington, in Yorkshire, has been closely studied by Aveling, who has shown that recusant families, like the Meynells, were able to survive and absorb recusancy fines by great efforts without facing ruin.[190] Yet the Meynells remained neutral in the civil war, and their constant persecution could go a long way towards explaining their apparent alienation from the king; Thomas Meynell and his son, Anthony, both compounded with the commissioners to pay jointly £100 a year and they paid this sum regularly.[191]

There are, however, a number of important exceptions to the thesis that Catholics who were burdened with recusancy fines during the Personal Rule subsequently remained neutral in the civil war. Two Yorkshire esquires, Henry Lawson of Brough and Stephen Tempest of Roundhay, compounded at £50 and £60 respectively and paid their fines regularly,[192] and yet they both became royalists. Similarly, Richard Massey of Rixton, in Lancashire, esquire, paid an annual fine of £40 from 1629,[193] and yet this did not deter him from joining the royalist party on the outbreak of war. In Somerset and Suffolk, however, the exceptions to the rough correlation between persecution during the Personal Rule and neutrality in the civil war are not particularly notable ones.

It can be argued, therefore, that the experience of a substantial number of Catholics during the Personal Rule was sufficient to alienate them from the king, with the result that, throughout the period of the war, only a minority of the king's Catholic subjects assisted the royalists. On the outbreak of the hostilities, the majority of Catholics wished to live in peace and to continue their regular way of life. Constant suspicion and persecution had taught Catholics the value of caution and they were reluctant to disturb the delicate *modus vivendi* they had established with their protestant neighbours. At the local level, some degree of understanding and tolerance, fortified by ties of kinship and neighbourhood, appears to have been developing between Catholics and protestants, a point which receives additional confirmation in a recent

190 H. Aveling, 'Recusancy Papers of the Meynell family', *Catholic Record Society* Vol. LVI, p. xxxvi.
191 *ibid.*; P.R.O., *Exchequer* 351/426–33.
192 P.R.O., *Exchequer* 351/426–33.
193 *ibid.* p. 426.

study of Staffordshire in this period.[194] Pym had no doubt seen
the dangers of this tendency towards a peaceful and charitable co-
existence when, on the 17 April 1640, he warned the House of
Commons that 'Wee must not looke on a Papist as hee is in himselfe but as hee is in the body of the Church.'[195]

The overwhelming majority of Catholics saw political quietism
as their safest course in the civil war. They had nothing to gain
from the victory of either party and their alienation from the king
appears to have balanced their fears of the consequences of a
parliamentarian victory.

In view of the large scale alienation of Catholics from the king
and the possible hostility of some Catholics to the royalist party,
a few Catholics may possibly have been led by that antipathy into
the parliamentarian camp. Leading royalists, like the Earl of
Newcastle and Lord Herbert, accused the parliament at the time
of hypocritically welcoming and employing Catholics in its
armies,[196] and parliament itself periodically examined reports that
the Catholics were being allowed to join its army. At least one
parliamentarian propagandist acknowledged in January 1643 that
parliament's armies were not absolutely free from papists,[197] and
as late as the 28 November 1644, the House of Commons ordered
the Lord General to examine Captain Buller 'concerning the
Information given that he doth employ Papists in his Troops.'[198]

Apart from the declarations of royalists and parliamentarians,
there are some more positive indications that Parliament may have
received assistance from some Catholics. The case of Thomas
Stich of Fetter Lane, London, a Catholic esquire, is of particular
significance, for not only was Stich still acting as one of the attor-
neys in the office of the Treasurers Remembrancer as late as the
4 December 1644, but he also appears to have lent parliament £300,
and constitutes, therefore, the case of a Catholic lending the parliament material support.[199]

194 J. T. Pickles, 'Studies in Royalism in the English Civil War 1642–1646,
with Special Reference to Staffordshire University of Manchester M.A.
thesis (1968) p. 211.   195 P.R.O., S.P.D. 16/450, f. 108.
196 J. Webb, op. cit. Vol. I, p. 193; A Declaration made by the Earl of New-
Castle for his resolution of Marching into Yorkshire (London, 1642).
197 A Confutation of the Earle of Newcastles Reasons for taking under his
command divers Popish Recusants in the Northerne parts (London, 1643).
198 C.J. Vol. III, p. 707.
199 House of Lords Archives, 4 December 1644: Copy of an order; 21
November 1646: Annexed papers.

There are also a number of instances of parliamentarians having Catholic wives, or coming from Catholic families. Richard Edwards of London, for example, who was married to a Catholic, was a soldier in the parliament's army.[200] Similarly, Edward Saltmarshe of Saltmarshe, in Yorkshire (the second son of Philip Saltmarshe who, originally a Catholic, subsequently changed his religion) was a captain in the parliament's army and, after the war, married Gerard Ireland, the Catholic widow of Thomas Meynell of North Kilvington, esquire. Two of their sons became priests and Edward Saltmarshe was presented as a recusant for the first time in 1671.[201] Whether Edward had been a secret Catholic before that date or whether he had had Catholic sympathies would, however, be sheer speculation.

An account of a conspiracy against the Lord Protector published in 1654 reveals the surprising possibility that even the Protector's own regiment was not free from Catholics.[202] Two soldiers from the Protector's regiment were involved in the conspiracy, John Hippon and one Copley, and the former, examined before a Westminster justice of the peace on the 21 June 1654, confessed to being a Catholic.[203] Although Hippon played down his own part in the conspiracy, the fact remains that he appears to have been both a Catholic and a parliamentarian soldier in Cromwell's own regiment until 1654.

It is, therefore, by no means improbable that there were a few Catholics in the parliament's armies. There are no indications, however, that there was a substantial number of Catholic parliamentarians or that the parliament actually encouraged their assistance.

The statistical analysis undertaken in this essay shows quite clearly that the great majority of Catholics in every county studied remained neutral in the civil war. A total of 1,511 Catholics has been examined of whom nearly eighty-two per cent were found to be neutrals; or, conversely, only between a fifth and a sixth of all sequestered Catholics were royalists. When related to the total number of royalists, Catholic royalists formed a very small proportion indeed, comprising only about thirteen per cent of the royalists

200 P.R.O., *S.P.D.* 18/129, f. 103.
201 *Catholic Record Society* Vol. IV, p. 382; Vol. XI, p. 576; Vol. LVI, p. xvi.
202 *The Harleian Miscellany* (London, 1813) Vol. X, pp. 210–15.
203 *ibid.* p. 245.

The behaviour of the Catholic gentry requires special attention and table 4.7 below sets out the totals of Catholic gentry from earlier county tables.

table 4.7

Catholic royalists		Neutral Catholics	
Knights and above	25	Knights and above	24
Esquires	68	Esquires	81
Gentlemen	94	Gentlemen	190
Total	187	*Total*	295

The table shows quite clearly how the tendency to royalism was stronger among the upper gentry and weaker among the lower gentry. Just over a half of the Catholics of knightly status and above were royalists, while about forty-six per cent of Catholic esquires, and thirty-three and a half per cent of Catholic gentlemen, were royalists. Furthermore, of all the Catholic gentry counted, about two-fifths were royalists. If the counties studied are regarded as a good sample of the whole country, and the two-fifths is seen as a national proportion, then Catholicism is not all that much less a characteristic, or major element, of the royalist party, than puritanism is of the parliamentarian party.[204]

Recent studies of the civil war in Kent and Staffordshire show that substantial numbers of Catholic neutrals are to be found in other counties besides the sample chosen for this study. Everitt, in his study of Kent, has concluded that, although 'several' of the royalists in Kent were Catholics, 'in general the recusants of the county kept their heads low and endeavoured to remain neutral.'[205] Similarly, Pickles, in his recent study of Staffordshire, states that the 'Catholics as a body did not flock to the king's banner' and that 'in quantity and quality, there was a substantial number of Catholics who remained neutral during the war.'[206] Catholic neutrality would appear, therefore, to have been widespread and, bearing in mind the variety of the sample, the results obtained from the county studies might be regarded as an indication of the national position.

204 J. T. Cliffe shows that about half of the Puritan gentry families of Yorkshire supported the Parliament. (J. T. Cliffe, *op. cit.* p. 421.)
205 A. M. Everitt, *The Community of Kent and the Great Rebellion 1640–60* (Leicester, 1966) p. 118.
206 J. T. Pickles, *op. cit.* pp. 196, 257.

In the long term, neutrality proved a wise choice for the Catholics. The Commonwealth did not inaugurate a period of intense Catholic persecution; on the contrary, the Catholics received a degree of toleration far greater than any previous Stuart leniency. Catholic inactivity in the civil war showed up the popish menace for the bogey it was, and enabled Catholic apologists like Birchley to beg the Protectorate for toleration for his fellow Catholics on the grounds that most Catholics had not supported the royalists in the civil war.

5

The Reactions of Women, with special reference to women petitioners

Patricia Higgins

Preface

The political and religious controversies, and the outbreak of civil war, disturbed women as much as men. It required them to play unusual roles and it impelled some of them to adopt unconventional attitudes. Women came to play such a large part in religious and political movements, that it is a very one-sided view of the civil war that ignores their existence. In seventeenth-century English society a wife had to obey her husband, a daughter her father, a maidservant her master: wives, daughters and maidservants were not expected to have opinions of their own and they were represented for all public and political purposes by the male head of the household. Politics was a man's business and a woman's place was in the home. It is an index of the intensity of the crisis in English affairs that it spurred women to act in politics independently of men (though no doubt generally under the influence of men and assisted by men). They participated in the popular demonstrations which tried to make king, parliament and the ruling groups more responsive to the demands of the people over whom they ruled. Excluded from ruling, women might well sympathize with the ruled. They were intensely involved in religious movements and it is probably as a result of their concern for spiritual matters that they were forced to take account of state affairs as well. But it may be that the religious inspiration for the political activities of women has been overemphasized, and that secular motives are no less important. There are signs before 1640 that women were becoming dissatisfied with their inferior status, and were potentially yet one more discontented element in English society. The intervention of women in politics in the 1640s and 1650s marked stirrings of the movement for the emancipation of women, and produced tentative claims to equality with men.

BRIAN MANNING

AS long ago as 1909 Ellen A. McArthur studied 'Won Petitioners and the Long Parliament'.[1] She provided a framework for the study of the attempts of women to influence parliamentary decisions—following, in the main, S. R. Gardiner's footnotes and expanding them.[2] One consequence of this method is that her account of the role of women in the Leveller movement is incomplete. Moreover, a scrutiny of newspapers (other than those specifically mentioned by Gardiner) would have led her to revise her chronology for some of the episodes. She was almost exclusively concerned with women's demands as they were stated in their petitions and how these demands reflected on the status of women. Further, she did not inquire whether these petitions might have been written by men, but seems to assume that their authors were female.

This short essay tries to fill in some of the gaps in Ellen McArthur's article, to present a fuller account of the role of women in expressing their opinions and attempting to impose them on others by demonstrations. It must be stressed, however, that these women were merely an active minority of the total female population of civil war England. For most women, especially those living outside London, life continued as usual or with only minor interruptions.

It is possible that the picture of women in the civil war presented by their masculine contemporaries may be somewhat stereotyped in certain respects. For example, there was a tendency for men to regard women whose deeds they found extraordinary or admirable as women of a 'masculine spirit', or comparable with the exceptional women of mythology, rather than just as women.[3] John Lilburne, the Leveller, remarked of his wife, Elizabeth, that

1 *English Historical Review* Vol. XXIV (1909) pp. 698–709.
2 S. R. Gardiner, *History of England* (1883–4) and *History of the Great Civil War* (1909–11).
3 For example, C. F. Aspinall-Oglander, *Nunwell Symphony* (1945) pp. 94, 99; John Lilburne, *Jonahs Cry* (1647) p. 4, J.R.L.; William Prynne and Clement Walker, *A True . . . Relation of . . . Tryall . . of Nathaniel Fiennes, late Colonel and Governor of the City and Castle of Bristoll* (1644) p. 54, J.R.L.; 'An account of the Sieges of Brampton Castle and the Massacre of Hopton Castle by Captain Priamus Davies', *Manuscripts of the Marquis of Bath* Vol. I, H.M.C. (1904) p. 27; *A perfect Relation of . . . the Apprehending . . . Mistris Phillips* (1643) p. 3, B.M. E.247(13); James Strong, *Joanereidos* (1645) B.M. E.287(1).

'though a Femimine' she was 'yet of a gallant and true Masculine
Spirit'.[4] The women petitioners for peace in August 1643 were
called 'Medeans', and one of them a 'Medusa' or a 'Hecuba'.[5] The
women involved in the Leveller petitioning of April 1649 were
'Amazones',[6] and in May they were likened to 'gallant Lacedemonians, or bold Amazons'.[7] Indeed, there were 'whole Troopes
of Amazons . . . marching with confidence to encounter Tyrannie,
and with abundance of courage exceeding the ordinary sort of
Womens demanding [in] high Tearmes Freedome for their
Levelling Brethren. . . .'[8] That is to say these women did not
conform to the masculine idea of what women were normally like.
It is impossible to say whether that idea conformed to pre-civil
war reality or not. If it did, it would mean that the civil war was
important in the history of women in England in that it saw the
appearance of a new type of woman. Yet it seems more probable
that the civil war was simply the occasion which permitted latent
female potentiality to be expressed. This view is strengthened by
the fact that in the late sixteenth century,[9] and very possibly much
earlier also, this convention was observed in the reporting of
out-of-the-ordinary behaviour of women.

Again there seems to be a convention whereby the women of
the London 'mob' are described by opponents as fishwives,
Billingsgate women,[10] or simply 'scum'. William Prynne had
decided views and prejudices about fishwives. He said of Fiennes's
reply to Clement Walker that it was 'so fraught with lies, a base
lye and such like uncivill ignoble language in the margin as better
became an Oyster-woman at Billinsgate, than a Souldier or man
of Honour. . . .'[11] Speaking of sectarian railings against the
Westminster Assembly he wrote—they 'libell against them in
publike with such unchristian, uncivill, approbious Billinsgate

4 Lilburne, *Jonahs Cry* p. 4.
5 B.M. E.65(4).   6 B.M. E.552(12).
7 B.M. E.556(22).   8 B.M. E.552(16).
9 For example, on 8 August 1588 when Queen Elizabeth was at Tilbury to
review her army which was expecting an invasion from the Armada,
an observer remarked of her that 'full of princely resolution and more than
feminine courage . . . she passed like some Amazonian empress through
all her army'. On the following day the queen herself told her troops: 'I
know I have the body of a weak and feeble woman, but I have the heart
and stomach of a king. . . .' (J. E. Neale, *Queen Elizabeth I* (reprinted,
Pelican Books, 1961) p. 302.)
10 For example, about women petitioners, B.M. E.65(8), (11); E.552(12).
11 Prynne and Walker, *op. cit.* p. 3.

termes',[12] and he concluded: 'I shall rake no more in this Pamph-leters nasty Kennel which abounds with such filthy stincking stuffe, and Billingsgate Language as this.'[13] *Mercurius Britannicus* said of a royalist news-sheet: 'This new Aulicus is one so full of lying and railing, that I think he is assisted by all the Pimps, Players, Poets and Oyster Women in the Towne.'[14] *Mercurius Prag-maticus* twitted the Levellers saying 'Why don't you fight . . . it is base for you to deale like Billingsgate wenches with nothing but words.'[15] One tract-writer described the Billingsgate women in verse:

> Assist Mol Cut-Purse, and ye warlike bands,
> That march towards Bellingsgate with eager hands,
> And tongues more loud than bellowing Drums, to scale
> Oyster or Herring ships, when they strike saile
> In that Creekes bosome . . .[16]

The first example given by the *Oxford English Dictionary* of the use of 'fishwife' in such a fashion is in 1662: 'They abuse one another like Fishwives.' As for Billingsgate, references in the seventeenth century to the abusive language of this market are said to be so frequent that foul language comes to be called 'Billingsgate'. The first example given of such usage is in 1652; and the first of 'Billingsgate women' used in a derogatory sense is from Marvell in 1672: 'There is not a scold at Billinsgate.' As by the early Restoration era these expressions are found in literary works, it is safe to assume that they were commonplace in general conversation by the time of the civil war. It is possible that on seeing a crowd of petitioning women, a hostile observer would be tempted to call them 'fishwives', whether or not this were descriptive of their social and economic position, in order to express his feelings against women doing such things; or he might feel that they must be 'Oyster-Wenches' because only the lowest people in society could be capable of such acts.[17] More-over, if he wished to play down the importance of a crowd he

12 William Prynne, *A Fresh Discovery of Some New Wandring Blasing Stars* (1645) p. 17, M.C.R.L.
13 *ibid.* p. 40. 14 B.M. E.71(10).
15 Quoted by Eduard Bernstein, *Cromwell and Communism* (London, 1930) pp. 150–1, *n.* 1.
16 Strong, *op. cit.*
17 For Butler says 'from ladies *down to* Oyster-wenches', *Hudibras* ed. A. R. Waller (Cambridge, 1905) p. 149.

would say that it consisted only of the basest sort of people, such as 'fishwives', since only the better sort of people carried any weight.

These masculine accounts of women's activities in the civil war are coloured very largely by their preconceptions of the nature of women and of their true place in society, as well as by partisanship. This makes the interpretation of their descriptions of female actions rather difficult.

Women in bodies showed their disapproval of the decisions of authority by demonstrations, hoping that these would persuade those in authority to reverse their policies. Their actions have to be seen within the context of the long tradition of women's involvement in enclosure and other riots.[18] Indeed in 1641 and 1642 they were involved in enclosure and fen riots. There was a riot 'at Buckden, in the county of Huntingdon upon the lands of the Bishop of Lincoln'[19] on 18 June 1641 in protest against enclosure. Although this was not a recent enclosure 'some Hundreds of Women and Boys, armed with Daggers and Javelins, in a very tumultuous . . . manner, entered upon the Grounds, threw open the Gates, and broke down the Quicksets of the said Inclosure, and turned in great Herds of Cattle upon the Premises to the disquieting of the present Possession, and to the great Damage and Loss of the now Bishop of Lincolne. . . .' The rioters were to be dealt with at the next quarter sessions but their leaders were 'sent for as Delinquents' to the House of Lords.[20] However, when a Huntingdon justice of the peace on 8 July went to estimate the damage that had been done, he 'found there a crowd of about 100 persons, chiefly women and boys, who had broken down the fences . . . and when he asked them . . . to drive out their cattle until the matter should be lawfully determined, they only answered him with contemptuous words, and refused to obey the orders of the House though three times read over to them.'[21] On the same day, in response to their petition,[22] and at the request of the Bishop of Lincoln, the rioters, named as 'Mary Shelley, Henry

18 For example, vide Dorothy Owen, 'Lincolnshire Women', The Lincolnshire Historian Vol. 2, No. 6 (1959) p. 33; Eric Kerridge, 'The Revolts in Wiltshire against Charles I', Wiltshire Archaeological Magazine Vol. 57 (1959) p. 69.
19 H.M.C. Fourth Report (1874), Appendix, 'Lords' Manuscripts', p. 76.
20 L.J. IV, 22 June 1641.
21 H.M.C. Fourth Report (1874), Appendix, 'Lords' Manuscripts', p. 85.
22 ibid.

Longeland, and Mary his Wife, John Laundell and Marriann his wife, and Francis Bradshawe', were ordered to be released from the Fleet prison.[23] There had been earlier disputes between the Shelley family and the Bishop of Lincoln.[24]

In the same year 'On Aug. 30, most of the justices being gone to the Assizes at Lincoln, great numbers of people, both men and women, to the number of 200 . . . forcibly entered about 100 acres of land in Mr Walrond's possession, wounding his servants; and though Sir Thomas Bishop commanded them in his Majesty's name to keep the peace, and made proclamation for their departure, yet they did not wholly depart, but carried thence a great quantity of Mr Walrond's wheat. And the day following . . . men and women assembled in great multitudes, and by force carried from the lands of George Kirke great quantities of wheat and other grain belonging to his tenants, notwithstanding they were then required by Sir Thos. Bishop to desist and depart.'[25]

Moreover, in May 1642 Margaret Eure wrote to Sir Ralph Verney: 'I wish you all take heed of women, for this very vermin have pulled down an enclosure, which some of them were put in prison for it by the justices, they had their pipe to go before them, and their ale and cakes to make themselves merry when they had done their feats of activity.'[26]

During the civil war women also demonstrated in an entirely different fashion in London. They formed part of the London 'mob' and took a leading role in demonstrations, the aim of which was to bring pressure to bear upon the Lords and Commons. Indeed they intervened *as women* in politics. There was what it might be permissible to call in modern terms an identifiable female 'lobby' or 'pressure group'.

Captain Venn, a member of parliament for the City of London, was accused of collusion with his followers in the City to put pressure on the House of Commons, especially during the debate

23 *L.J.* IV, 8 July 1641.
24 B. Dew Roberts, *Mitre and Musket: John Williams 1582–1650* (Oxford, 1938) p. 174.
25 *C.S.P.D. 1641–1643* pp. 116–17 (Certificate of Wm. Cony and Rutland Snoden, justices of peace in co. Lincoln to the House of Commons, concerning the disturbances and rioting in the Fens. 6 September, 1641).
26 *H.M.C.* Seventh Report, Appendix, 'Verney Manuscripts' (1897) p. 439 (writing from Malton in Yorkshire); F. P. Verney, *Memoirs of the Verney Family* (4 vols., 1892–9) Vol. II, p. 86 (Margaret Eure to Sir Ralph Verney, 21 May 1642).

on the Grand Remonstrance.[27] Clarendon asserted that another member of the Commons offered to prove 'that the wife of Captain Venn . . . had with great industry solicited many people to go down with their arms to Westminster upon a day that was named, [25 November 1641] when, she said, her husband had sent her word that in the House of Commons they were together by the ears, and that the worser party was like to get the better of the good party, and therefore her husband desired his friends to come with their arms to Westminster to help the good party, and that thereupon very many in a short time went thither.'[28] Further inquiries into this story were apparently shelved. However, a writer recalled in 1643 that Venn sent 'his Summons by his Wife to assemble the . . . City',[29] referring, presumably, to this occasion.

In January 1642 Charles I was attended by the Lord Mayor when he came to the City to demand the arrest of the Five Members for treason. After the king departed 'the citizens' wives fell upon the Lord Mayor, and pulled his chain from his neck, and called him traitor to the liberties of it, and had like to have torn him and the Recorder in pieces'.[30] A later account says that this deed was done by 'a Zealous sister'.[31]

Women were associated with petitions to parliament expressing strong views on matters of state. In retrospect Samuel Butler wrote:

> The Oyster-women lock'd their Fish up,
> And trudg'd away to cry No Bishop.[32]

Nehemiah Wallington remarked on the fact that women as well as men went up to Westminster with petitions;[33] and, speaking of the numerous petitions against bishops, Milton wrote: 'the meanest artizans . . . also women . . . assembling with their complaints, and that sometimes in a lesse humble guise than for

---

27 *Journal of Sir Simonds D'Ewes* ed. W. H. Coates (New Haven, 1942) p. 215.
28 Edward, Earl of Clarendon, *The History of the Rebellion* (reprinted, Oxford, 1958) Book IV, 120.
29 *A letter from Mercurius Civicus to Mercurius Rusticus* (Oxford, 1643) p. 9 B.M. E.65(32).
30 *Manuscripts of Lord Montagu of Beaulieu*, H.M.C. (1900) p. 141.
31 *A letter from Mercurius Civicus to Mercurius Rusticus* p. 18.
32 Butler, *op. cit.* p. 42.
33 Nehemiah Wallington, *Historical Notices of Events Occuring Chiefly in the Reign of Charles I* ed. R. Webb (2 vols., London, 1869) Vol. II, p. 42.

petitioners, have gone with confidence, that neither their mean-
nesse would be rejected, nor their simplicity contemn'd, nor yet
their urgency distasted either by the dignity, wisdome, or moderation of that supreme Senate; nor did they depart unsatisfi'd.'[34]

It is interesting to note that as early as 10 December 1641
Thomason acquired a satire, purporting to be a '. . . Petition of
the Weamen of Middlesex Which they intended to have presented
to the High Court of parliament. . . .'[35] However, the first
example of women on their own petitioning parliament appears
to come from 31 January 1642: 'there was . . . a Petition delivered
to the Lords by a company of women, containing therein their
wants and necessities by reason of the great decay of trading, and
the present distractions and distempers of the state, the Composing of differences between the two houses of Parliament,
That the Commons House they conceive did what in them lay to
relieve them, and redresse their grievances; but that such opposition being made in the Lords House, which is a great hindrance
to their reall intentions in their proceedings, to perfect the same;
That Religion may be established, and present aid and assistance
transported into Ireland for the reliefe of the distressed Protestants.'[36] On the next day Palace Yard was thronged by a crowd of
women who declared 'We had rather bring our children, and
leave them at the Lords' door, than have them starve at home'.[37]
Moreover on this day another petition was delivered to the Lords
'by a company of Women, about the number of 400, desiring an
answer of their petition delivered the day before, and attending
there for the delivery thereof, the Duke of Lenox coming to the
House, they presented him their petition, who answered: "Away
with these women, wee were best to have a parliament of
Women."[38] Whereupon some of the Women interrupting his
passage, catched hold of his staffe, humbly desiring him to receive

34 Milton, *An apology against a Pamphlet call'd a modest Confutation of the
   Animadversions upon the Remonstrant against Smectymnuus* (1642) p. 40, J.R.L.
35 B.M. E.180(17).   36 B.M. E.201(13).
37 Salvetti's newsletter 4 (14) February 1641 (1642) quoted by Gardiner,
   History of England Vol. X, p. 162.
38 It is interesting to speculate on the familiarity of Lennox with Aristoph-
   anes's *Parliament of Women.* The bible and the classics were the two great
   educative influences in the seventeenth century, hence the facility with
   which protagonists quoted the former or alluded to the latter. It is
   reasonable to suppose that the idea of a parliament of women was not
   entirely novel to Lennox. (See below, notes 212, 213, 215.)

their petition, upon which the Duke being moved, offered to draw back his staffe, but they holding it so fast between them, it was broken, whereupon the said Duke was enforced to send for another staffe; after which they delivered their petition to the Lord Savage, who presented it to the Lords, and upon reading, and some debate thereof, they gave order that twelve of the petitioners should be called into the House, to declare their grievances, which was done accordingly.'[39] Wallington also noticed the women petitioners of 1 February 1642: 'in the Lords House there was a petition delivered to the Lords by a company of women, containing their wants and necessities, by reason of the great decay of trading, occasioned by the present distempers and distractions of the State, and composing of differences between the two Houses of Parliament; that the Commons' House they conceive have done what in them lay to relieve them, and redresse their grievances; but, that such opposition being made in the Lords' House, which is a great hindrance to their real intentions in their proceedings to perfect the same, that religion may be established, and present aid and assistance transported into Ireland for the relief of distressed Protestants.'[40] Wallington's account of the petition accords well with the original, which is entitled *To the Right Hon. the house of peeres now assembled in the Parliament. The humble petition of many poore distressed women in & about London*, and which is endorsed by the clerk on the back: '1 Feb. 1641 [i.e. 1642]. The petition of many poore women.'[41]

The Commons too were petitioned by women at this time. On 1 February 1642 Sergeant-Major General Skippon informed them that there were 'great Multitudes of Women at the Houses, pressing to present a Petition to the Parliament; and their Language is, that where there is One Woman now here, there would be Five hundred To-morrow; and that it was as good for them to die here, as at home'. The House desired him to use his 'Endeavours to pacify the Multitude, and send them Home in Quietness' as

---

39 B.M. E.201(13); *C.S.P.D. 1641–1643* p. 274 (3 February, 1642, Captain *Robert* Fox to Sir John Penington. McArthur, *op. cit.* p. 698, attributed this account to Captain *John* Fox and dated it 5 February 1642, and thus failed to see the connection with the events of 1 February 1642).
40 Wallington, *op. cit.* Vol. II, p. 6.
41 'Petition of Many Poor distressed women in and about London', House of Lords Papers, 1 February 1641 (2), House of Lords Record Office.

the House was 'now in Consideration of Matters of great Consequence; and will hereafter give such Directions as the Occasion
shall require'.[42]

On 4 February 1642 *True Diurnall Occurrences* related that 'This
day also there was a Petition delivered to the House of Commons,
by a company of Women, for an answer to the Petition which
they had formerly delivered with great clamour and out-cry
against Bishops.'[43] The women complained that 'great Danger
and Fear do still attend us, and will, as long as Popish Lords and
superstitious Bishops are suffered to have their Voice in the
House of Peers'.[44] They deplored the fact that 'that accursed and
abominable Idol of the Mass [is] suffered in the Kingdom, and
that Arch-enemy of our Prosperity and Reformation [i.e. Archbishop Laud] lieth in the Tower yet not receiving his deserved
Punishment'. And they declared that they had been moved to
petition the House because 'the Insolencies of the Papists and
Abettors raiseth a just Fear and Suspicion of sowing Sedition,
and breaking out into Bloody Persecution in this Kingdom, as
they have done in Ireland'.[45] The petition was presented by 'Mrs
Anne Stagg, a Gentlewoman and Brewer's wife, and many others
with her of like Rank and Quality',[46] and the House ordered that
'the Burgesses . . . for the Borough of Southwarke, Mr Pym,
Mr Strode, and Alderman Penington, are to go out to them, and
tell them, that this House has read their Petition;[47] and is very
apprehensive of the Calamities they suffer; and will use all the best
Care they can for the presenting and Remedying of them; and
desire . . . their Prayers for a good Success upon their Endeavours.'[48] Accordingly Pym did this, assuring them 'your

42 *C.J.* II, 1 February 1641 (2). See also a letter from Henry Oxinden of
    Deane to Henry Oxinden of Barham, not dated, but referring to women
    petitioning parliament, possibly on Tuesday 1 February 1642: B.M.
    Add. MS. 28000, f. 48b.
43 B.M. E.201(13).
44 ' . . . Petition . . . Feb. 4th 1641', *Harleian Miscellany* (1746) Vol. VII,
    p. 567. Cf. *A true copie of the Petition of Gentlewomen . . . Feb. 4 1641* (2),
    B.M. E.134(17).
45 '. . . Petition . . . Feb. 4th 1641', *Harleian Miscellany* (1746) Vol. VII,
    p. 567.
46 *ibid.* p. 569.
47 Valerie Pearl, *London and the Outbreak of the Puritan Revolution* (Oxford, 1961)
    p. 226, appears to be referring to this petition and says it was read at the
    suggestion of Henry Marten.
48 *C.J.* II, 4 February 1641 (2).

Petition . . . is thankfully accepted of, and is come in a seasonable Time'.[49] As indeed it had, for the next day the opposition of the Lords to the Bill for excluding Bishops from parliament was finally overcome.

On 10 February 1642 *Diurnal Occurrences* noted that there was 'read in the Lords House a Petition in the name of divers of her Majesties servants wives, whose husbands were to attend the Queen, and Lady Mary to Holland, which prayed for her stay, which after reading, and some debate thereupon a Message was sent to the House of Commons to desire a Conference, where it was moved and concluded on, that some of their Members should repair to the King's Majesty, to move him therein'.[50] There is a broadside in the Thomason Tracts of the 'Petition of many thousands of Courtiers, Citizens, Gentlemens and Trades-mens-wives, inhabiting within the Cities of London and West-minster, concerning the staying of the Queenes intended voyage into Holland . . .', which is said to have been 'presented and read in the House by the Lord Mandevill, the 10 of February, 1641'.[51] In this petition, however, the women do not mention the possi-bility of their husbands accompanying the Queen to Holland, but are concerned that on the Queen's departure there will follow 'an utter cessation and decay of all our trading': for 'your Peti-tioners, their Husbands, their Children, and their Families . . . have lived in plentifull and good fashion, by the exercise of sever-all Trades and venting of divers workes . . . All depending wholly for the sale of their commodities (which is the maintenance and very existence and being of themselves, their husbands and fam-ilies) upon the splendor and glory of the English Court, and principally upon that of the Queenes Majesty. . . .' And they go on to say that they 'have cause to fear that this sudden resolution in her Majestiee is occasioned by some just distaste taken at divers unusual and tumultuous assemblies, to the affright of her Royall Person, and at the unpunisht printing of many licentious and scandalous Pamphlets . . . wounding her sacred Majestie in the opinion of the vulgar. . . .' They therefore prayed the Lords to

49 '. . . Petition . . . Feb. 4th 1641', *Harleian Miscellany* (1746) Vol. VII, p. 569.
50 B.M. E.201(16).
51 *To the Right Honourable the House of Peeres now assembled in Parliament* B.M. 669 f. 4(59). This is identical with *Severall Petitions Presented to the Honorable Houses of Parliament now Assembled* (1642) B.M. E.135(31), except that the latter lacks the above address.

put down 'such seditious tumults and scandalls . . . and joyne with us in Petition for Her continuall residence amongst us. . . .'[52] It seems unlikely that the Commons would have acted upon a petition which was so friendly towards the queen and the royal point of view, so there may have been two different petitions to the Lords on the same day about the queen's proposed journey to Holland.

There were women who hated the war as such, perhaps because of the suffering that it caused. Jonathan Priestley related how his brother set off to join Fairfax in arms in Yorkshire soon after the outbreak of war, and his mother 'went along with him a quarter of a mile' and 'besought him with tears not to go'.[53] There are vague references to women petitioning parliament for peace,[54] and an interesting comment was made in January 1643: 'All sorts of persons unite in supporting the demand for peace . . . the petitions presented to parliament have been refused a hearing . . . To leave no moderate means of persuasion untried, the women are preparing to appear, in the hope that their sex may meet a more courteous hearing and a more pitiful heart, for repairing the ruin of this now wretched kingdom.'[55] It may be significant that Thomason has four mock petitions of late January, early February 1643,[56] all purporting to come from women desiring peace. But it is not until August that there is detailed information about women being involved in petitioning for peace. At this time the Commons were considering the Lords' peace proposals. A Common Council at Guildhall drew up a petition against acceptance of these proposals, which was received by the Lords on 7 August, when '. . . some thousands . . . went to the Parliament, and clamorously petitioned against peace. . . .' The

---

52 *Petition of . . . 10th Feb. 1641*, B.M. 669 f. 4(59).

53 'Some Memoirs concerning the Family of the Priestleys', in 'Yorkshire Diaries and Autobiographies in the Seventeenth and Eighteenth Centuries', Vol. II, *Surtees Society* Vol. 77 (1883) p. 26.

54 Clement Walker, *Relations . . . upon . . . Parliament begun . . . 1640* (1648) Vol. I, p. 49, M.C.R.L.; 'Memoirs of Denzil, Lord Holles 1699' in Francis, Baron Maseres, *Select Tracts* (1826) Vol. I, p. 292.

55 *C.S.P. Venetian 1642–1643* pp. 224–5 (Venetian Secretary to Doge. 9 January 1643).

56 *The Midwives just Petition* (1643) B.M. E.86(14); *The Virgins Complaint for losse of their Sweet-Hearts by these Present Wars* (1643) B.M. E.86(38); *The Humble Petition of Many Thousands of Wives and Matrons* (1643) B.M. E.88(13); *The Widowes Lamentation for the Absence of their deare Children and Suitors* (1643) B.M. E.88(26).

Commons rejected the peace proposals. According to one news-sheet claiming intelligence of so-called royalist activities, 'The Malignants upon this consulted what to doe, to worke their ends . . . They that Munday night put on those women that were Ring-leaders of the crew, to get such women in and about the City of London and Suburbs, as were desirous of Peace (as they pretended) to come to the Parliament house to cry for Peace, *which was to the women a pleasing thing, and thereupon some out of an earnest desire of Peace*, others out of the designe, came on Tuesday to Westminster, with white silke Ribbands in their hats, and cryed for Peace. . . .'[57] The wearing of white ribbons was the distinguishing mark of peace petitioners, just as the wearing of sea-green ribbons became that of the Levellers. Another news-paper also reported the activities of these women on 8 August: 'in the afternoone two or three hundred Oyster wives, and other dirty and tattered sluts, tooke upon them the impudency to come to the Honourable House of Commons, and cried for Peace and Propositions. . . .'[58] Laud commented that these women were 'as earnest for peace' as those were against peace who had petitioned the day before; and though he put their number at five or six hundred, ''tis but hundreds for thousands that came against it'.[59] Clarendon praised the women for petitioning for peace, when men were 'frighted from appearing in person to desire . . . those things upon which their hearts were most set'.[60] The Venetian Ambassador reported that 'the more moderate, and especially the women, who deplore the miseries of these times, appeared in equal numbers[61] with their children in their arms, to soften the hardest hearts and implore peace.'[62] But Sir Simonds D'Ewes in his diary gave a picture of a more violent demonstration, writing that 'a multitude of woemen . . . came downe in great confusion and came to the very doore of the house of Commons, and there cryed as in divers other places, Peace, Peace, and interrupted divers of the Members both as they went in and as they came out of the house . . . these indiscreet woemen . . . alsoe threatned to use violence to those in the house of Commons as were

57 B.M. E.65(11); William Laud, *Works* (Oxford, 1884) Vol. IV, p. 31.
58 B.M. E.65(8).   59 Laud, *op. cit.*, Vol. IV, p. 31.
60 Clarendon, *op. cit.* Book VII, 171.
61 i.e. equal to those men who petitioned against peace.
62 *C.S.P. Venetian 1643–1647* p. 8 (Venetian Secretary to Doge. 21 August 1643).

Enemies to Peace.'[63] *Certaine Informations* declared that the women 'so filled the staires' of the House of Commons 'that no man could passe up or downe, whereupon a man upon the top of the staires, drew his sword, and with the flat side stroak some of them upon the heads, which so affrighted them, that they presently made way and ran downe, and thereupon the Trained band that then waited, came and made a Court of guard upon the staires and so kept them off from further troubling the House'.[64] Another newspaper said that the women 'cryed for Peace, Committed no great disorder, but when they saw their own time, went home againe.'[65] Thomas Knyvett told his wife 'some verball satisffaction thay had and no hurt done that day.'[66] The Reverend John Lightfoot of the Assembly of Divines also agreed that '. . . they parted without any hurt.'[67] When the Venetian Ambassador reported that extraordinary violence was used against the women[68] he was probably confusing the events of this day with those of the next.

The next day, 'Wednesday Aug. 9, the number of women increased. . . .'[69] Rushworth said that they were 'two or three Thousand Women, of the meaner sort, with white Silk Ribbons in Their Hats';[70] but Clarendon, being sympathetic to their demands, described them as '. . . a great multitude of the wives of substantial citizens'.[71] Other accounts depicted the women as

---

63 D'Ewes, 'Diary', 8 August 1643, B.M. MS. Harl. 165, f. 149b. *Cf.* Rev. John Lightfoot, 'Journal of the Proceedings of the Assembly of Divines', *Works* (1824) Vol. XIII, p. 9.

64 B.M. E.65(8).

65 B.M. E.65(11).

66 B.M. Add. MS. 42153, f. 116 (Thomas Knyvett to his wife, 9 August 1643).

67 Lightfoot, *op. cit.* Vol. XIII, p. 9.

68 *C.S.P. Venetian 1643–1647* p. 8 (Venetian Secretary to Doge. 21 August 1643). On 9 August the use of violence was widely recorded, whereas on 8 August two commentators explicitly stated that there was no force used against the women, and of the other reporters of the events of 8 August, apart from the Venetian Secretary, only one described the treatment of the women as brutal. It is interesting to note that this was the account of a royalist newspaper, which reported 'You heard before how the good women flocked to Westminster on Tuesday last, to cry out for peace', and proceeded to describe the violence (B.M. E.65(26)). The Venetian Secretary may have jogged his memory about the events of these days by looking at this news-sheet.

69 Laud, *op. cit.* Vol. IV, p. 31. *Cf.* B.M. Add. MS. 42153, f. 116.

70 J. Rushworth, *Historical Collections* (1708) Vol. V, p. 143.

71 Clarendon, *op. cit.* Book VII, 171.

follows: 'about two or three thousand Women, most of them of the inferior sort, inhabiting about the City of London and the Suburbs thereof, gathered together at Westminster, under pretence of presenting a Petition to both Houses of Parliament for peace';[72] 'many conceived them five or six thousand, some say 500 of them were whores, they are all of the poorer sort, and most have their husbands *in the one or other Army*. . . .'[73] Some reports agreed that by noon there were 'near 5000';[74] 'five or six thousand at least' and '(except some few women) these women were for the most part, Whores, Bawdes, Oyster-women, Kitchenstuffe women, Beggar women, and the very scum of the Suburbs, besides abundance of Irish women.'[75] A graphic account of the demonstration of 9 August is given by *Certaine Informations*: '. . . there was such a fearfull Tumult and uprore raised by women about the Parliament House; as was never recorded by any Histories either ancient or moderne, which by eye witnesses is thus related. After the Trained Band was come into the Old Palace yard, and had set their Sentinell at the usuall places according to the custome, about an hundred women with white Ribbands in their hats pressed to make way through them, which the Sentinells opposing, more women come to second them, fell upon them and beate them away, and by violence made their way into the yard; then more women striving to land at the Parliament staires, were kept of there by the Sentinells, but they landing a little higher came in upon the West side of the yard, and then all of them cried out mainely, we will have Peace presently and our King, and this was their constant cry to all the Peers as they came to their House. . . .'[76] An interesting feature of this story is that it represented the women as coming to West-minister by water. One respect in which it differed from other accounts is in its description of opposition to the women's arrival made by the 'Trained Bands'. *The Kingdomes Weekly Intelligencer* was careful to point out that when the women came '. . . neither the Parliament, nor City' gave 'any order to the Trained Bands to hinder them, least it should be reported they would hinder any . . . for Peace.'[77]

Once at Westminster, besides crying out for peace, the women

72 B.M. E.65(4).   73 B.M. E.64(13).
74 Rushworth, *op. cit.* Vol. V, p. 143.
75 B.M. E.65(11).   76 B.M. E.65(8).   77 B.M. E.65(11).

were said to '. . . cry out for their slain and imprisoned husbands'.[78] 'When the Earle of Holland came, they began their cry
afresh,[79] and presented a Petition unto him, whereupon his Lordship wished them to be quiet, and he would do his best to procure
Peace. . . .'[80] Another account said that the women had '. . . a
petition for peace, which they presented to the House of Commons by the hands of one of the members of that House';[81] and
a third reported that '. . . some in the name of the rest came
and delivered their Petition, entituled the humble Petition of
Many civilly disposed women. . . .'[82] *Mercurius Civicus* repro-
duced the petition *in extenso*[83] and this is almost identical with an
undated petition in the Tanner MSS., the only important difference
being that the latter bears the additional information that the
petition was presented 'To the Honble ye Knts, Cittizens and
Burgesses of the House of Commons'.[84] The women addressed
the Commons as '. . . ye Phisitians that can restore this languishing
Nation, And that our bleeding Sister Kingdome of Ireland', and
they asked that 'the just Prerogatives and Priviledges of King and
Parliament' be maintained, 'the true Liberties and Properties of
the Subject' be restored, 'all honorable waies and meanes for a
speedie Peace' be endeavoured, and 'some speedie Course maie
be taken for ye settlemt of ye true Reformed Protestant Religion
. . . and ye renovation of Trade. . . .'[85] The House of Commons
'received and read' the petition '(there being little exception to
be taken unto it) and sent them out Sir John Hepsley [i.e. Hippis-
ley] and four or five more to returne them an answer, satisfactory
enough, if they had beene reasonable Creatures. . . .'[86] It is noted
in the Commons' Journals that six members (one of them being
Hippisley) were appointed to acquaint the women with the
House's desire for peace, that they would have the 'greatest Care

78 *Manuscripts of the Marquis of Bath* Vol. I, p. 17 (Sir John Scudamore to
   Brilliana, Lady Harley, 24 August 1643).
79 i.e. for 'Peace'.   80 B.M. E.65(8).
81 *Cowper Manuscripts*, Vol. II, H.M.C. 12th Report, Appendix II (1888)
   pp. 335–6 (Sir John Coke the younger to Sir John Coke, London,
   9 August 1643).
82 B.M. E.65(11).
83 B.M. E.65(4) ('The humble Petition of many civilly disposed Women
   inhabiting in the Cities of London, Westminster, the Suburbs and parts
   adjacent').
84 Bodleian Library, Oxford, MS. Tanner LXIV, f, 190.
85 *ibid.*   86 B.M. E.65(11).

of the Publick as may be' and would consider their petition further 'very speedily'.[87] Sir John Coke, the younger, called the answer 'fair', 'importing that the House was desirous of peace and would consider of their petition, and that in the meantime they should repair to their several dwellings.'[88] Rushworth confirmed that the women were asked to leave.[89]

With the reply to their demands the women 'were so farre from being satisfied that Sir John Hepsley and the rest received such course usage from them, that they desired no more of such imployment';[90] and 'with violence they would have pressed upon the outer doors. . . .'[91] They 'fell to be more unruly' than on the previous day,[92] and 'the tumult of women grew outrageous.'[93] Yet D'Ewes, while saying 'No man can excuse the indiscreet violence of these woemen', reported that when he left the House 'betweene eleauen and twelue of the clocke . . . I found a great throng of woemen both younger and older who were knocking at the doore and calling out that there might be peace, *they offering no violence at all to mee* but sufferred mee to passe quietly, and when I told them that I was for Peace, they bestowed some Benedictions upon mee.'[94] However, they fell 'upon all that have short haire and pull them both Ministers, Souldiers and others';[95] 'a Minister passing through the yard, they laid hands upon him, cried out a Roundhead, and tore his cloak and band';[96] 'the greatest part of them carrying themselves very uncivilly towards divers Members of the House, and others, using many horrid execrations, that they would have the blood of those (whom they in their furious zeale conceived to be averse to peace) . . .'[97] Yonge says the women 'kepte knockinge and beatinge of the outwarde dore before the parliament house, and would have violently forced the same open, and required Mr Pym, Mr Strode, and some other members . . . and threatened to take

87 *C.J.* III, 9 August 1643.
88 *Cowper Manuscripts* Vol. II, p. 336 (Sir John Coke the younger to Sir John Coke, London, 9 August 1643).
89 Rushworth, *op. cit.* Vol. V, p. 143.
90 B.M. E.65(11).
91 *Cowper Manuscripts* Vol. II, p. 336 (Sir John Coke the younger to Sir John Coke, London, 9 August 1643).
92 B.M. Add. MS. 42153, f. 116.
93 Lightfoot, *op. cit.* Vol. XIII, p. 9.
94 B.M. MS. Harl. 165, f. 150.
95 B.M. E.64(13).   96 B.M. E.65(8).   97 B.M. E.65(4).

the rounde heades of the parliament whome they saide they would caste into the Thames.'[98] '. . . From words they fell to blowes,'[99] for after noon the women 'came againe to the doore of the House at the upper staires head, as soone as they were past a part of the Trained Band that usually stood Centinell there, they thrust them downe by the head and shoulders, and would suffer none to come in or out of the Parliament house for two hours together, the trayned Band, advised them to come downe, and pulled them, but yet they would not goe, they then shot powder at them, for this they cared not, crying, nothing but powder, and having Brickbats in the yards, threw them very fast at the trained Bands, and disarmed some of them . . . these women were not any whit scared or ashamed of their incivilities, but cryed out so much the more, even at the doore of the house of Commons, Give us these Traytors that are against peace, that we may teare them in pieces, Give us Pym, in the first place, they were perswaded to forbeare to use such language of the Parliament, and to depart, but they cryed out so much the more; all this while the Parliament was in a manner Prisoners, the guard could not in two houres make way to the House, to bring them downe, being loath to offer violence to women, at last ten Troopers (some of them Cornets)[100] came to passe by the women, who had their Colours in their hats, which the women seeing, made 2 of them take their Ribbands out of their hats, not contented with that they offered to do the like to the rest, and laid violent hands upon them, whereupon they drew their Swords, and laid on some of them with their Swords flatwayes for a good space, which they regarded not, but enclosed them; upon this they then cut them on the face and hands, and one woman lost her nose, whom they say is since dead, as soon as the rest of the women saw blood once drawne, they ran away from the Parliament House, and dispersed themselves in smaller numbers, into the Churchyards, Pallace, and other places; and about an houre after the House was up, a Troope of horse came, and cudgelled such as staid, with their Kanes, and dispersed them. . . .'[101]

98 Walter Yonge, 'Diary', B.M. Add. MS. 18778, f. 13b (ascribed wrongly by McArthur, op. cit. pp. 702–3, to 'Longe').
99 B.M. E.64(13).
100 Rushworth, op. cit. Vol. V, p. 143, says that they were Waller's horse, whom the women abused as 'Waller's Dogs'.
101 B.M. E.65(11).

The various details of this account are corroborated, in whole or part, by other newspapers and eye witnesses.[102] Another news-sheet said that the Earl of Essex was responsible for sending the horse against the women,[103] while an entry in D'Ewes's diary alleged that it was contrived 'by the procurement of John Pym and some others who were enemies to all kind of Peace. . . .'[104] Coke declared that Pym was not in the House, though the women were 'threatening him very sore',[105] but Sir John Scudamore spoke of 'Mr Pym beaten by the women and with much difficulty escaped their fury by water'.[106] Yonge wrote that the women had cried before they left that they would return the next day 'with greater strengthe and would have swords and guns likewise. . . .' They 'gave out that they would demolishe all the workes aboute the towne', that is, the defensive fortifications around London.[107] The casualty figures varied from 'one',[108] 'two',[109] 'some',[110] 'divers'[111] women killed, to the Venetian Ambassador's exaggerated account of a 'bloody conflict' 'at the Houses of Parliament, which forced the lords to flee from their own chamber and some even from the city, ten persons being killed and more than a hundred injured, mostly women'.[112] One incident of the day that was widely noticed was the death of '. . . a maid servant, that had nothing to doe with the Tumult but passing through the Church-yard was shot.'[113] She was the daughter of a man who sold

102 B.M. E.64(13); E.65(4), (8); Rushworth, *op. cit.* Vol. V, pp. 143–4; Lightfoot, *op. cit.* Vol. XIII, p. 9; *Manuscripts of the Marquis of Bath* Vol. I, p. 17 (Sir John Scudamore to Brilliana, Lady Harley, 24 August 1643); *Cowper Manuscripts* Vol. II, p. 336 (Sir John Coke the younger to Sir John Coke, London, 9 August 1643); Thomas Knyvett to his wife, 9 August 1643, B.M. Add. MS. 42153, f. 116; Thomas Knyvett to his wife, 10 August 1643, B.M. Add. MS. 41253, f. 118; B.M. MS. Harl. 165, f. 150.

103 B.M. E.65(26).   104 B.M. MS. Harl. 165, f. 150.

105 *Cowper Manuscripts* Vol. II, p. 336 (Sir John Coke the younger to Sir John Coke, London, 9 August 1643).

106 *Manuscripts of the Marquis of Bath* Vol. I, p. 17 (Sir John Scudamore to Brilliana, Lady Harley, 24 August 1643).

107 B.M. Add. MS. 18778, ff. 13–14.

108 B.M. E.64(13); E.65(11); *Cowper Manuscripts* Vol. II, p. 336; Lightfoot, *op. cit.* Vol. XII, p. 9.

109 B.M. E.65(4).   110 Laud, *op. cit.* Vol. IV, p. 31.

111 B.M. Add. MS. 42153 f. 118; *Manuscripts of the Marquis of Bath* Vol. I, p. 17.

112 *C.S.P. Venetian 1643–1647* p. 8 (Venetian Secretary to Doge. 21 August 1643). *Cf.* Clarendon, *op. cit.* Book VII, 171.

113 B.M. E.65(11).

spectacles outside the gate of Westminster Hall on the east side.[114]

The Venetian Ambassador reported that 'Many of the women who went to implore peace have been imprisoned, as well as their husbands, the mere suspicion of desiring it being considered the last degree of criminality.'[115] Many were sent to Bridewell and 'one amongst the rest being a most deformed Medusa, or Hecuba, with an old rusty blade by her side, had her hands tied behind her with Match, and was guarded along by the trained Bands to prison. . . .'[116] The motive in imprisoning these women would seem to have been in order to examine them as to who prompted them to petition Parliament,[117] for there was a general feeling that the women's actions were not entirely spontaneous. Clarendon and Laud praised feminine courage, superior to masculine, in appearing for peace.[118] Yet the consensus of opinion was that men were behind it:[119] it was alleged that the women were instigated by '. . . some Men of the Rabble in Womens Clothes mixing among 'em',[120] while Yonge asserted that the women were 'sett on and backed by some men of rank and quality'.[121]

Some women when asked '. . . who put them on to this business, . . . said they were at such a Lords House, and he bid them go to the house of Commons, for they were against Peace.'[122] On 12 August a woman petitioned the Commons for leave to go to Holland '. . . for that she went in great Ieoperdy of her life here amongst her own Neighbours in that she refused to Ioyn with them in their tumultuous rising against Parliament on the Wednesday before. . . .' She repeated some hearsay that 'many of the Woemen had been with a great Earle in this Kingdome, who encouraged them in that tumultuous manner to come downe to the Parliament under pretence for peace . . . and that if they came downe in that manner but 3 or 4 dayes . . . these propositions for peace would passe the Houses and they would then have

114 B.M. MS. Harl. 165, f. 150. *Cf.* B.M. Add. MS. 42153, f. 118.
115 *C.S.P. Venetian 1643–1647* p. 11 (Venetian Secretary to Doge. 28 August 1643).
116 B.M. E.65(4).
117 B.M. E.65(8).
118 Clarendon, *op. cit.* Book VII, 171; Laud, *op. cit.* Vol. IV, p. 31.
119 For example B.M. E.65(8); Lightfoot, *op. cit.* Vol. XIII, p. 9.
120 Rushworth, *op. cit.* Vol. V, p. 143.
121 B.M. Add. MS. 18778 f. 14.
122 B.M. E.65(11).

peace. . . .' This is a reference to the Earl of Holland, and accordingly the Commons set up a committee to examine him,[123] only to find that he had left for Oxford.[124] This mention of Holland is interesting because *Certaine Informations* said that the women had handed their petition to him and he had assured them of his endeavours to secure peace.[125]

The Kingdomes Weekly Intelligencer developed the fullest conspiracy theory of the women's activities. It asserted that the 'Malignants' enlisted the women to cry for peace and that the women themselves confessed that '. . . they had those to countenance them, in this businesse that would not desert them; being asked where they got so many hundred yards of silke Ribbin to were in their hats, some said at the Lady Brunckhards house in Westminster, others that came from the other side of the water had some at a Ladies house in Southwarke, and so others at other Ladies houses in other parts of the Suburbs. The parties that appeared openly to countenance them: were Sergeant Francis; who is sent to the Lord Generall to be tried by a Counsell of War, another one was Master Pulford whom the Parliament hath likewise committed, upon Information of his countenancing these women, at the house of Commons doore. . . .'[126] *The Parliament Scout* may be allowed the final comment on the women petitioners for peace of August 1643: 'Thus we see, to permit absurdities, is the way to increase them; Tumults are dangerous, swords in womens hands doe desperate things; this is begotten in the distractions of Civill War.'[127]

There were isolated displays of women's hostility to the war after 1643,[128] but, notwithstanding their critics of whatever

---

123 B.M. E.65(21); *C.J.* III, 12 August 1643.
124 B.M. E.65(21).
125 B.M. E.65(8).
126 B.M. E.65(11); there is a notice of Francis's committal in *C.J.* III, 14 August 1643.
127 B.M. E.64(13).
128 For example *Portland Manuscripts*, Vol. I, H.M.C. 13th Report (1891) p. 289 (William Cawley to Robert Scawen. Chichester 13 October 1645). In 1645 women were involved in the Clubmen risings about Chichester, in which they incited inhabitants to refuse '. . . men or moneys for Sir Thomas Fairfax's army, or upon any other ordinance. . . .' So successful were they that '. . . not an £100—though above £4,000 due—being brought in since their first rising, no collector daring to distrain for fear of having his brains dashed out, 40 servants and women rising together armed with prongs and other weapons. . . .'

political complexion, the women petitioners of 1643 were remarkable in their efforts for peace. They were probably committed to neither side and genuinely anxious to end the war, though their desire for peace was no doubt exploited by peace party politicians in parliament and by royalist sympathizers in London.

Thomas Coleman had spoken in 1645 in general terms of the 'cryes of women' against Parliament,[129] but henceforth when the presence of women in Westminster is noticed it is usually in connection with Leveller demonstrations. In September 1646, armed with a petition, Lilburne's wife, 'with some scores of Gentlewomen her friends [and Lilburne's] . . . followed the House day by day, with importunate widowes cry for justice. . . .'[130] On the 23rd. she 'accompanied with divers other women presented printed papers to the Members of Commons as they passed into the house. . . .'[131] But the House of Commons had other business to spend the day upon.[132] In prison in March 1647 Richard Overton wrote a petition to the Commons on behalf of his wife and brother, who were held for breaking the press laws, and this petition was presented 'by a competent number of women. . . .'[133]

Women were next around parliament during August and October of 1647. On 26 August, when a petition was presented on behalf of Lilburne,[134] 'to avoid all disturbance in the Houses of Parliament[135] it was ordered . . . that the guards that do attend the house . . . should observantly keep all the passages, and with all to clear them from those clamorous women, which were wont to hang in clusters on the staires, and before the doores of the Parliament'[136] and in Westminster Hall.[137] On 15 October more severe measures were taken, for it was 'Ordered by the Commons . . . that the Serjeant at Armes . . . be required . . . to

129 Thomas Coleman, *Hopes Deferred and Dashed* (1645) p. 32, B.M. E.294 (14).
130 John Lilburne, *The Iuglers Discovered* (1647) p. 2, B.M. E.409(22).
131 B.M. E.513(12).
132 B.M. E.355(12).
133 *Appeale . . . Mary Overton* (1647) B.M. E.381(10); Richard Overton, 'An Appeale' (1647) in *Leveller Manifestoes of the Puritan Revolution* ed. D. M. Wolfe (New York, 1944) p. 166.
134 B.M. E.518(24).
135 A subsidiary reason was the danger of the plague. B.M. E.405(13).
136 B.M. E.405(3). *Cf.* B. Whitelocke, *Memorials of English Affairs* (1732) p. 267 (26 August 1647).
137 B.M. E.518(24).

apprehend, all such women . . . that he shall be informed of, who clamour about the Houses, and speake any scandalous words against the Parliament, and carry them to the next justice of the peace, who is required to send the said persons so apprehended to the House of Correction, and to give order that they may be there punished, according to Law and justice. . . .'[138] On 1 August 1648 'ten thousand citizens of London, men and women, petitioned that Lilburne be set free or have a legal trial.' They persuaded the Lords and Commons to liberate him and cancel his fine.[139]

The high point, however, of the intervention of women in political movements came in April and May 1649 when petitions for the release of the four Leveller leaders—Lilburne, Walwyn, Prince and Overton—poured into the Commons.[140] Lilburne recalled later how '. . . abundance of . . . the feminine sex' had been among these petitioners.[141] *Mercurius Pragmaticus* announced in April that '. . . the lusty lasses of the levelling party are drawing to a generall Rendezvous at Westminster, to present a Petition.'[142] It was noted that on Sunday 22 April 'a Petition was promoted at Severall Congregationall Meetings in and about the the City of London, for women to subscribe to a Petition to be presented to the House of Commons the next morning in behalfe of Lieut. Col. John Lilburne, and the rest of their friends in prison, in some places many signed it, in other places none at all, and in some places it was disputed.'[143] Indeed, 'Copies of the Petitions were sent to all parts about London, To desire that all those women that are approvers thereof should subscribe it, which accordingly many did, and delivered in their Subscriptions to certain women appointed in every Ward and Division to receive the same.'[144] Moreover, the women were ordered on 23 April 'to meet at Westminster Hall . . . betwixt 8 and 9 of clock in the forenoon'.[145] They came, bearing this petition,

---

138 B.M. E.518(46). *Cf.* B.M. E.411(14); *C.S.P.D. 1645–1647* p. 574; *C. J.*, V, 15 October 1647.
139 Bernstein, *op. cit.* pp. 59–60.
140 B.M. E.551(10); E.552(16); E.555(9).
141 William Cobbett, *State Trials* (1809) Vol. IV, p. 1280.
142 B.M. E.551(15).
143 B.M. E.529(21).
144 B.M. E.529 (20). *Cf.* B.M. E.529(23).
145 *To the Supream authority. . . . humble Petition of divers wel-affected Women* (1649), B.M. E.551(14).

parts of which were printed in several news-sheets of t[
period.[146]

In their petition the Leveller women declared that parliament
was acting against Lilburne, Walwyn, Prince and Overton in a
tyrannical manner. They also complained that 'Trading is utterly
driven away, all kinds of Provision for Food at a most excessive
rate, multitudes ready to starve and perish for want of work,
employment, necessaries, and subsistance; Tythes, Excise,
Monopolies continued to the extreme disheartning of Tillage
and Trade, Taxes more and more than ever, and those rigorously
executed. . . .' They demanded the release of Lilburne, Walwyn,
Prince, Overton and also Captain William Bray and Mr William
Sawyer, and that if any proceedings were to be taken against
them, such should be according to 'the Law of the Land.' 'We
also intreat, that you will be pleased to declare particularly wherein the said Book laid unto their charge, tendeth to the hindrance
of the relief of Ireland, or the continuance of free-quarter, or is
treasonable in it self, because you have by your Declaration made
the same, and the abetting thereof in any person to be no less
than Treason.' 'Also, that you will be very wary in making
any thing to be treasonable, or a capital offence, that is not
essentially destructive to civil Societie: then which we know
nothing more, then the exercise of an arbitrary Power, or continuance of Authoritie Civil or Military, beyond the time limited
by Trust or Commission, or the perverting of either to unjust,
bloudy, or ambitious ends; things which our said Friends, with
others, have much complained of, and for which principally we
beleeve their lives are so violently pursued.' They concluded by
expressing the hope that the Leveller prisoners would be released, 'in preserving of whom you will preserve your selves,
your wives, children and the whole Nation from bondage and
misery . . . and become the joy and rejoycing of your Petitioners.'[147]

The women were at Westminster with their petition from 23 to
25 April and there is some confusion in the newspapers about the

146 B.M. E.529(20), (23), (25), (26); E.552(21). J. Frank, *The Levellers*
(Cambridge, Mass., 1955) p. 322, *n*. 50, states that the petition was
described in *The Moderate* No. 40, a week before its presentation, but
this is not true of the copy of *The Moderate* in B.M. E.550(28).
147 *To the Supream authority . . . humble Petition of divers wel-affected women*
(1649) pp. 6–8, B.M. E.551(14).

order of events. The consensus of opinion seems to be that on Monday 23 April several hundreds of women, 'nigh 500' according to one report,[148] brought the petition to Westminster,[149] which was signed by 10,000 women.[150] A sympathetic reporter described the women as 'civil' and their petition as 'clothed in humble yet high language'.[151] A hostile commentator said that their petition was 'reproachful and almost scolding';[152] and a bawdy account described the women as 'The Meek-hearted Congregation of Oyster-wives, the Civill-Sisterhood of Oranges and Lemmons, and likewise the Mealymouth'd Muttenmongers wives'.[153] 'The better to prepare a way' for their petition the women 'had a letter directed to Mr Speaker'.[154] '. . . Mr Speaker had not the manners to returne the curteous creatures thankes for their good affection to the Cause.'[155] It was indeed 'moved that their Petition might be called for but the House laid it aside'[156] and 'nothing done upon it'.[157] Various reasons were given for the House's attitude: one was that they were too preoccupied with '. . . the long debate upon the act for the sale of Dean and Chapters Lands.'[158] At any rate the House 'did not think fit to call them in . . .',[159] though 'they came up to the door but as women were sent doun again yet their Petition afterwards taken . . .'[160] for they returned the next day.[161] And on the Tuesday about 300 'holy sisters'[162] brought the petition, but 'The House gave no answer hereunto',[163] and they '. . . could not get it received'.[164]

On Wednesday the women returned again; this time 'The House of Commons sent out the Serjeant at Armes to the women to fetch in their Petition, concerning which, the House after debate, did not think fit to enter any thing about it in the Journall Booke; but sent them this answer by the Serjeant at Armes to tell them

148 B.M. E.529(20). *Cf.* B.M. E.529(23).
149 B.M. E.551(13). *Cf.* B.M. E.529(21), (26); E.551(20); Whitelocke, *op. cit.* p. 397.
150 B.M. E.551(13).
151 B.M. E.551(20). *Cf.* B.M. E.551(18).
152 Whitelocke, *op. cit.* p. 397.
153 B.M. E.552(12).   154 B.M. E.551(18).
155 B.M. E.552(12).   156 B.M. E.529(21).
157 B.M. E.529(26).   158 B.M. E.551(20).
159 B.M. E.529(23).   160 B.M. E.552(20).
161 B.M. E.529(22).   162 B.M. E.529(22).
163 B.M. E.529(22).
164 B.M. E.529(21). *Cf.* Whitelocke, *op. cit.*, p. 398.

by word of mouth . . . "Mr Speaker (by direction of the House) hath commanded me to tell you, That the matter you petition about, is of an higher concernment then you understand, that the House gave an answer to your Husbands; and therefore that you are desired to goe home, and looke after your owne businesse, an meddle with your huswifery.'[165] Two reports are agreed that the women then 'very civilly went away',[166] but *Mercurius Pragmaticus* claimed that after hearing the House's reply 'the storme began . . .' and the women's 'Tongues pelted hail-shot against the Members as they passed to and fro, whilst the Souldiers threw in squibs under their Coats . . . At length . . . Noll Cromwell laies his nose out at the dore . . . and sent forth Phillip Harbert . . . to baule them out of Westminster.' The women, however, 'rounded him in a Ring, til he swore he was for the Liberties of the People.'[167] *Mercurius Militaris* printed an account of the happenings at Westminster[168] supposedly on 23 April, which differed so much from other reports of that day, and agreed so much with *Pragmaticus*'s account of 25 April, that it most likely belongs to the latter date, although McArthur accepted *Mercurius Militaris*'s chronology. According to this version twenty women were admitted to the lobby with their petition, the soldiers not only threw squibs but cocked their pistols and forced the women down the Parliament stairs 'with files of Musquetiers'. Cromwell's cloak was seized by a woman who lectured him.[169] It was alleged that during this April petitioning 'the chief of the women who delivered the Petition to the House of Commons about Lilburn . . . hearing that these stood upon their Guard, opposing Commands, laughed, and said they were glad of it, and that the like would be in many other places sodainly.'[170]

On 29 April the funeral of Robert Lockyer, who had been executed by court martial for his part in a dispute over pay and his refusal to march to Mile End Green, provided a focus for a Leveller demonstration in which 'the Women brought up the Rear' of the impressive procession accompanying Lockyer's

165 B.M. E.529(21). *Cf.* B.M. E.529(26); E.552(15); Whitelocke, *op. cit.* p. 398. This answer noted without a date, or under a different date—Clement Walker, *op. cit.* p. 165 B.M. E.529(25); E.552(7), (8), (14), (16), (20); E.554(12), (18).
166 B.M. E.529(21); E.552(20).
167 B.M. E.552(15).   168 B.M. E.551(13).
169 *ibid.*   170 B.M. E.529(23).

coffin.[171] '. . . most of this great number that thus attended the Corps, had Sea-Green and black Ribbons . . . on their Brests.'[172]

At the beginning of May it was reported that the 'good women . . . are preparing to give another alarm at Westminster with a new Petition. . . .'[173] The 'bonny Besses In the Sea-green dresses' were described metaphorically as 'marching down in Batalia to give the Members of Westminster a second charge, with the artillery of a Petition. . . .'[174] Thomason acquired their petition on 5 May.[175]

In their May petition the women 'plead the Rights and Libertyes of all Peticoat Petitioners, and then demand Justice against all that had a hand in the murther of Mr Lockyer together with an inlargement of the rest of their Champions in the Tower and at Windsor, or else down go the supream Dagons with Ladles and Dish-clouts. . . .'[176] They were particularly concerned that Lockyer had been tried by 'Law Martial' in time of peace.[177]

Brailsford says that ten thousand women had signed the petition and that one thousand presented it.[178] One news-sheet reported that on 5 May there 'were also divers Women with a Petition in the behalf of M. Lilburn and the other three (with their Sea-green Ribbond, which they wore at the burial of Lockier their fellow Creature) their Petition was very high, and they very urgent for an Answer; not satisfied with that they had to their former. They have ever loved to meddle with what they should not from the beginning.'[179] On 7 May they were at the Commons again, and again wore 'on their breasts Sea-green Ribands'.[180] One paper likened these many, 'Levelling ladies'

171 B.M. E.553(1*).
172 B.M. E.529(34). *Cf.* B.M. E.552(20); Whitelocke, *op. cit.* p. 399; T. C. Pease, *The Leveller Movement* (1916) p. 280, gives as his source for this incident *The Army's Martyr* (1649) B.M. E.552(11), but there is nothing in this, or in a tract of the same title in B.M. E.554(6), about this occasion.
173 B.M. E.554(12).
174 B.M. E.554(13).
175 *To the Supreme Authority . . . Petition of divers well-affected Women* (1649) B.M. 669 f. 14(27).
176 B.M. E.554(12).
177 *To the Supreme Authority . . . Petition of divers well-affected Women* (1649) B.M. 669 f. 14(27).
178 H. N. Brailsford, *The Levellers and the English Revolution* (London, 1961) p. 317.
179 B.M. E.555(8).   180 B.M. E.554(14).

to 'a company of Gosops' because 'being frustrated of their expectations' to present the House with their petition 'they ran up and down . . . and shewed their petitions to every one'.[181] *The Moderate* printed a petition, identical with the broadside acquired by Thomason on 5 May,[182] under the date of 7 May.[183] On 8 May one journalist commented: 'There were this day, and 2 or 3 daies before, some Women tendring a Petition for liberty for Lieut. Col. John Lilburne, and the rest imprisoned of their friends; a Gentleman told them, That if they understood themselves they might be better occupied at home.'[184] Another sheet noted simply that these women petitioners '. . . are still unsatisfied'.[185] Later in the month one news-sheet recalled: 'Brethren . . . Petitions are odious to these Parliament vipers; for they reject the Petitions of your Levelling sea-greene Sisters . . . Ironically answering them that they might be better occupied at home. But I professe, that answer is not like to serve, for the bony lasses will try one touch more and if that will not doe they will scale the wall at Westminster, and with boyling water scald the Hornets out of their nests.'[186] Another commentator referred to the 'black-patched faces' of the women, whose desires were 'to raigne as Queenes': 'What's become of all my brave Virago's the Ladyes-errants of the Seagreen Order, devoted Vestals to the new erected Alcaron, so lately fluttering like flocks of wilde Geese, about the Parliaments eares, for liberty of their Champion Jack and his confederates, why doe ye not againe muster up your Pettycoates and white Apporns, and like gallant Lacedemonians, or bold Amazons advance your Banners once more in the Pallace yard and spit defiance in the teeth of Authority; tell the Parliament that it is liberty they fought for, liberty you come for. . . .'[187]

On 4 August 1649 the Council of State told Colonel Goffe that the officer of the guards must 'take care that no clamorous women nor spies be permitted to come within the walls of this House, and that no affront be offered to any members of Parliament or the Council of State'. But these women may have been

181 B.M. E.554(18).
182 *To the Supreme Authority . . . Petition of divers well-affected Women* (1649) B.M. 669 f.14(27).
183 B.M. E.554(15).
184 B.M. E.530(4). *Cf.* B.M. E.529(36).
185 B.M. E.529(37). 186 B.M. E.555(13).
187 B.M. E.556(22).

those 'who clamour upon the council upon pretence of debts due to them from the Parliament. . . .'[188] However, on Monday 27 October 1651 'a very notable Petition concerning Arrests, Prisoners, and Prisons . . . was presented to the Lord Gen. Cromwell. . . .' This newspaper account of this petition made no mention of its exclusively feminine nature, merely calling it 'The humble Petition of many thousands of . . . poor . . . Men and Women',[189] but another edition of this petition, almost identical with the newspaper version, gave it the title *The Womens Petition*.[190] The women remarked in this petition, 'We have for many yeers (but in especial since 1647) chattered like Cranes, and mourned like Doves; yea, with many sighs and tears have we presented our several complaints against God's and our enemies'.[191] The petition was permeated with Leveller language and its target was a favourite Leveller one, namely '. . . the impious, oppressive, delatory, and most chargeable practise of the Law, and destructive Imprisonment of Men and Women for Debt.'[192] This law 'was both harsh and inefficient, for, having deprived the debtor of all possibility of repayment by throwing him into prison, it kept him there till the arrival of the problematical date on which his debt could be paid.'[193] Parliament had attempted some reform in this sphere in 1641 and 1649[194] but the women were not satisfied with this and appealed to Cromwell to be their 'Deliverer from Oppression and Slavery'; for, although 'the Head of Tyrannie' had been cut off in 1649, tyranny 'still liveth in and by his ordained members of Injustice and Oppression'. However, the solution, obvious to them, namely the election of a new parliament, 'from which Lawyers, and all ill affected persons . . .' were to be excluded, not being practicable at that moment, they begged 'That in the mean time there may be such a course established, as that the Poor may by some easie and speedy way reap the fruit of Justice, and that their Persons may be acquitted from continual vexations and destructive Arrests and Imprisonment. . . .'[195]

188 *C.S.P.D. 1649–1650* p. 262.
189 B.M. E.791(1); nor did Whitelocke, *op. cit.* p. 512, mention its specifically feminine nature.
190 *The Women's Petition . . . to Cromwell 27 Oct. 1651* B.M. 669 f. 16(30).
191 *ibid.*   192 *ibid.*
193 Margaret James, *Social Problems and Policy during the Puritan Revolution* (London, 1930) pp. 328–9.
194 *ibid.* pp. 335–6.
195 *The Women's Petition . . . to Cromwell 27 Oct. 1651* B.M. 669 f. 16(30).

The women helped to keep this issue alive and in 1653 the Barebones Parliament set up a committee to consider the whole question of imprisonment for debt and passed an Act which gained the approval of the prisoners themselves.[196]

In 1653 the activities of radical women were concentrated upon the attempt to secure the release of Lilburne from imprisonment by petitioning parliament.[197] In the British Museum there is a petition entitled *To the Parliament of the Common-wealth of England. The humble Petition of divers afflicted Women, in behalf of M. John Lilburn Prisoner in Newgate*, which has been endorsed by Thomason 'June 25 1653'.[198] But there is no reference in the newspapers to a petition around this date, whereas in July two newspapers reported that 'The Women have drawn up an excellent Petition in behalf of M. Lilburn', and they printed a petition identical with the one attributed to 25 June by Thomason,[199] who may thus have written June in mistake for July. Then, in its next edition, the *Faithful Post* announced: 'In my last I presented you with the humble Petition of the afflicted women in behalfe of Mr John Lilburn; the rejection whereof occasioned a second Representation to every individual member of Parliament';[200] and it printed a petition[201] identical with one acquired by Thomason on 29 July and entitled *Unto every individual Member of Parliament. The humble Representation of divers afflicted Women-Petitioners to the Parliament, on the behalf of Mr John Lilburn.*[202] This second petition was probably presented on Wednesday 27 July, the day on which one newspaper noted that 'The Petition of many well affected women in and about the City of London, in behalf of Lieutenant Collonel John Lilburn was this day extant, but . . . they could obtain no answer. . . .'[203] 'On Wensday there came to the Parlt. about 12 women, with a petition in the behalf of Jo. Lilburne, it was subscribed by above 6000 of that sex, the chief of these 12 was wife to one Chidley a prime Leveller,[204] they boldly knockt at the doore, and the House taking notice that they were there, sent out Praise-God Barebones to disswade them from their enterprize, but he could not prevaile; and they persisting in their

196 James, *op. cit.* pp. 336–8.
197 Brailsford, *op. cit.* p. 616.
198 B.M. 669 f. 17(26).
199 B.M. E.707(6), E. 217(7).
200 B.M. E.217(13).
201 *ibid.*
202 B.M. 669 f. 17(36).
203 B.M. E.708(16).
204 Probably a reference to Mrs Chidley—*mother* of Samuel the Leveller according to Thomas Edwards.

disturbance another Member came out and told them, the House could not take cognizance of their petition . . .', but the women '. . . pressed for the receiving their Petition, which if they refused, they should know that they had husbands and friends, and they wore swords to defend the libertys of the People &c. and withall admonished them, to looke to themselves, and not to persecute that man of God, least they were also destroyed, as the late King, Bishops, Parlt. and all others that ever opposed him; who were all fallen before him.'[205] But the House would not receive their petition and the women 'proceeded to a new draught which will be presented (if they can get a Parliament mans hand to it) within a few days.'[206] It was noted on 30 July that 'Many hands were gathered to a Petition of a great number of women in behalf of Lieut. Col. John Lilburn.'[207] And thus there seems to have been a third petition, no copy of which has survived.

In the petitions of July 1653 the women were very concerned to assert their right to petition. In the first petition they warned parliament against laying its foundations in Lilburne's innocent blood; they reminded them that David had not been allowed 'to build a Temple for the Lord . . .' because he had dipped his hands in blood, and they asked 'Whether the ready pronenesse to the spilling of blood in the last Parliament . . . were not the maine cause that God forsook them. . . .' They warned that 'if God spared not the natural branches take heed lest he also spare not you. . . .' They begged parliament not to imitate the 'natural branches' 'in pride, in keeping at distance with other People, or in Apparel, Diet, housing, and Fantastique Fashions, complements, couches and congees, Cloathing in Scarlet, and Faring deliciously every day, or in covetousnesse, advancing their estates, Families and Relations, upon the ruins of the People, taxing them without measure, laying also of heavy burdens upon them, whilst Pharisee-like, they felt not the weight with one of their fingars. Scorned information, and despised Petitions. . . .' They warned them to guard against the shedding of innocent blood, and especially that of Lilburne, whom they had now imprisoned and put on trial for his life for returning from a banishment imposed by the previous parliament: they begged

205 Bodleian Library, Oxford, MS. Clarendon Vol. 46, ff. 131b–132a ('Advertisement from London, 29 July 1653').
206 B.M. E.708(16).   207 *ibid.*

parliament 'to put a stop to M. Lilburns Tryal, and to make full inquiry into the whole matter upon which the late Parliament grounded their unjust Sentence and Act.'[208] In their second petition the women protested that they had 'attended several days at your House-door with an humble Petition, desiring the making null of the most unrighteous, illegal Act made against Mr Lilburne by the late Parliament . . .' without being heard. They revealed their fear that 'what is done or intended against him (being against common right and in the face thereof) may be done unto every particular person in the Nation'. They concluded with the hope '. . . that you will not suffer any further proceedings to be had upon that most unrighteous Act against Mr Lilburne.'[209]

The unusual part played by women in petitioning and in politics, Leveller and non-Leveller, challenged generally accepted ideas about the place of women in seventeenth-century English society. Women asserted that they had some political rights, not excluding the right to express their views and influence important decisions by means of petitions to parliament. This unrest among some women was reflected in the writings of satirists.[210] A royalist ballad described the differing views expressed by women at an imaginary meeting to settle the government and religion of the country, which meeting was summoned by the cry:

> Come Clowns, and come Boys, come Hoberdehoys,
> Come Females of each degree,
> Stretch your throats, bring in your Votes,
> And make good the Anarchy.[211]

A political squib among the Conway papers represented the House of Commons as consisting of women.[212] This idea of a

208 *To the Parliament of the Commonwealth . . . petition of afflicted women in behalf of Lilburne* (1653) B.M. 669 f. 17(26).
209 *Unto every individual Member of Parliament, the . . . Representation of . . . women . . . on behalf of Mr John Lilburn* (1653) B.M. 669 f. 17(36).
210 For example *Three Speeches* (1642) B.M. E.240(31); *The Resolution of the Women of London to Parliament* (1642) B.M. E.114(14); *Mrs Wardens Observations* (1642) B.M. E.115(20); *Women will have their Will* (1648) B.M. E.1182(12); *A Tragicomedy called Newmarket Fair* (1649) B.M. C.34 b.35.
211 *Rump: or an exact collection of the choycest Poems 1639-61* (1662) Vol. I, p. 291, M.C.R.L.
212 *C.S.P.D. 1641-1643* p. 229; also in Henry Nevile, *The Parliament of Ladies* (1647) pp. 13-14, J.R.L.

parliament of women was a popular theme. In 1640 a petition to the Commons complained of 'The swarming of lascivious, idle and unprofitable books and pamphlets . . . as namely . . . the Parliament of Women. . . .'[213] The Duke of Lennox's reaction to women petitioners was to exclaim: '. . . wee were best to have a parliament of Women.'[214] Ribald scribblers produced mock petitions that were alleged to have been presented to parliament by women.[215] In one of these the women are made to say: 'we do engage our selves under penalty of being committed with or by any Justice of the Peace, to abandon all uncivil meetings . . . not committing any unnaturall or unlawfull exploit by way of ryot.'[216]

Women petitioners felt obliged to explain themselves, and their justifications of their novel activity are a noteworthy feature, particularly for the Leveller period, of the petitioning. The authorship of the petitions which the women presented to parliament is unknown, but even if they were penned by men, they are of interest for the light which they throw on the status of women. Moreover, the women petitioners are reported as answering their critics orally as well, and presumably spontaneously.

The women accepted the view that they were inferior to men: speaking, in 1642, of their 'frail Condition';[217] describing them-

---

213 W. M. Clyde, *The Struggle for the Freedom of the Press from Caxton to Cromwell* (St Andrews, 1934) pp. 53–4. *Cf. The Parliament of Women* (1646) B.M. E.1150 (5); Henry Nevile, *The Ladies Parliament* (1647), B.M. E.1143; *A Parliament of Ladies* (1647) B.M. E.384(9); *An Exact Diurnall of the Parliament of Ladyes* (1647) B.M. E.386(4); *Hey Hoe for a Husband or, the Parliament of Maides* (1647) B.M. E.408(19); *The Ladies, a second Time Assembled in Parliament* (1647) B.M. E.406(23); *Match me these two . . . An Answer to a Pamphlet entituled a Parliament of Ladies* (1647) B.M. E.400(9).

214 B.M. E.201(13).

215 For example *The Petition of the Weamen of Middlesex* (1641) B.M. E.180(17); *Midwives Just Petition* (1643) B.M. E.86(14); *Virgins Complaint* (1643) B.M. E.86(38); *Petition of . . . Wives . . . for cessation . . . civill wars* (1643) B.M. E.88(13); *Widowes Lamentation* (1643) B.M. E.88(26); *Virgins Complaint* (1646) B.M. E.351(5); *Midwives Just Complaint* (1646) B.M. E.355(20); *The Maids Petition* (1647) B.M. E.401(26) (its demands may have been genuine); *A Remonstrance of the Shee-Citizens of London* (1647) B.M. E.404 (2); *The City Dames Petition* (1647) B.M. E.409(12) (noted by Whitelocke, *op. cit.* p. 54); Henry Nevile, *Ladies a second time . . . in Parliament* ('Petition of Citizens Wives') p. 7, J.R.L.

216 *The Maids Petition* (1647) p. 2 B.M. E.401(26).

217 '. . . Petition . . . Feb. 4th 1641', *Harleian Miscellany* (1746) Vol. VII, p. 568.

selves as the 'weaker sex' in 1643;[218] and referring, in 1649, to the 'weak hand of Women'.[219] They emphasized that they were acting 'not out of any Self-conceit or Pride of Heart, as *seeking to equal ourselves with Men, either in Authority or Wisdom*', but merely 'following herein the Example of the Men, which have gone . . . before us',[220] thus admitting the superior wisdom of men and accepting subjection to them. The former point is reiterated by the petitioners of 1653 who declared 'the thing is so gross, that *even Women* perceive the evil of it'; adding, 'neither do we hope that your Honours . . . will have the less regard unto our Petition *although Women*.'[221] However, in the petition which they presented in May 1649 the Leveller women gave as one reason for their actions, dissatisfaction with the earlier answer given by parliament to their husbands,[222] but they do not seem to have thought out the implications of this line of reasoning, failing to push it to the logical conclusion, namely political action by wives independently of their husbands; for on 27 July 1653 when about twelve petitioners under the leadership of Katherine Chidley came to the House with a petition for Lilburne, and a member 'came out and told them, the House could not take cognizance of their petition, they being women, and many of them wives, so that the Law tooke no notice of them,' . . . 'they replyed, that they were not all wives, and therefore pressed for the receiving their Petition. . . .'[223] The logic of their reply is immediately apparent:[224] they were implicitly accepting the traditional notion that when it came to expressing political views, the wife's were included in, and became explicit only through her husband's. This was, consciously or unconsciously, a retreat from the position of 1649 when the women had declared: 'we

218 Bodleian Library, Oxford, MS. Tanner LXIV, f. 190.
219 *To the Supream authority . . . humble Petition of divers wel-affected Women* (1649) p. 4, B.M. E.551(14); *To the Supreme Authority . . . Petition of divers well-affected Women* (1649) B.M. 669 f. 14(27).
220 '. . . Petition . . . Feb. 4th 1641', *Harleian Miscellany* (1746) Vol. VII, p. 569.
221 *To the Parliament of the Commonwealth . . . petition of afflicted women in behalf of Lilburne* (1653) B.M. 669 f. 17(26); B.M. 669 f. 17(36).
222 *To the Supreme Authority . . . Petition of divers well-affected Women* (1649) B.M. 669 f. 14(27).
223 Bodleian Library, Oxford, MS. Clarendon Vol. 46, f. 131b ('Advertisement from London July 29 1653').
224 *Cf.* Pauline Gregg, *Free-Born John: A Biography of John Lilburne* (London, 1961) p. 215, who cannot explain the logic of the women's reply.

are no whit satisfied with the answer you gave unto our Husbands. . . .'[225]

Further, the women were very conscious of the unusual nature of their activities, saying, 'we confess it is not our custom to address our selves to this House in the Publick behalf . . .',[226] and that indeed to do so 'may be thought Strange and unbeseeming our Sex. . . .'[227] And, in fact, they frequently met with hostility and ridicule.[228] For example, on 1 February 1642 the Commons asked Skippon to dismiss the women petitioners '. . . as the House was . . . now in Consideration of matters of great Consequence',[229] as though the women's petition was of little importance; and, since its contents were undeniably important, it must have been the sex of the petitioners that made their petition trivial. Indeed, as we have seen, actual physical violence was used against the peace petitioners of 9 August 1643.[230] In the Leveller period of petitioning masculine hostility became much more overt and its language more violent. On 23 April 1649 the women petitioners were '. . . as women . . . sent doun again . . .' and their petition not accepted; though it was accepted two days later, despite a member of parliament's remark that 'it was strange that women should petition.'[231] But when the House did condescend to consider the petition their reply to the women was 'That the matter you petition about, is of an higher concernment then you understand, that the House gave an answer to your Husbands; and therefore that you are desired to goe home, and looke after your owne businesse, and meddle with your huswifery'.[232] This was interpreted by one commentator as meaning 'in effect, that they should go home and spin; it being the usuall work of women either to spin or knit and not to meddle with State Affaires.'[233] Another newspaper alleged that the women

---

225 Just as servants were included in their masters; *To the Supreme Authority . . . Petition of divers well-affected Women* (1649) B.M. 669 f. 14(27).

226 *To the Supream authority . . . humble Petition of divers wel-affected Women* (1649) p. 4, B.M. E.551(14).

227 '. . . Petition . . . Feb. 4th 1641', *Harleian Miscellany* (1746) Vol. VII, p. 569. *Cf.* B.M. E.551(13).

228 *Cf.* above nn. 210–16. This is also a feature of the news-sheets of the period, For example B.M. E.556(22), and the Duke of Lennox's comments reported in E. 201(13).

229 *C.J.* II, 1 February 1641 (2).

230 See above nn. 100–14. For example B.M. MS. Harl. 165, f. 150a.

231 B.M. E.551(13).   232 B.M. E.529(21).

233 B.M. E.554(18).

petitioners were really demanding 'let women weare the breeches'. Reflecting on the activities of these women it concluded: 'It is fitter for you to be washing your dishes, and meddle with the wheele and distaffe'; 'we shall have things brought to a fine passe, if women come to teach the Parliament how to make Lawes.' 'It can never be a good world, when women meddle in States matters . . . their Husbands are to blame, that they have no fitter imployment for them.'[234]

These comments were echoed on 8 May 1649, when 'a Gentleman told them [i.e. the women petitioners] That if they understood themselves they might be better occupied at home.'[235] And this particular incident seems to have been in the mind of the writer of a news-sheet later in the same month when he wrote: 'Brethren . . . Petitions are odious to these Parliament vipers for they reject the Petitions of your Levelling Sea-greene Sisters . . . Ironically answering them that they might be better occupied at home'; and he added, 'But I professe, that answer is not like to serve; for the bony lasses will try one touch more, and if that will not doe they will scale the wall at Westminster, and with boyling water scald the Hornets out of their nests.'[236] And up again they did bob, of course, only to be told on 27 July 1653, that '. . . the House could not take cognizance of their petition, they being women, and many of them wives, so that the Law tooke no notice of them. . . .'[237]

In the reception accorded to women petitioners it is possible to observe the appearance of the age-old caricature of women as loquacious busybodies. It was of the women petitioners of April 1649 that it was written: 'If their tongues must be pratling they may finde other talke'—i.e., other than 'State matters'.[238] And of those of 5 May: 'They have ever loved to meddle with what they should not from the beginning.'[239] On 7 May the Leveller ladies were likened to 'a company of Gosops'.[240]

The fact that women knew that they would provoke these almost reflex reactions from men and yet were prepared to face

234 B.M. E.529(23).
235 B.M. E.530(4).
236 B.M. E.555(13).
237 Bodleian Library, Oxford, MS. Clarendon Vol. 46, f. 131b ('Advertisement from London July 29 1653').
238 B.M. E.529(23).   239 B.M. E.555(8).
240 B.M. E.554(18).

them in the course of doing what they felt they had to do, argues some degree of female emancipation. Women could contemplate defiance of convention. Moreover these acts of defiance were not single isolated incidents, taking place on the actual day of petitioning, for the well-organized activity of the feminine part of the Leveller movement in collecting signatures for the petition of 23 April 1649 has been noted.[241] Women were prepared to leave the home and come into the forum, and, short of locking them up, there was little their husbands or fathers could do about it.

Despite the obligatory curtsy to custom and convention in the protestations of inferiority with which the women prefaced their petitions; when it came to explaining their actions the women forgot their modesty and came out with bold arguments to justify their activities. They drew on the Bible and secular history for support. In the petitioning of 4 February 1642 the women declared: 'Neither are we left without Example in the Scripture', and they cited the 'Woman of Tekoa'[242] and Esther appearing before Ahasuerus.[243] Esther was recalled in the second Leveller petition of 1653 also, when the women hoped that parliament would not 'be worse unto us, then that Heathen King was to Esther, who did not onely hear her Petition, but reversed that Decree or Act gone forth against the Jewes.'[244] The Leveller ladies in their April 1649 petition reminded their readers that 'God hath wrought many deliverances for severall Nations, from age to age by the weake hand of women. By the counsell and presence of Deborah, and the hand of Jaell, Israell was delivered from the King of Canaan, Sisera and his mighty Host, Judges 4.'[245] Lilburne's female sympathizers wrote in a similar vein in 1653: 'That seeing nothing is more manifest then that God is pleased often times to raise up the weakest means to work the mightiest effects, and in as much as the holy prophet David himselfe was prevented, by the timely addresses of a weak woman,[246] from a most resolved purpose of shedding of Blood . . . we could

241 See above *nn*. 143, 144.
242 2 *Sam*. 14.
243 ' . . . Petition . . . Feb. 4th 1641', *Harleian Miscellany* (1746) Vol. VII, pp. 568, 569.
244 *Unto every individual member of Parliament: the . . . Representation of . . . women . . . on behalf of Mr John Lilburn* (1653) B.M. 669 f. 17(36).
245 *To the Supream authority . . . humble Petition of divers wel-affected Women* (1649) pp. 4–5, B.M. E.551(14).
246 i.e. Abigail, 2 *Sam*. 23.

not forbeare to make this our humble application unto you.'[247]
However, these Biblical arguments seem to be justifications for
occasional 'unfeminine' behaviour on special occasions, when
divine intervention reversed the natural order or course of
things, and deliverances were wrought by God through the
instrument of weaker vessels; they did not offer a basis for a
sustained feminist movement.

Similarly, secular history offered Boedica, who was represented
to parliament in 1653 in the following manner: 'Your Honours
may be pleased to call to minde that never-to-be-forgotten
deliverance obtained by the good women of England against the
usurping Danes then in this Nation.'[248] The Leveller women also
appealed to this precedent in April 1649: '. . . by the British women
this land was delivered from the tyranny of the Danes (who then
held the same under the sword, as is now endeavoured by some
Officers of the Army) and the overthrow of Episcopall tyranny
in Scotland was first begun by the women of that Nation.'[249]

The women began to use arguments which implied equality of
the sexes when they turned to justifying their actions by reference
to an equal interest of men and women in religion and in the
church. In some respects this was a fairly conventional claim, but
nevertheless an important one. Moreover, puritan insistence on
individual salvation and on the equality of man and woman in
Christ, which had been taken up and further stressed by the
sectaries in the civil war period, had given it a new vigour and
freshness. In their petition of 4 February 1642 the women remarked: 'It may be thought strange . . . to shew ourselves by Way
of Petition, . . . but [considering] the Right and Interest we have,
in the common and publick Cause of the Church, it will . . . be
found a Duty commanded and required'. 'First, Because Christ
hath purchased us at as dear a Rate as he hath done Men; and
therefore requireth the like Obedience for the same Mercy, as
of Men'. 'Secondly, Because in the free Enjoying of Christ in his
own Laws, and a flourishing Estate of the Church . . . consisteth
the Happiness of Women as well as Men'. 'Thirdly, Because

247 *To the Parliament of the Commonwealth . . . petition of afflicted Women in
behalf of Lilburn* (1653) B.M. 669 f. 17(26).
248 *Unto every individual member of Parliament: the . . . Representation of . . .
women . . . on behalf of Mr John Lilburn* (1653) B.M. 669 f. 17(36).
249 *To the Supream authority . . . humble Petition of divers wel-affected Women*
(1649) p. 5, B.M. E.551(14).

Women are Sharers in the common Calamities that accompany . . .
Church . . . when Oppression is exercised over the Church . . .
wherein they live, and an unlimited Power hath been given to the
Prelates, to exercise Authority over the Consciences of Women,
as well as Men; witness Newgate, Smithfield, and other Places of
Persecution, wherein Women, as well as Men, have felt the Smart
of their Fury'. 'We do it . . . according to our Places, to discharge
that Duty we owe to God, and the Cause of the church. . . .'[250] In
May 1649 the Leveller women lamented: ' . . . since we are assured
of our Creation in the image of God, and of an Interest in Christ
equal unto men . . . we cannot but wonder and grieve that we
should appear so despicable in your eyes as to be thought unworthy to Petition. . . .'[251] 'We hope . . .', reads the second
petition of Leveller women in 1653, ' . . . that . . . your Honours
will not slight the persons of your humble Petitioners, nor with-
hold from us *our undoubted right of petitioning*, since God is ever
willing and ready to receive the Petitions of all, making no
difference of persons. The ancient Laws of England are not
contrary to the will of God: so that we claim it as our right to
have our Petitions heard; you having promised to govern the
Nation in righteousness. . . .'[252]

The third tack which the women petitioners took in arguing
for their right to petition was to claim as citizens an equal interest
in the Commonwealth and in legal rights and privileges. This
was foreshadowed in the petition of 4 February 1642 when the
women spoke of their interest 'in the common Privileges', in a
flourishing Commonwealth, and in the 'Calamities that accompany . . . Commonwealth, when Oppression is exercised over . . .
[the] Kingdom',[253] and it was developed by the Leveller petitioners. Indeed, the transference of claims to equality from the religious to the secular sphere was a specifically Leveller contribution
to this development. This growth of political activity and political
beliefs out of religion is well illustrated by the fact that the

250 ' . . . Petition . . . Feb. 4th 1641', *Harleian Miscellany* (1746) Vol. VII,
pp. 568, 569.
251 *To the Supreme Authority . . . Petition of divers well-affected Women* (1649)
B.M. 669 f. 14(27).
252 *Unto every individual member of Parliament: the . . . Representation of . . .
women . . . on behalf of Mr John Lilburn* (1653) B.M. 669 f. 17(36).
253 ' . . . Petition . . . Feb. 4th 1641', *Harleian Miscellany* (1746) Vol. VII,
pp. 568, 569.

Leveller women's petition of 23 April 1649 was '. . . promoted at Severall Congregationall Meetings in and about the City of London . . .' on the previous Sunday.[254] In this petition the women affirm that they had decided on this course of action 'considering, That we have an equal share and interest with men in the Commonwealth.'[255] By May of this same year the women petitioning in the Leveller cause have fully developed the view that as they have an equal share with men in the church, so '. . . we are assured . . . also of a proportionable share in the Freedoms of this Commonwealth, we cannot but wonder and grieve that we should appear so despicable in your eyes as to be thought unworthy to Petition or represent our Grievances to this Honourable House. Have we not an equal interest with the men of this Nation, in those liberties and securities contained in the Petition of Right, and other good Laws of the Land? Are any of our lives, limbs, liberties or goods to be taken from us more than from Men . . . ? And can you imagine us to be so sottish or stupid, as not to perceive, or not to be sencible when dayly those strong defences of our peace and welfare are broken down . . . ?

'Would you have us keep at home in our houses, when men . . . as the four prisoners . . . are . . . forced from their Houses . . . to the affrighting and undoing of themselves, their wives, children, and families? Are not our husbands, our selves, our children and families by the same rule as lyable to the like unjust cruelties as they?

'. . . and must we keep at home in our houses, as if we our lives and liberties and all, were not concerned? . . . must we show no sence of their sufferings . . . nor bear any testimony against so abominable cruelty and injustice?

'No . . . Let it be accounted folly, presumption, madness or whatsoever in us, whilst we have life and breath, we will never . . . cease to importune you . . .

'And therefore again, we entreat you to review our last petition . . . *For we are no whit satisfied with the answer you gave unto our Husbands and Friends*, but do equally with them remain lyable to those snares laid in your Declaration. . . .'[256]

254 B.M. E.529(21).
255 *To the Supream authority . . . humble Petition of divers wel-affected Women* (1649) B.M. E.551(14).
256 *To the Supreme Authority . . . Petition of divers well-affected Women* (1649) B.M. 669 f. 14(27).

The possibility that Mrs Chidley, who was the mother of Samuel Chidley, Treasurer of the Leveller party, may have been the author of this petition,[257] points to the link between the religious sects and radical politics, for Mrs Chidley was a keen sectary, and the author of religious tracts, as well as being extremely active in the Leveller movement; and it also suggests that notions of equality between men and women in the state were derived from notions of equality between men and women in the church.

In stating in their May petition that they were petitioning because of dissatisfaction with the answer given to their husbands and 'Friends', the women reached the most extreme 'feminist' position of the period. They seem to be challenging the very basis of the patriarchal society in which they lived, and in which the father/husband was the head of the household and the rest of the family was, as it were, 'included in him'. These women were claiming the right to speak and act for themselves, to have an existence and rights apart from their husbands, and not to be included automatically in an answer that had been given to their husbands. Perhaps they were not wholly conscious of the implications of their claim, for in 1653 they seem to have conceded the point that the wives have no right to be petitioning when the husbands have already been given an answer.

Lastly, women petitioners asked for an equal hearing with men on the basis of the contribution that women had made to the 'Cause'. This line of argument draws attention to the unusual roles that women undertook during the civil war and the extent to which the opportunities for women to undertake roles outside the home and to perform tasks previously done by men contributed to their emancipation.[258]

One of the petitioners of April 1649 complained to Cromwell that they could not get their petition read, though 'time hath been when you would readily have given us the reading of Petitions, but that was when we had mony, plates rings and bodkins to give you: You think we have none now. . . .'[259] She spoke accurately of the material contribution of women to the Cause. Thomas

257 Brailsford, *op. cit.* p. 317.
258 *Cf.* the influence of the First and Second World Wars in emancipating women.
259 B.M. E.551(13).

May wrote: 'The parliament . . . were very able to raise forces, and arm them well, by reason of that great mass of money and plate which to that purpose was heaped up in Guildhall, and daily increased by the free contribution of those that were well-affected to the parliament cause; . . . the poorer sort, like the widow in the gospel, presented their mites . . . insomuch that it was a common jeer of men disaffected to the cause, to call it the thimble and bodkin army.'[260] Howell declared: 'Unusual voluntary collections were made both in town and country. The sempstress brought in her silver thimble, the chambermaid her bodkin . . . into the common treasury of war. . . . And observed it was that some sort of females were freest in those contributions, as far as to part with their rings and ear-rings.'[261] Other writers noticed the contribution of women to the raising of parliament's forces.[262] In London,[263] Canterbury,[264] Norwich [265] and Coventry women formed committees and provided funds to raise troops of horse for parliament,[266] which became known as the 'Virgins Troopes'.[267] The troop financed by the young women of London served in the Earl of Essex's army,[268] and the Norwich troop was taken by Cromwell into his own regiment where it saw good service.[269]

Women worked on the building of fortifications, especially in London. Butler asserted that women

> March'd rank and file, with Drum and Ensign,
> T'entrench the City; for defence in[270]

A royalist ballad declared that 'Isaac our L. Maior' had built his trenches with the help of women.[271]

260 T. May, *The History of the Parliament of England* (Oxford, 1854) p. 212.
261 Quoted in C. Hill and E. Dell, *The Good Old Cause* (London, 1949) p. 278.
262 For example *Lord Have Mercie Upon us* (1643) p. 11, B.M. E.75(5); Whitelocke, *op. cit.* p. 61; *The Loyal Convert . . . or some annotation on this book* (1644) p. 19, J.R.L.; *Political Ballads of the 17th and 18th Centuries* ed. W. W. Wilkins (1860) Vol. I, p. 47; Butler, *op. cit.* p. 149; *Rump: or an exact collection of the choycest Poems 1639–61* (1662) Vol. I, p. 71, M.C.R.L.; Clement Walker, *History of Independency* (1648) p. 165, M.C.R.L.
263 Butler, *op. cit.* p. 149.   264 *Mercurius Aulicus* p. 487, J.R.L.
265 Wallington, *op. cit.* Vol. II, p. 171.
266 *Mercurius Aulicus* pp. 769–70, J.R.L.
267 *Hulls managing of the Kingdoms Cause* (1644) p. 15, B.M. E.51(11).
268 T. Carlyle, *Letters and Speeches of Cromwell* (1904) Vol. I, p. 145, *n.* 2.
269 C. H. Firth, *The Regimental History of Cromwell's Army* (Oxford, 1940) Vol. I, pp. 11–12.   270 Butler, *op. cit.* p. 149.
271 'On the Demolishing the Forts', *Rump: or an exact collection of the choycest Poems 1639–61* (1662) Vol. I, p. 246.

Indeed it was alleged by the royalists that the Lady Mayoress, Mrs Penington, armed with an entrenching tool, was present at the fortifications.[272] In fact women from all classes of society were involved in this war work in London,[273] especially between August and November 1642 and during the four months preceding June 1643.[274] Thus the London women who spoke in 1649 of their contribution to the Cause were speaking with much justification.

Women were involved, on the parliamentary side, in siege work in Gloucester,[275] Bristol[276] and Hull[277] in 1643, and in Lyme in 1644;[278] and on the royalist side in Worcester,[279] Hereford,[280] Nantwich and Maidstone.[281] There were examples of women playing the part of soldiers,[282] regular and otherwise. Women not infrequently became garrison commanders when

272 *ibid.* p. 246.
273 For example *C.S.P. Venetian 1642–1643* p. 273; W. Lithgow, 'The Present Surveigh of London and Englands State' (1643), *Somers Tracts* (1810) Vol. IV, p. 538; N. G. Brett-James, *The Growth of Stuart London* (London, 1935) pp. 275–6; Jacob Larwood, *The Story of the London Parks* (n.d.) pp. 27–8; Butler, *op. cit.* p. 149; May, *op. cit.* p. 330.
274 C. V. Wedgwood, *The King's War 1641–7* (London, 1958) p. 139; Whitelocke, *op. cit.* p. 63; Brett-James, *op. cit.* pp. 270, 279; *C.S.P. Venetian 1642–1643*, pp. 192, 273; May, *op. cit.* p. 330; Lithgow, *op. cit. Somers Tracts* (1810) Vol. IV, p. 538; B.M. E.249(2), (3), (6), (10); B.M. E.104(25).
275 John Dorney, 'Briefe . . . Relation of . . . Passages . . . in Seige Before Glocester 1643', *Bibliotheca Gloucestrensis* ed. John Washbourn (Gloucester, 1825) Vol. II, p. 227. *Cf.* John Corbet, 'An Historical Relation of the Military Government of Gloucester', *ibid.* Vol. I, p. 48.
276 Prynne and Walker, *op. cit. passim.*
277 *Hulls managing of the Kingdoms Cause* (1644) pp. 14–15, B.M. E.51(11).
278 Whitelocke, *op. cit.* p. 88; Strong, *op. cit. passim.*
279 D. R. Guttery, *The Great Civil War in Midland Parishes* (Birmingham, 1951) pp. 35, 36; B.M. E.105(17); *Mercurius Aulicus* p. 288, J.R.L.
280 John Webb, *Memorials of the Civil War in Herefordshire* (1879) Vol. II, p. 387.
281 *A Famous Victory . . . the Raising of the Siedge of Namptwich* (1644) B.M. E.31(6); H. F. Abell, *Kent and the Great Civil War* (Ashford, 1901) p. 213.
282 For example, *Mercurius Aulicus*, p. 844, J.R.L.; *The Resolution of the Valiant Danes . . . with the Valiant Resolution of Lady Sanders* (1642) B.M. E.128(6); *A True and Exact Relation of All the Proceedings of the Marquesse Hartford etc. in Publishing of the Commission of Array in Somerset* (1642) B.M. E.112(33); B.M. E.202(21); *C.S.P.D. 1639*, pp. 146, 282 (Edward Norgate to Robert Reade, 9 May and 5 June); A. C. Wood, *Nottinghamshire in the Civil War* (Oxford, 1937) p. 102, n.1; C. H. Firth, *Cromwell's Army* (reprinted, London, 1962) pp. 298–9.

their houses were besieged.[283] Some acted as couriers[284] ar
spies;[285] others assisted in escapes.[286] Women were used ex-
tensively for disseminating the tracts and news-sheets which
were such an important aspect of communication and propaganda;[287] and a few of them were involved in the printing
of unlicensed and subversive material.[288] They tended the
wounded;[289] managed the family estates in the absence of their
husbands, and dealt with the new officialdom thrown up by the
civil war, such as the Committee for Compounding.

This expansion of women's field of activity, and their contribution to the war effort, could not be ignored, and the women
petitioners used it as a bargaining point in April 1649,[290] and
again in 1653, when they reminded the Commons of 'the readi-
ness and willingness of the good women of this Nation, who
did think neither lives, nor their husbands and servants lives
and estates to be too dear a price for the gaining of yours and
the Nations ancient Rights and Liberties out of the hands of
incroachers and oppressors'. 'And therefore we hope,' they concluded, 'that . . . your Honours will not slight the persons of
your humble Petitioners, nor with-hold from us our undoubted
right of petitioning.'[291]

283 For example, Eliot Warburton, *Memoirs of Prince Rupert and the Cavaliers*
(1849) Vol. II, pp. 426-9; Guttery, *op. cit.* pp. 35, 40; *H.M.C.* Second
Report, Appendix, p. 147; *Manuscripts of the Marquis of Bath* Vol. I,
pp. 1-32; *Portland Manuscripts*, Vol. III, *passim*; *H.M.C.* Ninth Report,
Appendix Part II, p. 387.
284 For example B.M. E.105(24); *A True Discoverie of . . . the . . . Plot to ruine
the Citie of London* (1643) B.M. E.105(31). Cf. *C.S.P. Venetian 1642-1643*
p. 237; *C.S.P.D. 1645-1647* p. 260.
285 For example, M. A. E. Green (ed.), *Letters of Henrietta Maria* (1857) p.
122; Wallington, *op. cit.* Vol. II, p. 225.
286 For example, 'An Account of King Charles I's escape from Worcester',
ed. Edmund Goldsmid, *Bibliotheca Curiosa* (Edinburgh, 1883) pp. 19-20;
D.N.B. Jane Whorwood.
287 Joseph Frank, *The Beginnings of the English Newspaper 1620-1660* (Cambridge, Mass., 1961) p. 39; C. V. Wedgwood, *op. cit.* pp. 163-4;
C.S.P.D. 1648-1649 p. 310.
288 For example, *L.J.* V, 4 October 1642; *H.M.C.* Sixth Report, Appendix,
Part I, 'Lords' Manuscripts', p. 130.
289 For example Firth, *Cromwell's Army* p. 258; Mary Coate, *Social
Life in Stuart England* (London, 1924) pp. 159-60; Anne, Lady Halkett,
'Autobiography', *Camden Society* New Series, Vol. 13 (1875) pp. 62-3, 66.
290 *To the Supream authority . . . humble Petition of divers wel-affected Women*
(1649) p. 5, B.M. E.551(14).
291 *Unto every individual member of Parliament: the . . . Representation of . . .
women . . . on behalf of Mr John Lilburn* (1653) B.M. 669 f. 17(36)

There appears to be a contradiction between the female petitioners' admissions of the inferiority of their sex and the intellectual case they made out for the equality of the sexes. It would be fair to say that this contradiction was more than apparent, it was real. However, it is not wholly surprising, for the society in which these women lived, and the air they breathed, was excessively patriarchal. The religious and political crisis caught up women, stimulated them into undertaking unconventional actions and into forming their own opinions on religion and politics. In such an atmosphere, strange speculations and new ideas germinated and flourished riotously. While not overtly challenging masculine superiority, women tentatively put forward justifications for the involvement of women in politics based on the equal rights of men and women. They did not abandon their customary deference to men and to a male-dominated society, but they perceived that 'ye weaker Sex' had rights which in a crisis of church or Commonwealth it could assert; so that it was said of one woman during the civil war that she had been '. . . found playing the good huswife at home (a thing much out of fashion). . . .'[292]

[292] *A Perfect Relation of . . . the Apprehending . . . Mistris Phillips* (1643) p. 2, B.M. E.247(13).

6

The Levellers and Christianity

J. C. Davis

Preface

The intensity and significance of the crisis that English society was undergoing is well illustrated by the outburst of radical ideas and radical movements after the civil war. Englishmen before 1640 were divided into 'the gentleman' and 'the people'—the rulers and the ruled —and the latter were not expected to have political opinions or to take part in politics. But the political and religious controversies, and the collapse of traditional authorities, brought into politics men who had been previously only on the fringes of the governing class, or entirely outside it. They became as critical of parliament as they had been of the king. The ideas of Christianity meant one thing to a well-established aristocrat or squire, but something different to a poor peasant or artisan. Christianity provided the means of measuring the arrangements in this world by the standards of the next, by which they were inevitably found wanting. Thus Christianity supplied a reservoir on which the discontented could draw for criticism of the existing order of things, and for inspiration to rebel. All the radical movements of this period, from the religious fanaticism of the Fifth Monarchists to the legalism and rationalism of the Levellers, drew their basic intellectual inspiration from Christianity. Men outside the governing class tended to develop religious opinions that differed from those of their rulers, and their struggle for religious liberty—liberty to hold, practise and propagate their own religious beliefs—was a struggle against the ruling order, 'The Establishment'. This struggle brought the religious radicals into politics, because they could not obtain religious freedom without political power. So long as the state, whether in the form of king or parliament, controlled the church, and compelled men to conform to a single state-church, whether that church was episcopalian or presbyterian, the struggle for religious liberty was a political struggle. Since religion provided the sanction for secular authority— kings, magistrates, fathers, masters, employers must be obeyed because god commands it and will punish those who disobey—the struggle for the separation of the church from the state and for the toleration of different views in religion, was bound to undermine the authority of kings, magistrates, fathers, masters, employers. And the inspiration for radicalism was not exclusively religious. Men who lived in different ways and have different needs, have different ideas. A village community of small farmers, or an urban community of small merchants and craftsmen, conducted its affairs with a sense of communal responsibility and good neighbourliness, and they translated their ideas from the local to the national community. Their

THE relationship between religious and political thinking in the seventeenth century seems to grow more problematic rather than less, as time goes on. Not only are the traditional religious categories called in question[1] but what has been taken as the substance of specific political theories is shown never to have existed.[2] As interpretations of both the politics and the religion are challenged, relating the two becomes increasingly dangerous.

The influence of religious belief on the Levellers as a group of political thinkers has been seen in three main ways. Most commentators perhaps have followed William Haller in seeing religion as a secondary influence within the movement. 'Its leaders were animated by religious convictions and they were experienced in the organization of religious dissent, but the movement was not a religious but a secular one, aiming to secure certain positive rights and benefits by political action.'[3] Others, however, have seen religion as a primary influence either through the Christian liberty, individualism and egalitarianism professed within the sects or through the example of the voluntaristic and contractual organization of the sectarians' gathered churches.[4]

1 See, for example, C. H. George, 'Puritanism as History and Historiography', *Past and Present* No. 41 (1968), pp. 77–104.
2 For this process in relation to the Levellers see, C. B. Macpherson, *The Political Theory of Possessive Individualism* (Oxford, 1962) Ch. iii, 'The Levellers: Franchise and Freedom'.
3 W. Haller and G. Davies, *The Leveller Tracts, 1647–53* (Columbia, 1944) p. 7. *Cf.* D. M. Wolfe, *Leveller Manifestoes of the Puritan Revolution* (New York, 1944) p. 3; H. N. Brailsford, *The Levellers and the English Revolution* ed. C. Hill (London, 1961) pp. 549–51; H. Holorenshaw, *The Levellers and the English Revolution* (London, 1939) pp. 35–6; D. W. Petegorsky, *Left-Wing Democracy in the English Civil War* (London, 1940) pp. 25, 82; W. Schenk, *The Concern for Social Justice in the Puritan Revolution* (London, 1948) pp. 35, 36, 38; Gertrude Huehns, *Antinomianism in English History* (London, 1951) p. 115.
4 See, for example, P. Zagorin, *A History of Political Thought in the English Revolution* (London, 1954) pp. 12, 14; G. P. Gooch, *English Democratic Ideas in the Seventeenth Century* (Cambridge, 1927) Ch. III; T. C. Pease, *The Leveller Movement* (Washington, 1916) p. 363; D. M. Himbury, 'The

conceptions of democracy, in the form of the limitation of power and social responsibility, were derived from the ideals of local self-governing communities and were applied to the state. In many ways it appears that the ideas of the 'godly middle sort of people' found their fullest expression among the Levellers.

BRIAN MANNING

Yet a third group see the influence of religion as varying over time or from one individual to another within the group.[5]

This essay attempts to show that religion was a primary influence on the Levellers but that the current way of describing that influence is unsatisfactory and produces an unwarranted emphasis on idealism in the political writings of the Levellers.

The main problem for those who have seen the Levellers as a religiously oriented group has been reconciling an apparently élitist religious position with their apparently democratic view of civil society and individual rights. A second problem, and one not so often attempted by historians, is that of explaining how the Levellers' extreme religious individualism did not lead to an anarchist political position as it did, for example, in the early writings of Gerrard Winstanley.[6] Both problems have been resolved in terms of the segregation of the sphere of 'nature', to which man *as man* belonged, from the sphere of 'grace', to which the saints as the elect of God belonged, in Leveller thought.[7] Across the gulf between the two the Levellers are seen as carrying, unconsciously or by analogy, equality, individuality and liberty but not the élitism of election. The rule of natural law over the sphere of nature imposed limits on the application of divine precepts within civil society, just as it was itself relative, conditioned in its performance by the imperfection of natural man. Unfortunately, there is very little real evidence for any process of segregation and analogy in Leveller thought[8] and even less direct evidence for the inspiration of congregational organization.

Religious Beliefs of the Levellers', *The Baptist Quarterly* Vol. 33 (1954); R. M. Jones, *Mysticism and Democracy in the English Commonwealth* (New York, 1932) Ch. V; D. B. Robertson, *The Religious Foundations of Leveller Democracy* (New York, 1951); Howard Shaw, *The Levellers* (London, 1968) p. 4; A. D. Linday, *The Essentials of Democracy* (London, 1935) p. 11.

5 Joseph Frank (*The Levellers* (Cambridge, Mass., 1955)) appears to see religion as a diminishing influence on the Levellers and Richard Overton's 'secularized and pragmatic humanism' as increasingly important (p. 129). Pauline Gregg (*Free-Born John: A Biography of John Lilburne* (London, 1961)) contrasts the religiously motivated Lilburne with Overton, 'the complete rationalist' (p. 113). On Overton as a rationalist see Keith Thomas, *Religion and the Decline of Magic* (London, 1971) p. 313.

6 See D. B. Robertson's discussion of this point, *The Religious Foundations of Leveller Democracy* pp. 105–9.

7 A. S. P. Woodhouse, *Puritanism and Liberty* (London, 1950), Introduction.

8 See L. F. Solt, *Saints in Arms* (London, 1959) Ch. IV; Robertson, *The Religious Foundations of Leveller Democracy* p. 92.

Those who see the Levellers as primarily a secular group do not, of course, have this problem of explaining the transference of values from grace to nature. Nevertheless, these historians insist that the Levellers segregated the two spheres and lay emphasis on the Levellers' argument from natural law. Here the difficulty can be the Levellers' preoccupation, especially in their early works, with religion and religious values in a social context. William Haller, for example, attempts to get round this by arguing that Lilburne confused natural and divine law and so was capable of being weaned from sectarian élitism by infusings of secularism.[9]

If the relationship between the Levellers' religious and political thinking is to be fully understood, however, it must be grasped that, in most important respects, the Levellers never distinguished between natural and divine law.[10] This essential point can be most clearly observed in their teaching on equity and in their inculcation of practical Christianity.

The concept of equity was used constantly throughout the Levellers' agitation and yet very little attention has been paid to it. They included it in their recurrent appeals to 'Justice, Equity and Conscience'.[11] 'I would have such a Government,' Lilburne proclaimed, 'that is founded upon the basis of Freedom, Reason, Justice and Common Equity. . . .'[12] 'Equity' seems to have meant two things to the Levellers. Less frequently and in their early days it was used in a quasi-juridical sense as the spirit rather than the letter of the law, as those general principles of justice by which the execution of the law should be moderated. In this sense, while equity may be above the letter of the law, it is at least related to it: 'for the Law taken abstract from its originall reason and end, is made a shell without a kernel, a shadow without a substance and a body without a soul. It is the execution of Laws according to their equity and reason, which is the spirit that gives life to Authority the Letter kills.'[13]

9 Haller and Davies, *Leveller Tracts* pp. 41-4.
10 *Cf.* Ernst Troeltsch, *The Social Teaching of the Christian Churches* (New York, 1960) Vol. I, p. 344. 'The sects rejected compromise with the world, and therefore also relative Natural Law.' See also Robertson, *Religious Foundations* pp. 50, 58-9, 71.
11 John Lilburne, *Englands Birth Right Justified* (1645) p. 8. See also, *Englands Freedom, Souldiers Rights* (1647) in Wolfe, *Leveller Manifestoes* p. 254.   12 John Lilburne, *Strength out of Weaknesse* (1649) p. 14.
13 Lilburne, *Englands Birth Right* p. 2. See also p. 5 for equity as the true sense or meaning or statute law. *Cf.* Richard Overton, *The Commoners*

Elsewhere, however, and more typically, equity was visualized as something entirely independent of the letter of specific legal enactments or judicial decisions. 'Yea, if the Law should comptroule and overthrow the equity, it is to be comptrouled and overthrowne it selfe, and the equity to be preserved as the thing, only legally, obligatory and binding.'[14] John Wildman saw the equity and the letter of the law as by no means complementary and insisted accordingly that equity be expressed in the wording of statute law.[15] Richard Overton expressed much the same idea in *A Remonstrance of Many Thousand Citizens*. 'Yee know, the Lawes of this Nation are unworthy a Free-People, and deserve from first to last to be considered, and seriously debated and reduced to an agreement with Common equity. . . .'[16]

Clearly, the Levellers were here using the term 'equity' not in a juridical sense but in the general sense of what is fair and right. Once, for example, Overton defined it as 'Justice and plaine dealing', to be contrasted with 'Policies and Court Arts'.[17] In this way the vagueness of the term was increased but at the same time the Levellers endowed it with moral imperatives which are of great significance in understanding the relationship between divine and natural law in their thinking.

The principle of equity frequently finds expression for the Levellers through the golden rule: do unto others as you would be done by.[18] The golden rule was, however, a divine injunction:

Complaint (1647) p. 8; Overton, *An Appeale from the Degenerate Representative Body* (1647) p. 159. Here Overton used almost exactly the same phrase, substituting 'Reason' for 'Equity' in the latter.

14 Overton, *An Appeale* p. 161. *Cf.* the almost identical wording in Overton's *The Hunting of the Foxes or the Grandie Deceivers Unmasked* (1649) in Wolfe, *Leveller Manifestoes* p. 362.

15 John Wildman, *Truths Triumph, or Treachery Anatomized* (1648) p. 11.

16 Richard Overton, *A Remonstrance of Many Thousand Citizens* (1646) p. 15.

17 *ibid.* p. 4.

18 See, for example, William Walwyn, *A Helpe to the right Understanding of a Discourse Concerning Independency* (1645) p. 3; Richard Overton, *The Araignement of Mr. Persecution* (1645) pp. 15, 22; Walwyn, *A Prediction of Mr. Edwards his Conversion and Recantation* (1646) p. 16; (?Walwyn), *No Papist Nor Presbyterian* (1648) in Wolfe, *Leveller Manifestoes* p. 307. In reply to the Levellers an interesting conservative twist on the golden rule was used. ' . . . justice is to render to everyone his owne, and not to do to another what you would not should be done to you'. *A Declaration of Some PROCEEDINGS of Lt. Col. John Lilburne, And his Associates* (1648) p. 39. The argument went on, 'The rich may be oppressed as well as the poor, property is to be preserved to all'.

'the scripture tells me, everyone ought to be fully persuaded in his own mind, and that whatsoever is not faith, is sin: it tells me I must doe as I would be done unto.'[19] In a highly significant phrase Lilburne declared that God had 'ingraved by nature in the soule of Man, this golden and everlasting, principle, to doe to another, as he would have another do to him.'[20] In addition God had provided a model of equitable law-making: 'So likewise, when he came to give a Law to the Israelites, as a Nation in whom he tooke a special delight, he doth not only give them a Law in plaine words without ambiguous termes, short and in their own tongue, unto which they were required to give their consent and gave it: but he also declares it universally given to al men and woemen, rich and poore, without any exception. All which is evident; plain and cleare in Exod. . . .'[21] Consequently it was possible for the Levellers to see the pursuit of equity as a religious obligation and its attainment as a worthy offering. They offered their final Agreement in the name of God, 'desiring the equity thereof may be to his praise and glory. . . .'[22]

But equity and the golden rule were also identifiable with reason. 'Reason is demonstrable of it self, and every man (less or more) is endued with it; and it hath but one ballance to weigh it in, or one touchstone to try it by viz. To teach a man to do as he would be done to.'[23]

In a most important passage in *An Appeale*, Richard Overton argued that reason was above precedent and superior to law; 'severall are its degrees, but its perfection and fulnesse is only in God.' Law had to be based in reason in accordance with three rational principles: self-preservation is a law of reason; 'necessity is the law above all laws'; the equity of the law is superior to the letter. 'Nothing which is against reason is lawfull, Reason being

19 William Walwyn, *A Whisper in the Eare of Mr. Thomas Edwards* (1646) p. 5.
20 John Lilburne, *London's Liberty in Chains* (1646), quoted in Zagorin, *A History of Political Thought in the English Revolution* p. 12. For scripture and law as the twin sources of equity see Lilburne, *The Legall Fundamentall Liberties of the People of England Revived, Asserted, and Vindicated* (1649) p. 20.
21 John Lilburne, *L. Colonel John Lilburne His Apologeticall Narration* (1652) pp. 17–18.
22 John Lilburne, Richard Overton, Thomas Prince, William Walwyn, *An Agreement of the Free People of England* (May 1649) p. 3.
23 Lilburne, *Strength out of Weaknesse* p. 14.

the very life of the Law of our Land: So that should the law be taken away from the Originall reason and end, it would be made a shell without a kernill, a shadow without a substance, a carkasse without life, which presently turns to putrifaction; and as Reason only gives it a legall Being and life, so it only makes it authoritative and binding.' Three pages later he restated the argument, substituting the term 'equity' for that of 'reason'.[24]

The moral imperatives behind equity in Leveller thinking are then both Christian and natural. Natural law is not made a clear concept and is never divorced from divine influence. As far as the notion of equity was concerned, there was no segregation between nature and grace, in fact the two are seen as complementary. 'I say no Power on earth is absolute but God alone, and all other Powers are dependants on him, and those Principles of Reason and Righteousnesse that hee hath indowed man with, upon the true Bassis of which all earthly power or Majestracy ought to be founded, and when a power of Majestracy degenerates from that Rule, by which it is to bee Ruled, and betakes it selfe to its crooked and innovating will, it is to be no more a Power or Majestracy, but an obnoxious Tyranny, to be resisted by all those that would not willingly have man to usurp the soveraigntie of God to Rule by his will and pleasure.'[25]

The explanation of how the Levellers could fail to distinguish between nature and grace and still avoid both secularism and also the political élitism of the presbyterians or Fifth Monarchists, is to be found in the influence of the doctrines of antinomianism and universal salvation on their writing and thinking. This is not to suggest that all of the Levellers were antinomians, but some of them were and their influence is paramount in this respect.[26]

24 Overton, *An Appeale* pp. 158–61.
25 Lilburne, *Strength Out of Weaknesse* pp. 21–2.
26 Lilburne shows evidence of antinomianism: see, for example, *A Copie of a Letter to Mr. William Prinne Esq.* (1645) p. 3. His protestations are usually of salvation rather than of élitist election. See, for example, *A Work of the Beast* (1638); *Come Out of Her my People* (1638) pp. 5–6; *A Coppy of a letter written by J. Lilburne, close prisoner in the wards of the Fleet, which he sent to Iames Ingram and Henry Hopkins* (1640?) p. 6. The influence of Walwyn on him was, as I shall argue, considerable. For Lilburne as rejecting the idea of the elect and tending in the direction of comprehensive grace see D. B. Robertson, *Religious Foundations* pp. 15–16. Overton also shows traces of antinomianism, see for example, *Mans Mortallitie* (1644) p. 5: ' . . . none can be condemned into Hell, but such as are actually guilty of refusing of Christ.' Gertrude Huehns emphasized the influence of

The idea that salvation was provided fully and freely for all men is a marked and consistent feature of Walwyn's writing. In an early tract he argued that the work of redemption was already perfected in Christ's death and that there was nothing more to do. '. . . we are all justified freely by his grace through the redemption that is in Jesus Christ.' '. . . neither infidelity, nor impenitency, nor unthankfulnesse, nor sinne, nor anything whatsoever can make void his purpose.' It was 'a worke perfected, depending on no condition, no performance at all', not even belief.[27]

Walwyn restated this theme in a later work, *The Vanitie of the Present Churches* (February 1649). He believed that the law had been replaced by the gospel and that 'the same Jesus whom the Jewes crucified, was Lord and Christ: That he is the propitiation for our sins, and not only for ours, but for the sins of the whole world, That it is the bloud of Christ which cleanseth us from all our sinne, That his love is so exceeding towards us, that even when we were enemies Christ died for us.'[28]

In April 1649 his enemies charged that 'he did not beleive [sic] that God would punish men for ever for a little time of sinning'.[29] In reply Walwyn proclaimed the importance of antinomianism to him, describing it as 'that *unum necessarium*, that pearle in the field, free justification by Christ alone'.[30]

For those like Walwyn, antinomians and believers in universal salvation, natural and divine law became indistinguishable. Since all men were saved, divine law, God's law made known to the elect, became the universal prescript. Thus natural law and divine law had to be seen as complementary, or rather as mutually inclusive, since both applied to all men.

The development of Lilburne's use of natural law argument illustrates well the influence of Walwyn's ideas, and the antinomian, free-grace views behind them, upon the general course of Leveller thinking. In 1638 Lilburne very sharply attacked the use of 'Philosophy and Logick' as being 'not the inventions or

---

antinomianism in Leveller thought, *Antinomianism in English History* pp. 109, 114. Leo F. Solt, on the other hand, believed that although Walwyn was an antinomian and a believer in universal salvation, he was untypical of the Levellers in these respects, *Saints in Arms* p. 67.

27 William Walwyn, *The Power of Love* (1643) pp. 24, 30–2.
28 William Walwyn, *The Vanitie of the Present Churches* p. 30; see pp. 29–31.
29 (? John Price), *Walwins Wiles or the Manifestators Manifested* (1649) p. 9.
30 William Walwyn, *Walwyns Just Defence* (1649) p. 10; see also p. 8.

Institutions of Jesus Christ nor his Apostles, but of the Divell and Antichrist, with which they mainly and principally have upheld and maintained their black, darke, and wicked King-dome: for Christ nor his Apostles in all their Disputes that ever they had with their Enemies ever made use neither of Logicke nor Philosophy but only of the Authority of the Scripture.'[31]

The problem here is how did Lilburne develop from this position to one where he could argue in terms of natural law and reason? William Haller saw Lilburne's progress to natural law, to an appeal to reason, as passing via the tuition of the legal theorists—St Germain, Henry Parker and above all Coke.[32] There are certainly signs of this in, for example, *Englands Birth Right Justified*, but the problem obviously still bothered Lilburne in that work for he appended to it a discussion of the relationship between natural and divine law. In this, divine law was described as superseding natural law, which was a minimal requirement.[33] Again, where he had ventured to use natural law argument in the body of the tract he had made it subservient always to divine law.[34]

In fact, however, it does not appear to have been the legal theorists who taught Lilburne to use natural law argument, but rather William Walwyn. In *Englands Lamentable Slavery* (which according to Thomason appeared only a few days after *Englands Birth Right Justified*) Walwyn urged Lilburne to drop his arguments from legal precedent and to appeal to natural law. He specifically attacked Lilburne's reliance on Magna Charta as interpreted by Coke. Magna Charta was a dupe, a 'messe of pottage', and 'when so choice a people . . . shall insist upon such inferiour things, neglecting greater matters, and be so unskilfull in the nature of common and just freedom as to call bondage libertie, and the rights of Conquerours their Birth rights, no marvaille such a people make so little use of the greatest advantages; and when

---

31 John Lilburne, *An Answer to Nine Arguments Written by T. B.* (1645) pp. 2–3. Although published in 1645, this tract was written in 1638.

32 Haller and Davies, *The Leveller Tracts* pp. 42–5.

33 Lilburne, *Englands Birth Right Justified* Postscript.

34 *ibid.* p. 7. The argument here was that examination on interrogatories was condemned by natural law but also by the conduct of Christ. The same argument had been used by Lilburne in an earlier work, *A Work of the Beast* (1638) p. 13.

they might have made a newer and better Charter, have falne to patching the old.'[35] Instead Walwyn urged Lilburne to appeal to equity '. . . for any man to be imprisoned without cause declared and witnessed (by more than one appearing face to face) is not only unjust, because expresslie against Magna Carta, but also against all reason, sense, and the Common Law of equitie and justice.'[36]

Although the legal theorists were important in the development of Lilburne's thought it appears to be Walwyn, with his identification of nature and grace, who pushed Lilburne in the direction of appeal to natural law. In January 1647 Lilburne published an attack on English law in the name of reason and nature. 'Observe from hence,' he wrote, 'from what a pure fountain our inslaving Laws, Judges, and Practices in Westminster Hall had their originall; namely from the will of a Conqueror and Tyrant. . . .' Nature taught man to defend himself, reason to do so in accordance with the golden rule of equity. '. . . nature tells me there is a God, reason dictates unto me, that I should speak honourably and reverently of Him.'[37]

Thus the Levellers' recurrent emphasis on equity illustrates a fusion of divine and natural law taking place in their thinking under the influence of antinomianism and in particular under William Walwyn's exposition of it. No doubt these ideas were transmitted with a great deal of vagueness and no small confusion. Nevertheless it is essential to be aware of them if one is to understand the Levellers' political pragmatism and their view of the individual.

The adoption of the idea of universal free grace meant that there could be no segregation between nature and grace in human affairs. Society became, as it were, the invisible church made visible. In Walwyn this produced a political concern with society as a whole and as a sum of individuals. '. . . love makes you no longer your owne but Gods servants, and prompts you to doe his will in the punishment of all kind of exorbitances, whether it be

---

35 William Walwyn, *Englands Lamentable Slavery* (1645) pp. 4–5. Thomason dated *Englands Birth Right Justified* 8 October 1645 and *Englands Lamentable Slavery* 11 October 1645. For a contemporary caricature of Lilburne's dependence on Magna Carta see *The Recantation of Lieutenant Collonel John Lilburne* (1647) p. 5.
36 Walwyn, *Englands Lamentable Slavery* p. 5.
37 John Lilburne, *Regall Tyrannie discovered* (1647) pp. 10, 16.

a breach of oaths, breach of trust or any kinde of injustice in whomsoever, and to be no respecter of persons; nor will any ones greatnesse oversway or daunt your resolutions, but you will be bold as Lions not fearing the forces of men, you will when need requires, that is, when tyrants and oppressors endeavour by might and force to pervert all Lawes, and compacts amongst men, and to pervert the truth of God into a lie. . . .'[38] Richard Overton was in fact suggesting much the same thing when he wrote, 'it is against the Law of Charity, not to doe as we would be done unto.'[39]

This emphasis on equity, blending reason and religion, natural and divine law, is paralleled by and related to another main theme of the Levellers, the theme of practical Christianity: 'were we all busied onely in those short necessary truths,' wrote Walwyn, 'we should soon become practical Christians; and take more pleasure in Feeding the hungry, Cloathing the naked, visiting and comforting the sicke, releeving the aged, weake and impotent; in delivering of prisoners, supporting of poore families or in freeing a Common wealth from all Tyrants, oppressors and deceivers, thereby manifesting our universal love to all mankind, without respect of persons, Opinions, Societies or Churches.'[40]

Like the other Leveller leaders, Walwyn believed that 'the essence of true religion is located in conduct.'[41] St James's definition of pure religion, with its injunction to be not only hearers but doers of the word, was repeated on numerous occasions by Walwyn.[42] But the Levellers as a whole were always 'earnestly desirous to make a right use of that opportunity God hath given us to make this Nation Free and Happy.'[43] Together they endorsed the primacy of practical religion. 'Though we were not so strict upon the formall and ceremoniall part of his service, the method, manner and personall injunction being not so clearly

38 Walwyn, *The Power of Love* p. 39.
39 Overton, *The Araignement of Mr. Persecution* p. 15.
40 Walwyn, *The Vanitie of the Present Churches* p. 43.
41 Zagorin, *A History of Political Thought* p. 25.
42 James 1, 27, see also Matthew 25, 35–9. *Cf.* Walwyn, *A Prediction of Mr. Edwards his Conversion* p. 18; *A Whisper in the Eare of Mr. Thomas Edwards* p. 9; *A Still and Soft Voice* (1647) pp. 7–9; *The Vanitie of the Present Churches* p. 23; *The Compassionate Samaritane* (1645) p. 37. Note also the reporting of Walwyn's holding this view in (?Price), *Walwins Wiles* p. 7.
43 Lilburne, Overton, Prince, Walwyn, *An Agreement of the Free People of England* p. 2.

made out unto us, nor the necessary requisites which his Officers and Ministers ought to be furnished withall as yet appearing to us in any that pretended thereunto: yet for the manifestation of God's love in Christ, it is clearly assented unto by us; and the practicall and most reall part of Religion is as readily submitted unto by us, as being, in our apprehensions, the most eminent and the most excellent in the world as proceeding from no other but that God who is Goodnesse it self.'[44]

The sanction of practical Christianity was both a standard for criticism of those already in power and a spur to renewed political concern and activity. Lilburne's denouncement of the apostasy of the parliamentary party is typical in its critical use of that standard. 'When I seriously consider how many men in the Parliament and else-where of their associates (that judge themselves the onely Saints and godly men upon earth) that have considerable (and some of them vast) estates of their own inheritance, and yet take five hundred, one, two, three, four, five, six thousand pounds per annum salaries, and other comings in by their places . . . when thousands, not onely of the people of the world, as they call them, but also of the precious and redeemed Lambs of Christ, are ready to starve for want of bread, I cannot but wonder with my self, whether they have any conscience at all within them or no, and what they think of that saying of the Spirit of God: that whoso hath this worlds good, and seeth his brother hath need, and shutteth up his bowels of compassion from him . . . how dwelleth the love of God in him?'[45]

In *The Power of Love* Walwyn attacked the lack of charity of the clergy; 'the wants and distresses of the poor will testify that the love of God they have not.' He found that, 'True Christians are of all men the most valiant defenders of the just liberties of their countrye.'[46] He explained his own involvement in politics in terms of 'true religion'. '. . . there is no man weake, but I would strengthen; nor ignorant, but I would informe: nor erronious but I would rectifie, nor vicious but I would reclaim, nor cruel, but I would moderate and reduce to Clemency: I am as

44 John Lilburne, Richard Overton, Thomas Prince, William Walwyn, *A Manifestation* (1649) p. 6.
45 Lilburne, *Legall Fundamentall Liberties* p. 59.
46 Walwyn, *The Power of Love* 'To the Reader', see also p. 37 and *Walwyns Just Defence* pp. 22–4. Lilburne was of the same opinion, see for example, *The Just Defence of John Lilburne* (1653) p. 2.

much grieved that any man should be so unhappy as to be cruel and unjust, as that any man should suffer by cruelty or injustice . . . it is from this disposition in me, that I have engaged myself in publick affairs.' 'I esteeme it a high part of true religion to promote common justice. . . .'[47]

Lilburne saw the spread of practical Christianity as a way of reducing litigation,[48] and the Levellers generally sought in their specific proposals to practise 'true religion'. In the petition of March 1647, for example, they asked for 'powerful means to keep men, women, and children from begging and wickednesse that this nation may be no longer a shame to Christianity therein', and also for a 'just, speedy, plaine and unburthensome way for deciding controversies and suits in Law, and reduce all Lawes to the nearest agreement with Christianity'.[49]

Here, of course, one is very close to the relationship between the Levellers' views of practical Christianity and the religious sanction implicit in their view of equity. On occasion this relationship becomes explicit. In his narration in *A Picture of the Councel of State*, Richard Overton urged that his piety should not be judged by his 'personal infirmities' but by 'my Integrity and Uprightness to the Commonwealth, to whatsoever my understanding tells me is for the good of mankind, for the safety, freedom, and tranquillity of my Country, happinesse and prosperity of my Neighbours, to do to my neighbour as I would be done by, and for the freedom and protection of Religious people. . . .'[50]

The important point about practical Christianity was that, like the Levellers' notion of equity to which it was related, it was a vague and pragmatic concept, providing a strong moral imperative but no precise means of defining forms and procedures:

47 Walwyn, *A Whisper in the Eare of Mr. Thomas Edwards* pp. 3, 5. On occasion, Walwyn visualized socially radical effects arising from the practice of practical Christianity: ' . . . it will empty the fullest Baggs: and pluck downe the highest plumes.' *A Still and Soft Voice* pp. 8–9.

48 Lilburne, *Englands Birth Right Justified* p. 37.

49 *To the Right Honourable and Supreme Authority of this Nation, the Commons in Parliament Assembled* (March 1647) p. 6 clause 12, p. 5 clause 7.

50 John Lilburne, Richard Overton, Thomas Prince, *A Picture of the Councel of State* (1649) p. 43. See also Walwyn, *Walwyns Just Defence*, pp. 10–12. Walwyn here quotes Montaigne on the need for a practised Christianity and justifies himself by saying, 'I recite these passages, because I am in love with them [his adversaries], wishing them also of the same mind, for I wish them no worse then I wish to my self. . . .'

'. . . wherefore,' asked John Wildman, 'have God united people into a body or Society, or Nation? is't not for this that everyone should be helpful each to other and endeavour one anothers good mutually.'[51] The constitutional theorist might be forgiven for thinking that this answer was no answer. But it was precisely the type of answer that the Levellers kept on giving and its vague generality is indicative of their pragmatism.

The Levellers were true pragmatists in the sense that they were concerned about consequences rather than about forms in themselves.[52] Despite all that has been written about them as constitutional idealists and innovators, forms always remained secondary to them. They held with Henry Parker, John Goodwin and Roger Williams that God had endorsed government in general but not any particular form of government.[53]

This naturally had the effect of freeing them from adherence to traditional forms: 'now unto things in themselves disputable and uncertaine,' wrote Walwyn, 'as there is no reason why any man should be bound expressly to any one forme, further than his judgement and conscience doe agree thereunto, even so ought the whole Nation to be free therein to alter and change the publique forme, as may best stand with the safety and freedome of the people. For the Parliament is ever at libertie to make the people more free from burthens and oppressions of any nature but in things appertaining to the universall Rules of common equitie and justice, all men and all Authority in the world are bound.'[54] Here the limitation on pragmatism appears to be equity, which was itself, as applied by the Levellers, a pragmatic concept.

In *Strength Out of Weaknesse*, Lilburne asserted that 'the People may by a common consent alter their Government (for no Form of Civil Government is *Iure Divino*).'[55] Elsewhere the Levellers

51 Wildman, *Truths Triumph* p. 4.
52 See Frank, *The Levellers* Ch. X; Zagorin, *A History of Political Thought* p. 27.
53 John Wildman at the Putney debates declared 'we cannot find anything in the word of God of what is fit to be done in civil matters', but he added significantly that justice, mercy, peace and meekness are of God. Woodhouse, *Puritanism and Liberty* p. 108. *Cf.* Henry Parker, *Observations Upon Some of his Majesties late Answers and Expresses* (1642) p. 1; John Goodwin, *Anti-Cavalierisme* (1642) pp. 7–8; Roger Williams, *The Bloudy Tenent* (1644) p. 196.
54 Walwyn, *Englands Lamentable Slavery* p. 6.
55 Lilburne, *Strength out of Weaknesse* p. 12.

suggested that the life of all things was in their right use and application, not in the forms they took;[56] 'the just freedom and happiness of a Nation, being above all constitutions, whether of Kings, Parliaments or any other'.[57] This was felt to be so too in relation to church government. They repeatedly pronounced themselves prepared to accept an unspecified form of state-sponsored church provided that there was no coercion of individuals.[58]

Walwyn adopted the same pragmatic approach in his search for true doctrine. 'I carry with me in all places,' he wrote, 'a Touchstone that tryeth all things and labours to hold nothing but what upon plain grounds appeareth good and usefull: I abandon all niceties and useless things: my manner is in all disputes reasonings and discourses, to enquire what is the use: and if I find it not very materiall, I abandon it, there are plain usefull doctrines sufficient to give peace to my mind: direction and comfort to my life: and to draw all men to a consideration of things evidently usefull, hath been a speciall cause that I have applyed my selfe in a friendly manner unto all.'[59]

Many of the utterances of the Levellers appear obviously question-begging, expressive of the confused, good intentions of the apolitical: 'That as the Laws ought to be equal, so they must be good, and not evidently destructive to the safety and well being of the people.'[60] In A Manifestation, the Leveller leaders justified the efforts of their dying campaign on the grounds that 'if it produces not so good a settlement as ought to be, yet certainly it will prevent its being so bad as otherwise it would be.'[61] These rather callow statements become more readily understood if the essential Christian pragmatism which stands behind them be remembered.

This can also help to explain the Levellers' willingness to chop

56 Lilburne, Overton, Prince, Walwyn, *An Agreement of the Free People o, England* (1649) p.2.
57 Walwyn, *The Bloody Project* p. 13.
58 See, for example, Lilburne, *A Copie of a Letter to Mr. William Prynne* p. 7. As D. B. Robertson points out, 'Establishment *per se* was not the question', *Religious Foundations* p. 8.
59 Walwyn, *A Whisper in the Eare of Mr. Thomas Edwards* p. 10.
60 *An Agreement of the People for a firme and present Peace, upon grounds of common-right and freedome* (November 1647) clause IV, reserve 5, in Wolfe, *Leveller Manifestoes* p. 228.
61 Lilburne, Overton, Prince, Walwyn, *A Manifestation* p. 4.

and change the details of their programmatic statements, their little analysed but remarkable constitutional inconsistency.[62] It was possible for them to appear as republicans and as constitutional monarchists,[63] to take a democratic stance and then advocate a severely limited franchise,[64] or to say nothing about the franchise at all,[65] because these, while important, were not the essence. They were more concerned with the quality of administration than with constitutional forms, although they recognized that the former could be influenced by the latter: 'give us but Common Right, some foundations, some boundaries, some certainty of Law, and a good Government; that now when there is so high discourse of Freedom, we may be delivered from will, power, and meere arbitrary discretion, and we shall be satisfied.'[66] Like others, they were not 'wedded and glued to forms of government'.

Even the proposal of an Agreement of the People was only a device, never an article of faith with them. They might assert the correct way of introducing such an Agreement but, in itself, it was never a cardinal feature of their activity. The fact that they produced three different versions within a year and a half is indicative of their pragmatic attitude to it.

The importance of the Agreements in Leveller strategy and

62 See J. C. Davis, 'The Levellers and Democracy', *Past and Present* No. 40 (1968) p. 180.
63 For examples of the Levellers as republicans, see John Wildman, *Putney Projects or the Old Serpent in a new Forme* (1647) pp. 15–22; John Lilburne, *Englands New Chains Discovered* (1649) p. 159; as monarchists, John Lilburne, *An Impeachment of High Treason against Oliver Cromwel, and his son in Law Henry Ireton Esquires* (1649) p. 8; Lilburne, *Strength Out of Weaknesse* p. 12; Lilburne, *Come Out of her my People* p. 14.
64 For examples of the Levellers as democrats, see John Lilburne, *Rash Oaths Unwarrantable* (1647) p. 50; as exponents of a limited franchise, *To the Supream Authority of England, the Commons assembled in Parliament. The Earnest Petition of many Free-born People of this Nation* (January 1648), in Wolfe, *Leveller Manifestoes* p. 269. See also the discussion in Keith Thomas, 'The Levellers and the Franchise', in G. E. Aylmer (ed.), *The Interregnum: The Quest For Settlement 1646–1660* (London, 1972) pp. 57–78.
65 *To the Right Honourable the Commons of England in Parliament Assembled. The humble Petition of divers wel affected Persons* (September 1648) in Wolfe, *Leveller Manifestoes*, pp. 283–90. (Henceforth referred to as the petition of 11 September 1648.) This called for annual elections but said nothing on the franchise although it was subsequently considered by the Levellers to be a most important statement.
66 Walwyn, *Walwyn's Just Defence* p. 5.

thinking has been generally overrated. The Levellers never suggested that an Agreement of the People was the only means by which a national settlement could be attained. They appear to have seen the device in a more limited way, as a medium for joint action with the army and in fact the army was indispensable to the strategy of the Agreement because it offered the only feasible means of popular subscription on a national basis. The third Agreement of 1 May 1649 is the only Leveller Agreement addressed directly to the nation and even here the document appeals over the heads of the officers to the mutinous regiments of the army. Lilburne and Wildman, the main exponents of the Agreement idea among the civilian Levellers, had also the strongest military connections and background. The idea itself may have originated in the example of the army's Solemn Engagement of June 1647, rather than in covenant theology. Rainborough asked significantly, at the Putney debates, that the Levellers' first Agreement be judged by the standard of the Solemn Engagement.[67] The idea of an Agreement appears to have had no independent appeal to the Levellers. As early as April 1645, Overton had suggested a national covenant to engage everyone in public freedom,[68] but during the next two and a half years there was no response from his colleagues.

The Agreement then was a compromise device used when the Levellers wished to work with the army. Their flexibility in relation to its details and implementation can best be illustrated by their changing attitude to the officers' Agreement, presented to the House of Commons in January 1649. In June 1649 Lilburne roundly condemned it and its presentation to parliament, as contrary to the whole spirit of an Agreement.[69] Yet two months earlier, in April, Lilburne and Overton had offered to be satisfied with the officers' Agreement, subject to some amendment of the clauses concerning religious liberty.[70] In A Manifestation, also published in April, the Leveller leaders had proclaimed that they would have accepted the officers' Agreement had it been put in

---

67 Woodhouse, *Puritanism and Liberty* p. 47. The whole issue involved in the preliminary dispute over engagements has to be seen against this background.
68 Overton, *The Araignement of Mr. Persecution* p. 30.
69 Lilburne, *Legall Fundamentall Liberties* pp. 35–41. See also Lilburne's detailed criticisms in *Engands New Chains Discovered.*
70 Lilburne, Overton, Prince, *A Picture of the Councel of State* pp. 22, 37.

execution.[71] As late as May 1652 Lilburne was still urging the
Grandees to go back to it.[72] Indeed the Levellers' rejection of
the officers' Agreement of January 1649, and the breach with the
Independent and Baptist congregations that this apparently
resulted in, has never been satisfactorily explained.

The use of Agreements remained an extraordinary device, and
the Levellers went on petitioning. After each of their failures to
negotiate an Agreement with the army they reverted to petitions.
Moreover, it was in their petitions that the Levellers advanced
their original constitutional ideas, as they did, for example, in
The Case of the Army and the great petitions of November 1647,
January 1648 and September 1648. The last of these, the petition
of 11 September 1648, has been rightly described as 'the most
important of the Levellers' proposals'.[73] The point here is that,
although it said nothing about the franchise, the Levellers appear
to have regarded it as in many ways more important than their
second (December 1648) and third (May 1649) Agreements.

In their petition of January 1649 they described themselves as
'Presenters and Promoters of the late Large Petition of September 11 MDCXLVIII' rather than as promoters of the Second
Agreement.[74] Again in March 1649 Lilburne, Overton and Prince
described themselves as 'presenters and approvers of the later
large Petition of the Eleventh of September 1648'.[75] Against the
charge of economic levelling readers were referred to the September petition rather than the second Agreement, although such a
purpose was disavowed in both documents.[76] Even later, after

71 Lilburne, Overton, Prince, Walwyn, *A Manifestation* p. 7.
72 Lilburne, *As You Were* (1652) cited in Haller and Davies, *Leveller
   Tracts* p. 32.
73 Brailsford, *The Levellers* p. 350. See also Haller and Davies, *Leveller
   Tracts* p. 147. Thomas May described it as the petition 'which broke the
   Ice' with regard to demands for justice against Charles I and the fomen-
   tors of the second civil war. Thomas May, *A Breviary of the History of the
   Parliament of England* (1655) in Maseres, *Select Tracts* (1815) Vol. I, p. 127.
74 *To the Right Honourable, the Supreme Authority of this Nation, The Commons
   of England in Parliament Assembled. The humble Petition of firm and constant
   Friends to the Parliament and Common-wealth, Presenters and Promotors of the
   late Large Petition of September 11 MDCXLVIII* (19 January 1649).
   Lilburne similarly described his followers on the title page of *Englands
   New Chains Discovered*, a petition presented to the Rump on 26 February
   1649.
75 John Lilburne, Richard Overton, Thomas Prince, *The Second Part of
   Englands New Chains Discovered* (March 1649) title page.
76 Lilburne, Overton, Prince, Walwyn, *A Manifestation* p. 4. See the Petition

the publication of their third Agreement (1 May 1649), the Leveller leaders were still appealing back to the petition of 11 September 1648 as the full and crucial statement.[77]

This process of appealing, beyond the second and third Agreements, back to the September petition may indicate that, in negotiating with the army, the Leveller leaders had risked alienating their London support and that in their breach with the Grandees they sought to appeal to a platform which had united that support. More important in this context, however, the willingness to shift tactics, the flexibility in relation to forms that the Levellers reveal, is symptomatic of their fundamental pragmatism.

That pragmatism, however, was conditioned by a morality basically Christian, expressed in terms of equity and practical Christianity. It was modified by a view of man which gave them their one element of formal consistency.

It has been rightly insisted by Macpherson that the Levellers' theory of possessive individualism or human self-propriety forms a key feature of their thought.[78] What has not been sufficiently emphasized is that the Levellers saw man primarily as a moral entity or agency and that their view of self-propriety was conditioned by this. It is true that, while a writer like Henry Robinson saw self-propriety only by analogy,[79] the Levellers saw it as rooted in the nature of man.[80] Nevertheless, for them a man's property in himself was a limited property, over which he could exercise only a limited control, the function of which was a moral and religious stewardship.[81]

---

of 11 September 1648 p. 6; *Foundations of Freedom; or an Agreement of the People* (December 1648) in Wolfe, *Leveller Manifestoes* p. 301.

77 Walwyn, *Walwyn's Just Defence* (May/June? 1649) p. 27; Richard Overton, *The Baiting of the Great Bull of Bashan Unfolded and Presented to the Affecters and approvers of the PETITION of the 11 Sept. 1648* (July 1649) p. 42; Lilburne, *An Impeachment of High Treason* (August 1649) pp. 1, 5; Lilburne, *Strength Out of Weaknesse* (October 1649) p. 2.

78 Macpherson, *The Political Theory of Possessive Individualism* Ch. III and pp, 3, 265–7.

79 See, for example, Henry Robinson, *Liberty of Conscience* (1644) pp. 19, 38, 40.

80 See, for example, Richard Overton, *An Arrow Against All Tyrants and Tyranny* (1646), p. 3: 'To every individual in nature is given an individuall property by nature . . .'; p. 5 'For by nature we are the sons of Adam, and from him have legitimately derived a naturall propriety, right and freedome. . . .'

81 *Cf.* Macpherson, *Possessive Individualism* p. 158. 'They can claim the

The Levellers did not conceive man's right of possession in his own person and capacities as absolute. Man, in relation to himself, had, as it were, a leasehold rather than freehold. His property was limited since in certain respects he could not alienate it. The most important of these inalienable prerogatives was his capacity for religious belief. Moreover, this was not only inalienable, but the individual himself was seen as having little control over it. In *A Compassionate Samaritane* Walwyn argued that man must *necessarily* follow his own reason and arrive at his own conclusions regarding religious belief.[82] Elsewhere, he wrote, 'I have no quarrell to any man, either for unbeleefe or misbeleefe because I judge no man beleeveth any thing but what he cannot choose but beleeve.'[83] Since 'whatsoever is not of faith is sin' man's property in his conscience was both naturally and morally inalienable.[84] It followed that 'no man can refer matters of religion to any other regulation. And what cannot be given cannot be received. . . .' Therefore the civil magistrate had no authority in matters of religion.[85]

Overton reached the same conclusion in a very similar way. There could be no compulsion in religion, 'for wee could not conferre a Power that was not in ourselves, there being none of us, that can without wilfull sinne binde ourselves to worship God after any other way, then what (to a tittle) in our owne particular understandings, wee approve to be just.'[86]

The limitations on one's rights to exploit one's capacity, to alienate aspects of one's property in oneself, also extended to man's capacity to injure himself and to injure others.[87] It was this inalienable and limited quality of self-propriety, that enabled Sexby at Putney to distinguish between it and real property: 'We

---

distinction of being the first political theorists to assert a natural right to property for which the individual owes nothing to society and which entails none of those duties entailed in the earlier doctrine of stewardship.'

82 Walwyn, *Compassionate Samaritane* p. 7.
83 Walwyn, *A Still and Soft Voice* p. 15.
84 Walwyn, *A Prediction of Mr. Edwards his Conversion* p. 4; *Compassionate Samaritane* p. 43.
85 Walwyn, *A helpe to the right understanding of a Discourse concerning Independency* p. 4. See Macpherson, *Possessive Individualism* p. 145.
86 Overton, *A Remonstrance* p. 12.
87 See, for example, Walwyn, *The Bloody Project* pp. 1–4; Overton, *An Arrow Against All Tyrants* p. 4.

have had little propriety in the kingdom as to our estates, yet we have had a birthright.'[88]

Most important, it was from this concept of limited self-propriety that the notion of limited government so characteristic of the Levellers was derived. Richard Overton demonstrated the link between the two most clearly. '. . . all iust humaine powers,' he argued, 'are but betrusted, confer'd and conveyed by ioynt and common consent, for to every individual in nature, is given an individuall propriety by nature, not to be invaded or usurped by any (as in mine Arrow against tyranny is proved and dis-covered more at large) for every one as he is himselfe hath a selfe propriety, else could not be himselfe, and on this no second may presume without consent.' But at the same time governments were impowered by men only 'for their severall weales, safeties and freedomes, and no otherwise: for as by nature, no man may abuse, beat, torment or afflict himself; so by nature, no man may give that power to another, seeing he may not doe it himselfe, for no more can be communicated from the generall then is in-cluded in the particulars, whereof the generall is compounded.'[89] This was what Overton called, on occasion, the 'defensive prin-ciple'. Against it 'no degrees, orders or titles amongst men can or may prevaill, all degrees, orders and titles, all Lawes, Customs and manners amongst men must be subject to give place and yeeld thereunto, and it unto none, for all degrees and titles Magisteriall, whether emperiall, regall, Parliamentarie, or other-wise are all subservient to popular safety . . . for without it can be no humane society, cohabitation or being, which above all earthly things must be maintained, as the earthly soveraigne good of mankind, let what or who will perish, or be confounded, for mankind must be preserved upon the earth and to this preserva-tion, all the Children of men have an equall title by Birth, *none to be deprived thereof*, but such as are enemies thereto, and this is the groundwork that God in nature hath laid for all commonwealths, for all Governours and Governments amongst men, for all their laws executions and administrations.'[90]

This last point brings out the third aspect of self-propriety as

88 Woodhouse, *Puritanism and Liberty* p. 69.
89 Overton, *An Appeale*, in Wolfe, *Leveller Manifestoes* p. 162, *Cf*. Overton, *An Arrow Against All Tyrants* p. 4.
90 Overton, *An Appeale*, in Wolfe, *Leveller Manifestoes* p. 178. (My italics.)

the Levellers saw it. Not only was it limited and in part inalienable. It was also God-given, a trust to be exercised with traditional Christian stewardship. 'From this fountain or root,' wrote Overton of self-propriety, 'all just humaine powers take their original; not immediately from God (as Kings usually plead their prerogative) but mediatly by the hand of nature, as from the represented to the representors; for originally, God hath implanted them in the creature, and from the creature those powers immediately proceed; and no further: and no more may be communicated then stands for the better being, weale, or safety thereof: and this is mans prerogative and no further, so much and no more may be given or received thereof: even so much as is conducent to a better being, more safety and freedome, and no more; he that gives more, sins against his owne flesh. . . .'[91] Walwyn believed that the right, the equitable exercise of a man's self-propriety would 'empty the fullest Baggs: and pluck downe the highest plumes'.[92]

The Levellers' recurrent emphasis on practical Christianity is itself illustrative of their belief that it was only as stewards that men held their own persons. '. . . no man is born for himself only,' they declared in 1648, 'but obliged by the Laws of Nature (which reaches all) of Christianity (which engages us as Christians) and of Publick Societie and Government, to employ our endeavours for the advancement of a communitative Happinesse, of equall concernment to others as ourselves. . . .'[93]

In consequence of this the individual had definite conscientious obligations which could not be delegated. Walwyn believed that those who sought true religion must try all faiths: ''tis your selfe must doe it, you are not to trust to the authority of any man, or to any man's relation: you will finde upon tryall that scarcely any opinion hath been truly reported to you.'[94] Or again, 'Whatsoever is not founded on faith is sin, and . . . every man ought to be fully persuaded of the trueness of that way wherein he serveth the Lord.'[95]

Similarly Lilburne argued that one of the two great evils facing

---

91 Overton, *An Arrow Against All Tyrants* p. 4.
92 Walwyn, *A Still and Soft Voice* pp. 8–9.
93 Lilburne, Overton, Prince, Walwyn, *A Manifestation* p. 3. See also Walwyn, *Power of Love* p. 39.   94 Walwyn, *Power of Love* p. 97.
95 Walwyn, *A Compassionate Samaritane* p. 43; Cf. Walwyn, *A Whisper in the Eare of Mr. Thomas Edwards* p. 5; *A Prediction of Mr. Thomas Edwards his Conversion* p. 40; *The Vanitie of the Present Churches* p. 50.

those who professed religion was 'living upon other mens light, takeing all for Gospel which Learned men say without tryall'. 'Carnal Professours' such as these were satisfied with forms only.[96] This attitude spilled over into Lilburne's political activity. He was reported by his enemies as insisting with his agents on the necessity 'to inform the people of their Liberties and Privileges; and not only to get their hands to the Petition, for (said he) I would not give three pence for ten thousand hands.'[97] Because of the commission with which he was entrusted man's activity had to be conscientious.

If this were to be so, however, if men were to act conscientiously in their relations with God and with other men, if they were to exercise their self-propriety as real stewards, then they must be free from compulsion or restraint in matters of conscience. The Levellers' demand for toleration thus sprang from their assumptions about self-propriety and its limited nature. Moreover, not only was this essential demand for freedom of belief and practice the most consistent feature of the Leveller programme, it was also the basis upon which were built in pragmatic fashion, all their further constitutional demands.

The consistency of the Levellers in demanding liberty of conscience is generally recognized. All three of their Agreements of the People set down as the first power withheld from government that of compulsion in religious observance. They were all equally clear against military impressment.[98] The fact that some of the Levellers seem to have believed that the fight for liberty of conscience was the primary purpose of the movement is not so frequently commented upon by historians.

'Of all liberty,' wrote Walwyn, 'liberty of conscience is the greatest; and where that is not a true Christian findeth none.'[99] In 1646 he believed that this was the main issue at stake. He held the same view three years later.[100] Captain Clarke, at the White-

96 Lilburne, *An Answer to Nine Arguments* 'To the Reader'; *Come Out of Her my People* p. 4. *Cf.* Walwyn's 'morall Christians', *A Still and Soft Voice* pp. 2–3.
97 *A Declaration of Some Proceedings* p. 14. See also Walwyn's, *The Bloody Project*, for instance, on this in relation to war service.
98 Wolfe, *Leveller Manifestoes* pp. 227, 300, 405.
99 Walwyn, *A Word More* p. 5, quoted in Schenk, *The Concern for Social Justice* p. 48.
100 Walwyn, *A Whisper in the Eare of Mr. Thomas Edwards* p. 12; *Walwyn's Just Defence* pp. 3–4.

hall debates, saw the important petition of 11 September 1648 as principally concerned with freedom of conscience.[101] Lilburne himself believed the same issue to have been the stumbling block in negotiations between the army, the Independents and the Levellers in late 1648.[102]

Even a superficial review of the early history of the Levellers reveals how their political programme grew out of their anxiety over freedom of conscience. The polemical careers of Lilburne, Walwyn and Overton all began, in the late 1630s and early 1640s, with demands for religious freedom and assaults on the pursuit of heresy by the established authorities. In 1645 the renewed threat from the Presbyterians and the imprisonment of John Lilburne drew those three together. In the first four months of that year, Walwyn produced *The Compassionate Samaritane* and *A helpe to the right understanding of a Discourse concerning Independency*; Lilburne published *A Copie of a letter to Mr. William Prinne, Esquire*,[103] and Overton, *The Araignement of Mr. Persecution*. All these tracts were concerned with religious liberty and the Presbyterian threat to it.

In May and June 1645, Lilburne was before the Committee of Examinations concerning his part in the controversy with Prynne, and more particularly for his remarks on the power of magistrates in religious matters. At this time, he and Walwyn appear to have been in direct association.[104] They were both involved in the action against Lenthall which led to Lilburne's arrest on 19 July.

From July to October 1645, Lilburne was in prison and this provided the second focus around which a 'coherent and purposeful' group developed.[105] When he published *Englands Birth Right Justified* in October, Lilburne still presented freedom of conscience as the central issue.[106] In order to defend it, however, he felt obliged to deal with the distinction between the equity and the letter of the law, with the logic of parliament's fight for freedom, the danger of vested interests, foremost among which

---

101 Woodhouse, *Puritanism and Liberty* p. 141.
102 Lilburne, *Legall Fundamentall Liberties* pp. 34–5.
103 Haller suggested that this was printed by Richard Overton or someone associated with him. *Tracts on Liberty in the Puritan Revolution* Vol. III, p. 179.
104 Gregg, *Free-Born John* pp. 116–19.
105 *ibid.* p. 134.
106 Lilburne, *Englands Birth Right Justified* Preamble.

was the monopoly of preaching, and the injustice of the Solemn League and Covenant. Thus an accretion of political and legal attitudes was building around the basic cause of liberty of conscience.

Similarly, in *Englands Lamentable Slavery* (October 1645) Walwyn argued that liberty of conscience was the main issue but that in order to secure it the authorities must be made accountable. His attitude to forms remained pragmatic. They were to be judged by the liberty they secured.[107]

In 1646 while the fight for liberty of conscience was still to the fore,[108] the imprisonment of Lilburne by the House of Lords in June, followed by that of Overton in August, renewed the Levellers' awareness that the issue of that fight was bound up with legal and constitutional problems. The relevance of these constitutional concerns to those of religious freedom and the Levellers' view of man's limited self-propriety is well illustrated in Overton's *A Remonstrance of Many Thousand Citizens* (July 1646). Here, after protesting against Lilburne's imprisonment, Overton argued that parliament was merely a convenience, chosen by the people for their welfare and endowed by them with a strictly limited trust. It followed that their powers in relation to church government must be limited too. 'Yee may propose what Forme yee conceive best, and most available for Information and well-being of the Nation, and may perswade and invite thereunto, but compell, yee cannot justly; for ye have no Power from Us to doe, nor could you have; for wee could not conferre a Power that was not in our selves, there being none of us that can without wilfull sinne bind our selves to worship God after any other way, then what (to a tittle) in our owne particular under-standings we approve to be just.'[109]

An Arrow Against All Tyrants (October 1646) was directed by Overton against the twin threats from the House of Lords' illegal claim to jurisdiction over commoners and from 'the most un-naturall, tyrannical, bloodthirsty desires and continuall endevours of the Clergy, against the contrary minded in matters of conscience'.[110] Although the tract was concerned primarily with the

107 Walwyn, *Englands Lamentable Slavery* pp. 6–7.
108 Walwyn wrote seven tracts on liberty of conscience between January and October 1646.
109 Overton, *A Remonstrance* p. 12.
110 Overton, *An Arrow Against All Tyrants* pp. 6, 12.

constitutional and legal threat emanating from the House of Lords, Overton thought it appropriate to begin with his fullest exposition of the concept of self-propriety.

This was merely carried a stage further in the Levellers' petition of March 1647. Here again the two most important areas of concern, religious freedom and legal rights, were seen as interconnected,[111] but specific constitutional reforms were now proposed. The burning of this petition by order of the House of Commons in May 1647 sealed the emergence of the Levellers as a movement of constitutional reform. They could now visualize England as returned to a state of nature and consequently accept as necessary the strategy of appealing to the army and through it to the people at large.

The constitutional proposals of the Levellers were thus in part derived from their fear that, without some such arrangements, freedom of conscience could not be guaranteed. At the Whitehall debates Clarke argued that, since the magistrate had always usurped power over conscience, they ought now to reserve it.[112] What D. B. Robertson has said of the third Agreement may be applied to the whole Leveller effort to find an acceptable constitution: it was 'an attempt . . . to prevent men from getting into a position to molest their neighbours.'[113]

That men in power would be tempted to excess, to violation of the self-propriety of others, was something that the Leveller leaders recognized early in their activity: 'standing water will speedily corrupt, if it have not fresh running springs to feed it, though it were never so pure at first'.[114] At Whitehall, Wildman argued that the magistrate was 'more probable to err than the people that have no power in their hands, the probability is greater that he will destroy what is good than prevent what is evil'.[115] 'We have proposed such an Establishment,' professed the Leveller leaders in one of their last joint statements, 'as supposing men to be too flexible and yeelding to world Temptations, they should not yet have a means or opportunity either to injure

---

111 To the Right Honourable and Supreme Authority of this Nation, the Commons in Parliament assembled (March 1647), in Wolfe, Leveller Manifestoes p. 136.

112 Woodhouse, Puritanism and Liberty pp. 141–2.

113 Robertson, Religious Foundations p. 104.

114 Lilburne, Englands Birth Right Justified p. 33.

115 Woodhouse, Puritanism and Liberty p. 161.

particulars, or prejudice the Publick, without extreme hazard and apparent danger to themselves.'[116]

In this respect, the third Agreement only epitomizes what is to be found elsewhere. The concern there shown for the details of representation, legislative quorums, the ineligibility of public officials for election, the restriction against the election of the same people to successive Representatives; the fundamental provisions against compulsion or interference in religion, against impressment, self-incrimination, legal injustice, trade restrictions and more besides; all these things stem from the fear that those in authority, if unchecked, would not leave individuals free to exercise their stewardship in their own persons: 'having by wofull experience found the prevalence of corrupt interests powerfully inclining most men once entrusted with authority, to pervert the same to their own domination and to the prejudice of our Peace and Liberties. . . .'[117]

William Haller once wrote that for the Levellers, 'there could be no liberty without toleration. . . .'[118] It would be truer to say that for them there could be no toleration without civil liberty. The distinction is more than a marginal one for without it one fails to appreciate the fact that their programmatic statements were pragmatically conceived; that their pragmatism was modified by Christian values expressed in their doctrines of equity and practical Christianity, and by their concept of man's limited self-propriety, that is to say by the fundamental place of traditional Christian stewardship in their social thinking.

116 Lilburne, Overton, Prince, Walwyn, *A Manifestation* p. 7.
117 Lilburne, Overton, Prince, Walwyn, *An Agreement of the Free People of England* p. 5.
118 Haller, *Tracts on Liberty* Vol. I, p. 87. *Cf.* Zagorin, *A History of Political thought* p. 7.

Select Bibliography

The Aristocracy

Aylmer, G. E., *The King's Servants: the Civil Service of Charles I, 1625–1642* (London, 1961)

Firth, C. H., *The House of Lords During the Civil War* (London, 1910)

Gardiner, S. R., *History of England from the Accession of James I to the Outbreak of the Civil War, 1603–1642* (10 vols., London, 1883–4)
History of the Great Civil War 1642–1649 (4 vols., London, 1893)

Hexter, J. H., *Reappraisals in History* (London, 1961): 'The Education of the Aristocracy in the Renaissance'; 'Storm Over the Gentry'.
The Reign of King Pym (London, 1941)

Hill, Christopher, *Economic Problems of the Church from Archbishop Whitgift to the Long Parliament* (Oxford, 1956)

Jones, G. F. Trevallyn, *Saw-Pit Wharton: The Political Career from 1640 to 1691 of Philip, fourth Lord Wharton* (Sydney, 1967)

Mathew, David, *The Age of Charles I* (London, 1951)
The Social Structure in Caroline England (Oxford, 1948)

Neale, J. E., 'The Elizabethan Political Scene', *Proceedings of the British Academy* Vol. XXXIV (1948), reprinted in *The Age of Catherine de Medici and Essays in Elizabethan History* (London, 1963)

Newton, A. P., *The Colonising Activities of the English Puritans* (New Haven, 1914) (reprinted New York, 1966)

Prestwich, Menna, *Cranfield: Politics and Profits under the Early Stuarts. The Career of Lionel Cranfield, Earl of Middlesex* (Oxford, 1966)

Snow, V. F., 'Essex and the Aristocratic Opposition to the Early Stuarts', *The Journal of Modern History* Vol. XXXII (1960)

Stone, Lawrence, *The Crisis of the Aristocracy* (Oxford, 1965)

Thomson, A., 'John Holles', *The Journal of Modern History* Vol. VIII (1936)

Willson, D. H., *The Privy Councillors in the House of Commons, 1604–1629* (Minneapolis, 1940)

Wormald, B. H. G., *Clarendon: Politics, History and Religion, 1640–1660* (Cambridge, 1951)

Zagorin, Perez, *The Court and the Country: the beginning of the English Revolution* (London, 1969)

The Middle Rank of the People

Campbell, Mildred, *The English Yeoman under Elizabeth and the Early Stuarts* (New Haven, 1942) (reprinted, London, 1960)

Cooper, J. P., 'Differences between English and Continental Governments in the Early Seventeenth Century', *Britain and the Netherlands* Vol. I, ed. J. S. Bromley and E. H. Kossmann (London, 1960)

Hexter, J. H., *Reappraisals in History* (London, 1961): 'The Myth of the Middle Class in Tudor England'

Hill, Christopher, *Society and Puritanism in Pre-Revolutionary England* (London, 1964)

Hill, Christopher and Dell, Edmund, *The Good Old Cause: The English Revolution of 1640–60* (London, 1949) (revised edition, London, 1969)

Hoskins, W. G., *The Midland Peasant* (London, 1957)
'The Rebuilding of Rural England, 1570–1640', *Past and Present* No. 4 (1953)

Howell, Roger, *Newcastle upon Tyne and the Puritan Revolution* (Oxford, 1967)

James, Margaret, *Social Problems and Policy during the Puritan Revolution 1640–1660* (London, 1930)

Laslett, Peter, *The World We have lost* (London, 1965)

MacCaffrey, Wallace T., *Exeter, 1540–1640* (Cambridge, Mass., 1958)

Macpherson, C. B., *The Political Theory of Possessive Individualism* (Oxford, 1962)

Mathew, David, *The Social Structure in Caroline England* (Oxford, 1948)

Notestein, Wallace, *The English People on the Eve of Colonization, 1603–1630* (London, 1954)

Pearl, Valerie, *London and the Outbreak of the Puritan Revolution* (Oxford, 1961)

Plumb, J. H., 'The Growth of the Electorate in England 1600–1715', *Past and Present* No. 45 (1969)

Stone, Lawrence, 'Social Mobility in England, 1500–1700', *Past and Present* No. 33 (1966)

Tawney, R. H., *Religion and the Rise of Capitalism* (London, 1926)

Unwin, George, *Industrial Organization in the 16th and 17th Centuries* (Oxford, 1904) (reprinted, London, 1957)

Wright, Louis B., *Middle-Class Culture in Elizabethan England* (Chapel Hill, 1935) (reprinted, New York, 1958)

The Puritans

Babbage, S. B., *Puritanism and Richard Bancroft* (London, 1962)

Cliffe, J. T., *The Yorkshire Gentry from the Reformation to the Civil War* (London, 1969)

Collinson, Patrick, *The Elizabethan Puritan Movement* (London, 1967)

'The Beginnings of English Sabbatarianism', *Studies in Church History* I (1964)

Crosse, Claire, *The Puritan Earl: the life of Henry Hastings, third Earl of Huntingdon, 1536–1595* (London, 1966)
The Royal Supremacy in the Elizabethan Church (London, 1969)

Dickens, A. G., *The English Reformation* (London, 1964)

Everitt, A. M., *The Community of Kent and the Great Rebellion 1640–60* (Leicester, 1966)

George, C. H., 'Puritanism as History and Historiography', *Past and Present* No. 41 (1968)

George, C. H. and Katherine, *The Protestant Mind of the English Reformation 1570–1640* (Princeton, 1961)

Hall, Basil, 'Puritanism: The Problem of Definition', *Studies in Church History* II (1965)

Haller, William, *The Rise of Puritanism* (New York, 1938)
Liberty and Reformation in the Puritan Revolution (New York, 1955)
Foxe's Book of Martyrs and the Elect Nation (London, 1963)

Hill, Christopher, *Economic Problems of the Church from Archbishop Whitgift to the Long Parliament* (Oxford, 1956)
Puritanism and Revolution (London, 1958)
Society and Puritanism in Pre-Revolutionary England (London, 1964)
Intellectual Origins of the English Revolution (Oxford, 1965)

Howell, Roger, *Newcastle upon Tyne and the Puritan Revolution* (Oxford, 1967)

Jordan, W. K., *The Development of Religious Toleration in England* (4 vols., London, 1932–40) (reprinted, Gloucester, Mass., 1965)
Philanthropy in England 1480–1660 (London, 1959)

Knappen, M. M., *Tudor Puritanism* (Chicago, 1939)

Lamont, William M., *Godly Rule: Politics and Religion, 1603–1660* (London, 1969)

Manning, R. B., *Religion and Society in Elizabethan Sussex* (Leicester, 1969)

Marchant, R. A., *Puritans and the Church Courts in the Diocese of York, 1560–1642* (London, 1960)

McGrath, Patrick, *Papists and Puritans under Elizabeth I* (London, 1967)

Miller, Perry, *The New England Mind: The Seventeenth Century* (Cambridge, Mass., 1939)

Morgan, E. S., *The Puritan Family* (Boston, Mass., 1944) (revised edition, New York, 1966)

New, J. F. H., *Anglican and Puritan: the basis of their opposition 1558–1640* (London 1964)

Richardson, R. C., *Puritanism in North-West England: A Regional Study of the Diocese of Chester to 1642* (Manchester, 1972)

Russell, Conrad, 'Arguments for Religious Unity in England 1530–1650', *Journal of Ecclesiastical History* Vol. XVIII (1967)

Solt, Leo F., 'Revolutionary Calvinist Parties in England under Elizabeth I and Charles I', *Church History* Vol. XXVII (1958)

Tawney, R. H., *Religion and the Rise of Capitalism* (London, 1926)

Trevor-Roper, R. H., *Archbishop Laud* (London, 1940) (second edition, London, 1962) *Religion, the Reformation and Social Change* (London, 1967)

Trinterud, Leonard J., 'The Origins of Puritanism', *Church History* Vol. XX (1951)

Walzer, Michael, *The Revolution of the Saints: A Study in the Origins of Radical Politics* (London, 1966)

The Catholics

Albion, G., *Charles I and the Court of Rome* (Louvain, 1935)

Aveling, H., *Post-Reformation Catholicism in East Yorkshire, 1558–1790* (York, 1960)
The Catholic Recusants of the West Riding of Yorkshire, 1558–1790 (Leeds, 1963)
Northern Catholics: The Catholic Recusants of the North Riding of Yorkshire, 1558–1790 (London, 1966)
Catholic Recusancy in the City of York 1558–1791 Catholic Record Society Publications, Monograph Series, II (1970)
'Documents relating to the northern commissions for compounding with recusants, 1627–1642' *Catholic Record Society* Vol. LIII (1960).
'The recusancy papers of the Meynell family' *Catholic Record Society* Vol. LVI (1964)

Basset, Bernard, *The English Jesuits from Campion to Martindale* (London, 1967)

Beales, A. C. F., *Education under penalty: English Catholic education from the Reformation to the fall of James II, 1547–1689* (London, 1963)

Bossy, John, 'The Character of Elizabethan Catholicism', *Past and Present* No. 21 (1962), reprinted in *Crisis in Europe 1560–1660* ed. T. Aston (London, 1965)

Caraman, Philip (ed.), *The years of siege: Catholic life from James I to Cromwell* (London, 1966)

Clancy, T. H., 'English Catholics and the Papal deposing power, 1570–1640' *Recusant History* Vol. VII (1963)

Clifton, R. 'The Popular Fear of Catholics during the English Revolution' *Past and Present* No. 52 (1971)

Dickens, A. G., 'The extent and character of recusancy in Yorkshire, 1604', *Yorkshire Archaeological Journal* Vol. XXXVII (1948)

Dickens, A. G. and Newton, J., 'Further light on the scope of Yorkshire recusancy in 1604', *Yorkshire Archaeological Journal* Vol. XXXVIII (1955)

Hardacre, Paul H., *The Royalists During the Puritan Revolution* (The Hague, 1956)

Havran, M. J., *The Catholics in Caroline England* (London, 1962)

Heyer, F., *The Catholic Church from 1648 to 1870* (London, 1969)

Jordan, W. K., *The Development of Religious Toleration in England* (4 vols., London, 1923–40) (reprinted, Gloucester, Mass., 1965)

Leys, M. D. R., *Catholics in England 1559–1829: a social history* (London, 1966)

Lindley, Keith, 'The lay Catholics of England in the reign of Charles I', *Journal of Ecclesiastical History* Vol. XXII (1971)
'The impact of the 1641 rebellion upon England and Wales, 1641–1645', *Irish Historical Studies* No. 70 (1972)

Magee, Brian, *The English Recussants* (London, 1938)

Mathew, David, *Catholicism in England, 1535–1935: portrait of a minority, its culture and tradition* (London, 1936)

McGrath, Patrick, *Papists and Puritans under Elizabeth I* (London, 1967)

Pugh, F. H., 'Monmouthshire Recusants in the Reigns of Elizabeth and James I', *South Wales and Monmouthshire Record Society* Vol. IV

Roebuck, P., 'The Constables of Everingham: the fortunes of a Catholic royalist family during the civil war and interregnum', *Recusant History* Vol. IX

Ryan, G. H. and Redstone, L. J., *Timperley of Hintlesham: a study of a Suffolk family* (London, 1931)

Trimble, W. R., 'The embassy chapel question, 1625–60', *The Journal of Modern History* Vol. XVIII (1946)

Watkin, E. I., *Roman Catholicism in England from the Reformation to 1950* (Oxford, 1957)

Wiener, Carol Z., 'The Beleagured Isle. A study of Elizabethan and Early Jacobean Anti-Catholicism' *Past and Present* No. 51 (1971)

Williams, J. Anthony, *Catholic Recusancy in Wiltshire, 1660–1791* Catholic Record Society Publications, Monograph Series, I (1968)

The Women

Ashley, Maurice, *The Stuarts in Love* (London, 1963)

Berens, Lewis H., *The Digger Movement in the Days of the Commonwealth* (London, 1906) (reprinted, London, 1961)

Bernstein, Eduard, *Cromwell and Communism: Socialism and Democracy in the Great English Revolution* translated H. J. Stenning (London, 1930) (reprinted, London, 1963)

Brailsford, H. N., *The Levellers and the English Revolution* ed. Christopher Hill (London, 1961)

Brown, Louise F., *The Political Activities of Baptists and Fifth Monarchy Men in England during the Interregnum* (London, 1911) (reprinted, New York, 1965)

Capp, B. S., *The Fifth Monarchy Men* (London, 1972)

Clark, Alice, *The Working Life of Women in the Seventeenth Century* (London, 1919)

Coate, Mary, *Social Life in Stuart England* (London, 1924)

Cohn, Norman, *The Pursuit of the Millennium* (London, 1957)

Frank, Joseph, *The Levellers: A History of the Writings of Three Seventeenth-Century Social Democrats: John Lilburne, Richard Overton, William Walwyn* (Cambridge, Mass., 1955)
The Beginnings of the English Newspaper, 1620–1660 (Cambridge, Mass., 1961)

Gibb, M. A., *John Lilburne, the Leveller* (London, 1947)

Gregg, Pauline, *Free-born John: A Biography of John Lilburne* (London, 1961)

Haller, William, *Liberty and Reformation in the Puritan Revolution* (New York, 1955)

Haller, William and Malleville, 'The Puritan Art of Love', *Huntington Library Quarterly* Vol. V (1942)

Hill, Christopher, *Intellectual Origins of the English Revolution* (Oxford, 1965)

James, Margaret, *Social Problems and Policy during the Puritan Revolution 1640–1660* (London, 1930)

Laslett, Peter, *The World We have lost* (London, 1965)

McArthur, Ellen A., 'Women Petitioners and the Long Parliament', *English Historical Review* Vol. XXIV (1909)

Macpherson, C. B., *The Political Theory of Possessive Individualism* (Oxford, 1962)

Morgan, E. S., *The Puritan Family* (Boston, Mass., 1944) (revised edition, New York, 1966)

Notestein, Wallace, 'The English Woman 1580–1650', *Studies in Social History: A tribute to G. M. Trevelyan* ed. J. H. Plumb (London, 1955)

Pearl, Valerie, *London and the Outbreak of the Puritan Revolution* (Oxford, 1961)

Pease, T. C., *The Leveller Movement* (Washington D.C., 1916) (reprinted, Gloucester, Mass., 1965)

Powell, C. L., *English Domestic Relations 1487–1653* (New York, 1917)

Robinson, R., 'Anticipations under the Commonwealth of Changes in the Law', *Select Essays in Anglo-American Legal History* Vol. I (Boston, Mass., 1907)

Rogers, P. G., *The Fifth Monarchy Men* (London, 1966)

Roots, Ivan, 'From the Lion's Den', *The Listener* 15 September 1963

Schenk, W., *The Concern for Social Justice in the Puritan Revolution* (London, 1948)

Schochet, G. J., 'Patriarchalism, politics and mass attitudes in Stuart England', *Historical Journal* Vol. XII (1969)

Stenton, D. M., 'Women in the English Revolution', *The English Woman in History* (London, 1957)

Stone, Lawrence, *The Crisis of the Aristocracy 1558–1641* (Oxford, 1965)

Thomas, Keith, 'Women and the Civil War Sects', *Past and Present* No. 13 (1958) reprinted in *Crisis in Europe 1560–1660* ed. T. Aston (London, 1965)

Veall, Donald, *The Popular Movement for Law Reform 1640–1660* (Oxford 1970)

Walzer, Michael, *The Revolution of the Saints: A Study in the Origins of Radical Politics* (London, 1966)

Wedgwood, C. V., *The Common Man in the Civil War* (Leicester 1957) *Poetry and Politics under the Stuarts* (Cambridge, 1960)

Williams, Ethyn Morgan, 'Women Preachers in the Civil War', *The Journal of Modern History* Vol. I (1929)

'Women in arms', *Times Literary Supplement* 14 January 1965

Zagorin, Perez, *A History of Political Thought in the English Revolution* (London, 1954) (reprinted, New York, 1966)

The Levellers

Brailsford, H. N., *The Levellers and the English Revolution* ed. Christopher Hill (London, 1961)

Davis, J. C., 'The Levellers and Democracy', *Past and Present* No. 40 (1968)

Frank, Joseph, *The Levellers: A History of the Writings of Three Seventeenth-Century Social Democrats: John Lilburne, Richard Overton, William Walwyn* (Cambridge, Mass., 1955)

George, C. H., 'Puritanism as History and Historiography', *Past and Present* No. 41 (1968)

Gooch, G. P., *English Democratic Ideas in the Seventeenth Century* ed. H. J. Laski (Cambridge, 1927)

Gough, J. W., *Fundamental Law in English Constitutional History* (Oxford, 1955)

Gregg, Pauline, *Free-born John: A Biography of John Lilburne* (London, 1961)

Haller, William, *Tracts on Liberty in the Puritan Revolution 1638–1647* (3 vols., New York, 1933–4) (reprinted, London, 1965)

Haller, William and Davies, Godfrey, *The Leveller Tracts 1647–1653* (New York, 1944) (reprinted, Gloucester, Mass., 1964)

Hill, Christopher, 'The Norman Yoke', *Puritanism and Revolution* (London, 1958)

Himbury, D. M., 'The Religious Beliefs of the Levellers', *The Baptist Quarterly* Vol. 33 (1954)

Holorenshaw, H., *The Levellers and the English Revolution* (London, 1939)

Howell, Roger and Brewster, David E., 'Reconsidering the Levellers: The Evidence of "The Moderate" ', *Past and Present* No. 46 (1970)

Huehns, Gertrude, *Antinomianism in English History* (London, 1951)

Jones, R. M., *Mysticism and Democracy in the English Commonwealth* (New York, 1932)

Lindsay, A. D., *The Essentials of Democracy* (London, 1930) (second edition, London, 1935)

Macpherson, C. B., 'The Levellers: Franchise and Freedom', *The Political Theory of Possessive Individualism* (Oxford, 1962)

Manning, Brian, 'The Levellers', *The English Revolution 1600–1660* ed. E. W. Ives (London, 1968)

Pease, T. C., *The Leveller Movement* (Washington D.C., 1916) (reprinted, Gloucester, Mass., 1965)

Petegorsky, D. W., *Left-Wing Democracy in the English Civil War* (London, 1940)

Robertson, D. B., *The Religious Foundations of Leveller Democracy* (New York, 1951)

Schenk, W., *The Concern for Social Justice in the Puritan Revolution* (London, 1948)

Shaw, Howard, *The Levellers* (London, 1968)

Solt, Leo F., *Saints in Arms: Puritanism and Democracy in Cromwell's Army* (London, 1959)

Thomas, Keith, 'The Levellers and the Franchise', *The Interregnum: The Quest for Settlement 1646–1660* ed. G. E. Aylmer (London, 1972)

Troeltsch, Ernst, *The Social Teaching of the Christian Churches*, translated Olive Wyon (2 vols., London, 1931)

Wolfe, Don M., *Milton in the Puritan Revolution* (London, 1941)
 Leveller Manifestoes of the Puritan Revolution (London, 1944) (reprinted, London, 1967)

Woodhouse, A. S. P., *Puritanism and Liberty* (London, 1938) (reprinted, London, 1950)

Zagorin, Perez, *A History of Political Thought in the English Revolution* (London, 1954)

Notes on Contributors

R. C. RICHARDSON is a graduate of Leicester and Manchester universities and since 1968 has taught at Thames Polytechnic, London, where he is now Senior Lecturer in History. He has published *Puritanism in north-west England: A regional study of the diocese of Chester to 1642* (Manchester, 1972), and is co-editor with W. H. Chaloner of a forthcoming bibliographical guide to British economic and social history. At present he is researching into the Presbyterian experiment in Lancashire, 1646–1660, and also preparing a study of agriculture and society in the late seventeenth and early eighteenth centuries for *The Agrarian History of England and Wales* Vol. V: *1640–1750*.

BRIAN MANNING was educated at Hurstpierpoint and Balliol. He graduated in the first class in the School of Modern History at Oxford in 1952. He was Harmsworth Senior Scholar at Merton 1952–1953, and assistant-lecturer in history at King's College, London, 1953–1957. Then he spent two years in the United States as a Commonwealth Fund Fellow; and since 1959 he has been lecturer in history at the University of Manchester. In 1967–1968 he was a Visiting Fellow at All Souls College, Oxford. He has published articles on 'The Nobles, the People, and the Constitution', in *Past & Present* No. 9 (1956) (reprinted in *Crisis in Europe 1560–1660* ed. Trevor Aston (London, 1968); 'The Levellers', in *The English Revolution 1600–1660* ed. E. W. Ives (London, 1968); 'The Outbreak of the English Civil War', in *The English Civil War and after, 1642–1658* ed. R. H. Parry (London, 1970). At present he is preparing for publication a book on *The English People and the English Revolution 1640–1649*.

KEITH LINDLEY was educated at the University of Manchester, where he obtained the degrees of MA and PhD. He was assistant-lecturer in history at Magee University College, Londonderry, and he is now lecturer in history at the New University of Ulster. He has published articles in the *Journal of Ecclesiastical History* and *Irish Historical Studies*. He is at present writing a book on riots in England 1603–1660.

PATRICIA HIGGINS was educated at Manchester University, where she graduated BA in 1964 and MA in 1965. She was an assistant librarian in Manchester University Library 1967–1969, and since 1969 she has been an Assistant Keeper in the Department of Manuscripts, British Museum. She is researching into the position of women in seventeenth-century England.

J. C. DAVIS was educated at Kingston High School, Hull, and the University of Manchester, where he graduated in the first class in the School of Modern History with Economics and Politics in 1962, and obtained the degree of MA in 1963. After a year spent working for the British Foreign Office, he taught history and economics in a Lancashire grammar school and worked as a history tutor for the WEA. In 1966 he was appointed lecturer in history at the newly-founded University of Waikato, New Zealand. Since 1971 he has been senior lecturer in history at the Victoria University of Wellington, New Zealand. He has published articles on the history of utopianism, Sir Thomas More, the Levellers, and the social interpretation of seventeenth-century English history. At present he is completing a book on English utopian thought in the early modern period.

Index of Subjects

Index of Persons and Places

Canterbury (Kent) 219
Capell, Mr 89
Carlisle, Countess of *see* Hay, Lucy
Carlisle, Earl of *see* Hay, James
Carter, Oliver 11(*note 25*)
Cary, Lorenzo 59
Cary, Lucius (?1610–43), 2nd Viscount Falkland, MP for Newport, Isle of Wight, in Long Parliament 59, 73, 77, 78, 79, 117
Case, Thomas 103
Castlemaine, Earl of *see* Palmer, Roger
Cavendish, William (1593–1676), 1st Earl of Newcastle, created Marquis of Newcastle 1643 61, 62, 65–6
Cecil, David (1604–43), 3rd Earl of Exeter 43
Cecil, Robert (1563–1612), 1st Earl of Salisbury 6
Cecil, William (1591–1668), 2nd Earl of Salisbury 65, 67, 68, 74, 75
Chaderton, Lawrence 12
Chaderton, William, Bishop of Chester 1579–95 3, 5, 8, 10, 12, 32
Charles I 18, 19, 20, 23, 32, 36, 37, 43, 45, 63, 65, 67, 68, 69, 70, 71, 73, 74, 75, 76, 78, 79, 80, 82, 83, 87, 93, 95, 106, 107, 112, 114, 122, 126, 128, 161, 166, 167, 168, 184
Charles, Prince of Wales 59, 76
Chester (Cheshire) 2, 3, 4, 6, 7, 12, 16, 18, 19, 25, 26, 30, 31, 32, 146
Cheynell, Francis 103
Chichester (Sussex) 13(*note 29*), 117
Chidley, Katherine 211, 218
Chidley, Samuel 207, 218
Chillingworth, William 91
Chudleigh, Sir George 61
Chudleigh, Captain James, son of above 61, 62, 63
Cirencester (Gloucestershire) 96, 118
Clare, Earl of *see* Holles, John
Clarendon, Earl of *see* Hyde, Edward
Clarke, Captain 246, 249
Clarke, James 137, 138
Cliffe, J. T. 139
Clifton, Thomas 142
Clotworthy, Sir John (d. 1665), MP for Maldon in Long Parliament 72
Coke, Sir Edward 232
Coke, Sir John (*c.* 1608–50), MP for Derbyshire in Long Parliament 194, 196
Coleman, Thomas 99
Colepeper, Sir John (1600–60), MP for Kent in the Long Parliament 73, 77, 78, 79
Compton, Spencer (1601–43), 2nd Earl Northampton 159

Constable, Henry, 1st Viscount Dunbar 143, 160
Constable, John, 2nd Viscount Dunbar 160
Constable, Sir Philip 144
Constable, Thomas 209
Conway, Edward (1594–1655), 2nd Viscount Conway 58, 61, 110
Conyers, Sir John 58
Coppinger, Edmund 9
Corbet, John 105, 113, 115, 116, 122, 159
Cosin, John 18
Cottington, Francis (1579–1652), 1st Lord Cottington 37, 43
Cotton, Edward 154
Courtenay, Sir William 155
Coventry (Warwickshire) 94, 95, 98, 99, 219
Crompton, Thomas 87
Cromwell, Oliver (1599–1658), MP for Cambridge in Long Parliament 85, 99, 118, 119, 138, 139, 174, 203, 206, 218, 219
Crosby, Sir Piers 49
Cross, John 166, 167

Daniell, Sir Ingleby 160
Davenant, William 40, 52, 53, 54, 61, 62, 64
Davies, William 138
Denbigh Castle 144
Derby, Earl of *see* Stanley, Henry and James
Derbyshire 116
Devereux, Robert (1591–1646), 3rd Earl of Essex 40, 41, 42, 43, 46, 47, 55, 56, 58, 62, 63, 64, 65, 66, 67, 68, 72, 74, 75, 93, 94, 97, 98, 99, 117, 123
Devonshire 118
D'Ewes, Sir Simonds (1602–50), MP for Sudbury in Long Parliament 85, 86, 190, 194, 196
Digby family 68
Digby, George (1611?–76?), Lord Digby, eldest son of 1st Earl of Bristol, MP for Dorset in Long Parliament 47, 68, 69, 73, 74, 76, 77, 78, 79
Digby, John (1586–1653) 1st Earl of Bristol 47, 55, 68, 69, 70, 73, 74
Dives, Sir Lewis 93
Dodd, A. H. 139
Dolman, Thomas 143
Dorset 118
Dorset, Earl of *see* Sackville, Edward
Dudley, Ambrose (1528–90), Earl of Warwick 9
Dudley, Robert (1533–88), Earl of Leicester 9